Choreographies of African Identities

Choreographies of African Identities

Négritude, Dance, and the National Ballet of Senegal

FRANCESCA CASTALDI

UNIVERSITY OF ILLINOIS PRESS
Urbana and Chicago

Cover photograph: Mural by Papisto Boy–Pape Mamadou Samb, depicting Léopold Sédar Senghor. The image is part of Samb's six-hundred-foot mural on an exterior factory wall in Bel-Air, Dakar. Photo by Mary Nooter Roberts and Allen F. Roberts, 1999. Reprinted by permission.

© 2006 by Francesca Castaldi
All rights reserved
Manufactured in the United States of America
∞ This book is printed on acid-free paper.
1 2 3 4 5 C P 5 4 3 2 1

Library of Congress Cataloging-in-Publication Data
Castaldi, Francesca, 1964–
Choreographies of African identities : négritude, dance, and
the National Ballet of Senegal / Francesca Castaldi.
p.   cm.
Originally presented as the author's thesis (doctoral)—
University of California, Riverside.
Includes bibliographical references and index.
ISBN-13: 978-0-252-03027-7 (isbn 13 - cloth : alk. paper)
ISBN-10: 0-252-03027-3 (isbn 10 - cloth : alk. paper)
ISBN-13: 978-0-252-07268-0 (isbn 13 - paper : alk. paper)
ISBN-10: 0-252-07268-5 (isbn 10 - paper : alk. paper)
1. Dance—Anthropological aspects—Senegal. 2. Blacks—
Race identity—Senegal. 3. National Ballet of Senegal. I. Title.
GV1588.6.C37   2006
793.31'09663—dc22   2005011094

Contents

Acknowledgments

Many experiences and people have made this writing possible. I wish I could thank you in a circle, in a merry-go-round. Please forgive the linearity of the page and the impression of beginning and ending that it imposes upon us. Read this not as a list but as the boomeranging spell that you sent my way. Thank you!

I salute the women who have nurtured writing in my daily life:

My mother, Adriana Schiavoni, who first placed the pen in my hand and taught me how to read and write; who whispered stories into my ears and into my dreams from a very early age, feeding them to me as often as bread was on the table; and who made up her own stories, for us, her children, and who wrote them down.

My grandmother, Matilde Bertoni, who aged as a happy intellectual and spent the last days of her life writing her autobiography. Holding her book in my hands was the first intimate sense I had of a "familiar" author.

My grandmother, Wanda Catapano, who has been such a magical presence as a spirit at my side, fanning tears out of my eyes when I was too sad to move and too angry to breathe deeply.

My aunt, Serena Castaldi, who taught me to think with the sharpness of hot tongue and to create new words that like secret passages birth like women birth.

Professor Marta Savigliano, who, as the chair of my dissertation committee, was my closest mentor and adviser, offering constant guidance, trust, and inspiration. She has taught me the art of writing as gardening: searching for the resilient seeds of the wild, planting and protecting them in fertile ground, watering the tendrils, and later trimming and cutting with a decisive but gentle touch. Her teaching has permeated this text with definite, profuse, and diffuse influences; she has prodded me to shift perspective to avoid sore muscles and stale arguments, to follow and undo the margins by decentering and recentering, to go where pain lives without fear, to question myself beyond what is comfortable, and to walk my ideas in public.

Professor Susan Foster, whose contagious obsession with choreography as a metaconcept allowed me to view social practices as choreographed interventions on the stage of life, and whose ability to deconstruct the most natural-looking motion into a narrative of agentive interventions reminded me that where there is a dance there is always a subject who dances!

Professor Bennetta Jules-Rosette, who welcomed me at the University of California at San Diego for many series of the Popular Music Workshop with the African and African-American Studies Research Project, and who thus gave me the opportunity to develop my ideas in dialogue with a committed and talented group of international scholars and artists. The sponsoring of my postdoctoral research as a fellow of the African and African-American Studies Research Project in fall 2001 and winter 2002 enabled me to turn my dissertation into the bulk of this book and to further develop my ideas in dialogue with students and faculty. Her insights on Négritude have deeply influenced my understanding of Léopold Sédar Senghor's literary and political project, and her commitment to crossing disciplinary boundaries and challenging the arbitrary linguistic barriers imposed by colonial histories has greatly enhanced my understanding of the African Diaspora.

Joan Catapano, the editor-in-chief of the University of Illinois Press, whose support has been crucial in making this writing public.

My friend and colleague Riselia Duarte Bezerra, who engaged me in conversations that carried through the years of my doctoral studies and have allowed me to develop my ideas in dialogue with hers.

Paula Seniors, who kindly hosted me in her home in San Diego and shared friendship and intellectual camaraderie.

I thank the women who have sustained another kind of daily writing, that which takes place on my body.

Professor Susan Rose, who nurtured my understanding of choreography well beyond theory and who has been a model of punk kindness—that love for anarchy, because it creates freedom without hierarchies.

Carol Zeitz, Sara Shelton Mann, Terry Sendgraff, Susan Murphy, and Anna Halprin—mentors in healing in motion, who have injected curiosity and fierce experimentation into the alchemy of transforming the self through falling, flying, spinning, reversing, repeating, and twisting in body and fantasy.

Giulia Castaldi, my sister, whose youthful transgressions in social geography have taught me to go where we are not supposed to go.

I also want to thank these male relations:

My father, Giorgio Castaldi, who taught me that to question is more important than to obey, and whose supportive help has come at crucial times in my life, which he detected with an intuitive cunning worthy of a woman-witch!

Professor Jeff Tobin, an enduring friend, who has made me laugh when I was at my stiffest and most disheartened intellectual moments, and whose ideas have nurtured mine with generosity.

Nilo Cayuqueo, my companion and husband, whose heart-roots run deep in *ñukemapu,* and who anchored me to Abya Yala at those crucial moments when I risked being swept across the ocean, providing the nurturance and love that I can call home.

I also want to thank Professor Christopher Waterman, whose book on Jùjú music was one of the first inspirations for this project, and who later welcomed me as a postdoctoral researcher at the Department of World Arts and Cultures at the University of California at Los Angeles in the spring of 2002 and as a visiting scholar during the winter and fall of 2003. I am grateful for the opportunity to present some of these ideas in my course on African politics and performance.

I thank Allen and Mary Roberts, also at the University of Californa at Los Angeles, for the picture on the cover—part of Papisto Boy's spectacular mural in an industrial area of Dakar.

John and Jean Comaroff at the University of Chicago guided my first steps of engagement in African anthropology with a commitment and acumen that has sustained me for many years past our encounter. John MacAloon, also at the University of Chicago, provided me with the experience of the richness that comes from engaging in interdisciplinary research, an experience that has fundamentally shaped my scholarly attitude.

Professors Ray Kea and Sterling Stuckey guided my studies in African history and aesthetics at the University of California at Riverside, where I carried out my doctoral studies. George Lipsitz at the University of California at San Diego was an inspiration for his political integrity and commitment and his capacity to weave narratives of music, identity, and politics into moving scholarship. I also thank him for his kind words of encouragement and his always-provocative questions.

The department of dance at the University of California at Riverside supported my doctoral studies in dance history and theory. The Social Science Research Council, Africa Program, and the UCR Humanities Graduate Student Research Grant provided funding for the initial phase of research in Dakar. The Gluck family generously supported the presentation of the resulting research to local communities of students.

Sandor Diabankouezi with gentleness and grace led my steps toward Africa before I ever set foot on the continent, and thus acted as a human bridge to my research in Senegal.

I want to thank the Diallo family, who so generously hosted and protected me in Dakar. I am particularly thankful to Anta and Marie Diallo for sharing their room with me, to mother Aminata for her skillful maneuvers at the food bowl, always flickering morsels of fish and meat toward my side of the dish, and to Vieux Màgget Diallo, who was a patient and devoted guide to the world of Dakar.

Bouly Sonko welcomed me to the daily rehearsals of the National Ballet of Senegal and to the joking atmosphere of the company. His daily dance lessons offered a constant refrain in my research and allowed me to sweat my way through under his guidance.

Xalifa Guéye of the Ballet Mansour allowed me enter the well-guarded walls of the company studio in Ñaari Tali and offered me his trust. For this I thank him. I also thank Adama Diallo and Ndiuwar Thiam for sharing their work with the Ballet Kaddu gi. I am grateful to Mahommed Ngom, to Sedou Massaly, and to Awa Sene for their friendship.

Leigh Swigart, who directed the West African Research Center at the time of my research, recommended two wonderful Wolof teachers: Ibu Sarr and Sidi (whose last name I have forgotten). I have never had such capable and exciting language teachers.

Finally, I thank Mareme Faye, Malick Sow, Oumar Mboup, Malang Bayo, and Aziz and Alicia Faye for keeping Senegal alive in Los Angeles.

Choreographies of African Identities

Introduction: Positionality and the Choreography of Theory

They call us men of cotton, coffee, and oil
They call us men of death
But we are men of dance, whose feet grow stronger
As we pound upon firm ground.

—Léopold Sédar Senghor

Dance and Africans have a long-standing association that has been nurtured through the last two centuries by colonial histories and anticolonial struggles. On the colonial side of history, the coloring of the African body with the heavy tones of racist discourse and the devaluation of dance as a prediscursive form of expression concurred to make African dance a powerful icon of primitivism. On the anticolonial side, African dance allowed for the articulation of indigenous cultural beliefs and the expression of historical continuities, making dance also a powerful medium of indigenous resistance against the European colonizers.

The space between personal and social histories is the territory from which I write and the ground on which I dance. And here I stand, not at the beginning of it all, not at the end, but at a start. Colonized Africa confronts me with phantasmagoric creatures—powerful Africans scantily dressed, savage people of great strength—that engage in battle with dancers in flesh and blood. They fight for my attention on the stage and pull me between reality and fantasy, between the present and the specters of history. *Here I stand.*

I turn white as I step into African dance; I turn white like my dead ancestors who invented the tones of racialized discourse. This color sticks to my skin and cannot be brushed away by a blissful forgetfulness. The sweat of ecstatic dancing cannot wash out the whiteness on my body and erase the memory of four centuries of slavery, over half a century of colonial domination, and its permutation into neocolonial yokes. This memory designs a space with its own choreographic imperatives: it pulls me back to a place of beginnings, of roots, of movements into the past, never stepping forward. Africa, the mother of humanity. At the beginning there was also dance, the mother of the arts, the most primitive of artistic expressions. Thus, Africa and dance make a good duet, supporting each other in the making of stereotypes of primitiveness.

We used to say that Africans have no history and only we, the white ones who possess written language, have a history worthy of mention. We now say that Africa has no future, a whole continent of hopelessness, with perhaps the exception of its tip—South Africa. Through this writing I question this choreography, this movement backwards, and at the same time I account for its origin.

With arrogance and stubbornness—no, with humbleness and cowardice, I presume to write about Senegalese dance.

The single term "dance" hides within it the struggles of dance makers over the control of their products; the circulation, consumption, and proliferation of dances beyond an original locus of production; and the gaps in age and cultural and social background between artists, producers, and audiences. The term "Senegalese" covers an even more heterogeneous ensemble of religious, political, economical, ethnic, generational, and gendered identities and histories. "Senegalese dance" as such does not exist, yet I have sutured the plurality of the uneven strands covered in the fictional singular by taking the National Ballet of Senegal as the official embodiment of Senegalese dance, invested by the state to construct, represent, and preserve the cultural patrimony of the nation. I thus began and ended this research project seated at the Irvine Barclay Theater in California, watching the National Ballet of Senegal perform in 1995 and again in 1998. Between these two events I labored to acquire the resources to interpret the performance of the Ballet not only as a spectator/critic but also as an ethnographer.[1] From January to March 1996 and from September 1996 to March 1997, I conducted ethnographic research in Dakar, the capital of Senegal, interrogating the activities of the National Ballet of Senegal and of three other African Ballet companies operating in the city.

Central to my ethnographic approach to the work of African Ballets in Senegal has been the concept of choreography, which I define in the context of the dance practices under analysis as a form of historical writing that foregrounds the corporeal dimension of social subjects as the means and object of writing. This conceptualization is intended to disturb the association of dance with the ephemeral and the nonverbal that has until recently dominated the discipline of dance studies in Euro-America. The association of dance with a form of expression that vanishes at the moment in which it is performed and that at the same time, because of its ephemerality, does not possess a history contrasts with dominant West African conceptualizations of dance practice. All over West Africa, the circle of social actors gathered to dance has been conceived as the paradigmatic spatiotemporal formation that locates dancers outside the ephemerality of quotidian life. The circle stands as a metaphor of historical time, which is not an abstract and linear category but rather is conceived through the living memory of a collective body in dialogue with past generations. Dance becomes a privileged space where communication with the ancestors is enacted: The dancing body proclaims the continuity between the material and the spiritual, which in turn links the past and the present. Dance is memory, a memory that is not static and does not exist outside the moment of remembrance. Rather, it needs to be activated and made meaningful through the embodiment of ancestral spirits and the repetition of performances. The relation with the ancestors is a two-way relation: The ancestors (the past) depend on the living (the present), just as the living depend on those who came before them (Abilogu 1982; Stuckey 1987; Diabankouezi 1992). At the same time, the continual redefinition of the relationship between the past and the present carries implications for the construction of a meaningful future. Thus, past, present, and future are continually transformed in the dancing circle, which delimits the boundaries of manipulable space-time: History is reinterpreted and rewritten through performance and through the fusion of bodies and spirits.

Similarly to the association of dance with ephemerality, the conceptualization of dance and words as mutually exclusive domains represents a Eurocentric perspective that does not resonate with West African conceptualizations. As Mark Franko (1995) has argued, Euro-American dance criticism has until recently assumed a modernist aesthetic that constructs a narrative in dance history that is tautological to the aesthetic of modern dance itself. Expressive theory has allowed scholars and dancers to conceive of a dancing subject that is at the same time private and depersonalized, expressive of a subjective interiority and universal. The passage from affect, to feeling, to gesture characterized modernist readings of the process of artistic creation performed by modern dance choreographers (Franko 1995:8).[2] Within this tripartite model of creation (and the subsequent variations introduced by successive generations of modern dance choreographers) language was excluded from dance making and was rather conceived as a radical externality to dance practice. While the externality of words to dance was contested by successive generations of dancers, nevertheless it found theoretical coherence in relation to the analysis of canonical modern dance figures like Isadora Duncan and Martha Graham. The Cartesian split between mind and body gave further historical weight to the separation between dance and verbal practice. Dance was associated with the body and the natural, alternatively conceived as the instinctual or the unconscious, but always nonverbal, rather than with the cultural, the willed, and the conscious, which were understood to belong to the mental domain of linguistic expression. In the West African context, dancing and speaking are not conceived as two radically separate domains of action. The association of words with dance has a long history that goes back to precolonial West African empires and the social practices of the griots who performed as musicians, oral historians, and dancers. In chapter 6 I analyze this connection between music, poetry, and dance, not so much in relation to the griot caste and precolonial history but for its relevance in the context of African Ballet companies and their contemporary practice. I argue that dance can be understood as a form of orality in which rhythm mediates between music, speech, and dance. It is precisely as a form of orality, rather than as essentialized movement, that contemporary Senegalese dance displays continuities with precolonial dance practices and with the larger Pan-African world across the Black Atlantic.[3] By looking at choreography in its specific performance context I argue that the relationship between drumming, singing, and dancing calls for a definition of choreography in "African dance" that addresses the relationship between the aural and the kinetic as one of the constitutive elements of dance making and delivery. Choreography can then be thought of as the organizing principle of performance, while dance becomes the specific instantiation of choreographic principles.

The definition of choreography as a form of historical writing, while pointing to the abstract and enduring quality of performance principles, is also meant to implicate my writing on dance as a form of choreography. I mean to draw attention to the fact that the staged presentation of characters and events displayed on the pages of this book follows its own history: a genealogy of academic interests that have defined the object under consideration. These interests, and the specific mode of representation that expresses them, have most strongly been inscribed by the discipline of anthropology. The relevance of anthropology for this study does not simply rest in the fact that my position vis-à-vis the National Ballet of Senegal was that of ethnographer. It also rests on the observation that anthropology has historically maintained a monopoly over the study and representation of African cultures in Euro-America at least into the 1960s and has influenced Léopold Sédar Senghor's culturalist arguments in his Négritude ideology (a point I explain in chapter 2).

In this context my own body has acted as a visible sign of mediation between anthropology's past (its colonial context) and present (the pretense to a postcolonial status), a mediating nexus between theory and practice, history and utopia, and personal contingencies and macropolitical processes. I call this body that extends beyond the confines of physical presence, extending vertically in time and horizontally in space, the corpo-real. My own body, as the single body of a contemporary ethnographer, is thus inserted into a corporeal field, *a corpus of histories* that reaches back to previous generations of ethnographers and to the historical cradle of ethnographic practice: colonialism.

The removal of the body of the ethnographer from ethnographic accounts, which until recently has characterized ethnographic monographs, signaled a historical blind spot in the discipline of anthropology: to recover the original "native" mode of life, the colonial presence was to be silenced from ethnographic accounts. The body of the ethnographer, rendered invisible in the ethnographic text, stood as a methodological silencing of the colonial project, which nevertheless defined the very existence of the ethnographic field. Thus we need to be cautious of naive solutions in new ethnographies that propose the simple reintroduction of the ethnographer's body within the writing of ethnographic monographs as a panacea to the conundrums of the ethnographic enterprise. Unless the body of the ethnographer is related to a body of histories that defines the interaction between social subjects and the networks of power in which they participate, the new ethnographies will contribute nothing new. I have attended to the corpus of knowledge relevant to this study by using V. Y. Mudimbe's theoretical framework (1988; 1994) to deconstruct the field of African anthropology into three conceptually framed periods. In presenting the discourses dominant in each period, I have focused on the slippery shifts between definitions of African identities through ethnic, racial, or national categories and how these shifts have historically configured interpretations of African dance. Following the cultural logic inscribed within these different conceptions of African dance, I construct intersecting narratives and interpretations of the choreographic work of the National Ballet of Senegal, narratives that parallel the three theoretical paradigms identified by Mudimbe.

According to Mudimbe, the first paradigm supporting the constitution of specialized knowledge on and about Africa extends from the end of the nineteenth century through the first quarter of the twentieth century and is defined by the preoccupations of colonial anthropologists and the protagonism of European scholars. Following Mudimbe's characterization, I call it the "Order of the Same." The Order of the Same refers to the use of Africa as a trope in which "nonwestern otherness" is reduced to "western sameness" as European conceptual and political frameworks generate and define the antinomies between African and European societies (Mudimbe 1988:72).

Under the Order of the Same, present notions of race and ethnicity coalesce into a single concept: the "tribe." The African tribe was defined through nineteenth-century social evolution. Along an evolutionary line, the "tribal stage" indexed a level of sociocultural development one step above the (very primitive) bands of hunters-gatherers and far below the great European civilizations. The African tribe, as a homogeneous and essentialized social body (race) and as a political entity defined in sociocultural terms (ethnicity), sutured conceptions of race and ethnicity into one. Colonial administrators conceived of tribes paradoxically as both radically different from each other (separated by intractable cultural and religious differences) and as homologous entities vis-à-vis the colonial enterprise and its civilizing mission, each tribe the structural equivalent of others.

The Order of the Same was superseded by a new paradigm that I call (again in light of Mudimbe's analysis) the "Order of the Other." The Order of the Other began to dominate Africanist discourses in the 1920s and culminated in the 1960s with national-liberation movements sweeping across the African continent. African intellectuals, artists, and political masses engaged in anticolonial struggles and asserted themselves as the new protagonists of African history and scholarship, displacing colonial agents, reformers, and intellectuals from their role as Africa's planners and interpreters. Négritude was among the most important identity movements of the period. Léopold Sédar Senghor, one of the most fervent ideologues of Négritude, reworked the relationship between the categories of race, ethnicity, and national identity inherited from the previous order to galvanize the decolonization struggle. In Senghor's Négritude, ethnicity receded while race was wrenched from the narrow confines of the tribe to motivate political alliances over the continent of Africa and beyond. Senghor conceived of race as a sort of meta-ethnicity, indexing a cultural and biological unity that supersedes the diversity of individual African ethnicities. Race became the fundamental unit of action and analysis, much like the tribe had functioned in the previous order.

A third period, starting with the end of the 1960s and continuing to this day, ushered African anthropology into what I call the "Third Dis/Order." Two events symbolically mark the birth of this Dis/Order, with its shifting political and intellectual stakes in Africa: the African Studies Association meeting in Montreal and the Pan-African Cultural Festival in Algiers in 1969.

At the meeting in Montreal, African American and African scholars brought to the fore the covert connections between white hegemony in academia and larger patterns of U.S. supremacy in world politics, unmasking links between African scholars, the Central Intelligence Agency, and other government institutions like the State Department and the Agency for International Development (Wallerstein 1986:9). Black intellectuals thus revealed publicly the links between scholarly research and the new patterns of white control in postcolonial Africa, where the exigencies of the cold war shifted the axis of political control and intervention from the old colonial metropolises to Washington, D.C. The critique of the continued domination of foreign interests and scholars in African studies was paralleled by an internal critique among the African intellectuals gathered in Algiers. At the festival, Stanislas Adotevi and René Depestre denounced Négritude as a mystifying ideology that could no longer provide the basis for meaningful political action and organizing (Jules-Rosette 1998:7). These intellectuals saw Négritude as an ideological excuse mobilized by a privileged African elite to avoid engaging with the class antagonisms and historical specificities that configured the newly created African states. As African intellectuals evaluated the course to be taken after national independence, the relationship between classes and ethnicities within the space of the nation became a major concern. Race receded into the background as a political category connected to the colonial past and no longer meaningful to the postcolonial African world.

How did the reconfiguration of the meaning of "Africa" influence narratives about African dance? In chapter 2, I present the writing of dance scholars that falls within each of the paradigms outlined above. Under the Order of the Same, I examine the writing of Curt Sachs (in the late 1930s) with its related Eurocentric project of writing a history of world dance. I argue that Sachs's scholarly project configured a set of theoretical preoccupations and narrative themes around and about African dance that are still echoed in the work of some contemporary dance scholars. Under the Order of the Other, I focus on Senghor's contribution to dance studies around the time the Senegalese government hosted the first World Festival of Negro Arts in Dakar in 1966. Under the Third Dis/Order, I present the theoretical issues that have informed my own ethnographic writing on dance in Dakar (presented in chapters 4 through 7).

The overview of the theoretical structure of this book would be incomplete without a discussion of the concept of polyrhythms, which, through the teachings of the many dancers and drummers that I have encountered in the span of my research, has guided my thoughts and perceptions. Polyrhythms define not only a musical and choreographic strategy but also a theoretical model that articulates relationships of parts to a whole within a hierarchical structure.[4] This model contrasts with the hierarchical model in which relationships of power follow a linear and centralized mode of transmission and with a rhizomic model that conceptualizes a network of egalitarian relations without a center. A polyrhythmic model presents us with differentiated layers (nonhomologous relationships) within which different rules of improvisation apply (degrees of freedom) as well as with a circular (nonlinear) mode of connections that refer to each other without claiming an absolute point of origin.

Within a polyrhythmic structure, separate rhythms are necessary to create an interlocking whole. This whole is created by the active participation of players; it is not externally given. As John Chernoff has explained: "[T]he musicians do not find their entrances by counting from a main beat, but rather, they must find their entrances in relation to other instruments" (1979:47). Time is not externally given; it is created by the connection between players. These connections are organized through three layers of sound: one drum provides the time signature and the rhythmic base; another adds to the base, producing a complex interlocking of rhythms; and finally the master drum creates improvised variations or outstanding phrasing.[5] Three drums are enough to produce this polyrhythmic structure, yet often drum ensembles include a rhythmic complexity that accommodates four, five, or six rhythmic lines, as well as the replication of drum patterns by more than one drum.

Following the structure of a drum ensemble, I have taken the choreographic work performed by the National Ballet of Senegal at the time of my research as the base of a polyrhythmic ensemble. *Pangols*—the program that the company rehearsed day after day for more than six years and that it toured twice in the United States (1995 and 1998)—provides a stable reference point for analysis and interpretation. Like the base, the ensemble keeps playing on and on, establishing the time signature of the music, so the Ballet's recursive performance of *Pangols* creates a "choreographic present" that spans the passing of years and sustains the ethnographic present of my research, allowing me to interrogate and interpret the performance from different locations. These interpretative locations operate like the layers of sound in a polyrhythmic ensemble, articulating three interrelated narratives that shift not only the line of interpretation but the very object under analysis.

In a polyrhythmic ensemble, the process of interpretation does not follow the music but is a constitutive part of music making itself. Similarly, *Pangols* does not exist prior to interpretation as a separate entity (a pure truth), nor do different interpretations invalidate or displace one another (truer and falser interpretations). *Pangols* is defined as an object by the location from which it is interpreted, while relationality between the interpretative narratives defines the whole of the object, the whole of *Pangols,* that I present in this book. The three interpretative layers connect the spectacle on stage to different social and historical contexts and to different interpretations of African dance.

The first layer of analysis connects the National Ballet of Senegal to the historical context of independence and the appropriation of the nation-state by indigenous populations. The National Ballet of Senegal was founded only one year after Senegal acquired independence from France, and like other national dance troupes created all over Africa at the moment of decolonization, it implicated dance in the making of a national culture, reconfiguring local dance traditions as a vehicle of historical memory and continuity. African Ballets linked the newly independent state to the cultural patrimony of a pre-colonial past, uncontaminated and cleansed of the influences brought about by colonization. At the same time, they established a dialogue between western modernity and indigenous forms of art, like the new nation itself established continuity between the inherited colonial structure of the state and the Africanization of its personnel and goals. The fact that the French term "ballet" has been chosen to identify indigenous African dance troupes all over Francophone Africa is significant in this respect. The concept of African Ballet juxtaposes the western classical dance tradition to African dance, which for most Europeans evokes the tribal and the primitive. The term "African Ballet" stands as a challenge to European racist assumptions, suggesting that African dances are classical forms that offer their own aesthetic, equal in sophistication and beauty to the ballet tradition.[6]

Léopold Sédar Senghor—the first president of independent Senegal (1960–80)—promoted the Ballet as Senegal's cultural ambassador and called upon it to perform within the nation and in major theaters across the globe. Senghor, as the celebrated poet of Négritude and the president of Senegal for twenty years, gave an official voice to the cultural project embodied by the Ballet, a voice that has been historically relevant in its very constitution. For this reason I use Senghor's narrative on dance to provide the first line of interpretation of the performance of the Ballet at the Barclay Theater in California, a line explored in chapter 1 and then more fully historicized in chapter 2.

The second interpretative layer that I explore relates the performance of the Ballet of Senegal at the Barclay to the perspective of white spectators, who, like myself, consumed the onstage spectacle. The perspective of white spectators is presented through my own voice as a critic/spectator at the Barclay, recording my reaction to the performance while seated in the darkness of the orchestra section of the theater. In so doing I have shared in the arrogance of the dance critic by assuming that my interpretation of the performance speaks for and to other white spectators. Yet, unlike the modernist dance critic, I have deconstructed my own interpretation of the performance to make explicit the political and cultural references of my aesthetic judgments.[7] In uncovering the cultural resources at my disposal for interpreting the performance on stage, I have related the narrative of program notes to larger narratives outside the theater and to the spectacularization of African identities through racist imaginary.

A third location juxtaposes a new set of stories told to a different rhythm: I present Dakar as the heterogeneous cultural soundscape that reconfigures the interpretation of *Pangols* according to a new set of narrative frameworks. Rather than focusing on its reception by a white international audience, I interpret the performance from the point of view of its producers, interrogating the dance scene in the nation's capital following the meandering path of dance makers. My analysis, like the dancers themselves, moves back and forth between theater, streets, courtyards, and discotheques. The dances presented onstage by the National Ballet of Senegal acquire meaning from the disparate social spaces that the dancers traverse, referring to each other in a continual play of resonances and juxtapositions.

These three interpretative layers signal a new configuration of power between the three orders of knowledge and the respective narratives on African dance that they represent. In Mudimbe's theoretical schema, the Order of the Other is dependent on the Order of the Same. The Order of the Same is the central point of departure in Mudimbe's analysis, and as such it would occupy the position of the base in my polyrhythmic construction. In contrast, I metaphorically position Senghor's interpretation of the work of the National Ballet of Senegal, which belongs to the Order of the Other, at the base of the drum ensemble. In so doing I intend to displace the centrality that Mudimbe gives to colonialism and to argue that although the choreographic work of the Ballet, as a representative of neotraditional dance forms, has been shaped by colonial history, it is not contained by it. As Senghor has argued, the steady rhythm of the drums carries significant continuities with the precolonial past. The griots, as the guardians of dance traditions and as a caste that finds its origins in precolonial social formations, are a testament to historical continuities and Afrocentric realities that have interacted with the colonial experience but have not been created by it. I thus situate the racist narratives of world dance that depend on colonial history (and pertain to the Order of the Same) in the second layer of the ensemble, refusing to make the colonial experience the time signature of African history and its conceptual interpretive matrix.

Finally, by situating dance makers and performers in Dakar within the third layer of my polyrhythmic construction, I give them the position that belongs to the master drummer. The master drummer has the power to improvise, the freedom to break out of established patterns of action. As I argue in chapter 7, this creative freedom assumes great knowledge because it must respect the harmony of established interactions. An inexperienced drummer, if given the freedom to improvise, could ruin the harmony of the drum ensemble with a cacophony of incoherent sounds. This analogy allows me to argue that dance makers in Dakar, as masters of their own dance traditions, continually create new variations and forms, making tradition not a stable and ossified corpus of dances but a vibrant, ever-changing, pulsating reality. This reality pertains to the Third Dis/Order as an improvised intervention on the previous two orders. If the Order of the Same carries all the weight of the colonial experience, and the Order of the Other carries the weight of national culture, as the official ideology of the Senghorian state (and its successor Abdou Diouf), the Third Dis/Order marks the shift to unofficial culture. This culture can be understood as the mobile, survivalist tactic of the masses engaged in the informal economic sector and delinked from state control and protection. By calling this shifting mass culture the Third Dis/Order, I intend to underline its heterogeneity, which contrasts with the homogeneous narratives of the previous two orders, as well as the chronic reality of crisis that engenders it.

These three layers of interpretation of the work of the National Ballet of Senegal do not exhaust nor adequately represent the whole of *Pangols*. Most notably I have not addressed the meaning of the performance from a Pan-African perspective, nor have I tried to document historically the choreographic process by which the dances presented onstage were created and maintained among different communities. I hope that other scholars will bring forth these aspects of the work of the National Ballet, adding texture and depth to its cultural project. My own enduring preoccupation (as staged at the beginning of this introduction) has been defined by my positionality vis-à-vis the work of the Ballet, which has led me to confront the memory of white racism. The concept of polyrhythms helps clarify that "memory" does not imply that such racism is a thing of the past but rather that it depends on sedimentations centuries deep. The perniciousness and effectiveness of racism rests on its longevity and centuries of refinement and adjustments.

What do I mean by (white) racism? With the multiplicity of historical processes that have been analyzed under this heading and the plethora of discourses that have proliferated around this word, clarifications are necessary. My conceptualization of racism follows Frantz Fanon's (1963) and Etienne Balibar and Immanuel Wallerstein's (1991) preoccupation with the dialectical tension between racism, nationalism, and class. According to these scholars, racism refers to the naturalization of social differences that has been articulated in relation to Eurocentric representations of modern history and the related project of nation building. In this context, the continually unfinished process of peopling the nation has required the ideological externalization and internalization of political groupings independently from the configuration of territorial boundaries. Race and class have dialectically structured relations of production and social reproduction within and between nations, while simultaneously being manipulated by competing social groups as idioms in the ideological project of peopling the nation.

By contextualizing white racism within large historical processes rather than within psychological and culturalist discussions centered on individual attitudes, I intend to signal my own fundamental assumptions about race and racism. Like Fanon, Balibar, and Wallerstein, I give historical and ideological precedent to racism over race. While "racism" refers to the historical processes through which social relations are racialized (naturalized as inevitable), "race" is an objectified category that is itself the product of racialization. Thus, the objectification of race is precisely the work of racism, or a reaction to it. In the field of African art and African dance, a narrow culturalist focus has fed racialized readings of African arts leading to an endless proliferation of ethnic typologies. The field of dance ethnology, by assuming ethnicity to be the fundamental unit of analysis for African dance, failed to interrogate the processes of ethnic identity formation and their relation to artistic production. Rather, ethnicity functioned as an already given and self-evident matrix for the categorization of dances, giving rise to a discourse centered obsessively on "authenticity." Authenticity within this context operates to silence and aestheticize politics, just as racist discourse reduces social and political differences to visually detectable (aesthetic) differences. I make this point in chapters 1, 2, and 3, where I relate the ethnicization of African dance to a historical analysis of colonial racism. Beginning with chapter 4, I proceed to explore the analytical tensions between the categories of ethnicity, class, and nation vis-à-vis the dance practices of Dakar's inhabitants.

Chapter 4 addresses the central process of ethnic formation within postcolonial Senegal through a discussion of women's *sabar* dancing in the low-income quarters of Dakar and the related process of Wolofization. Wolofization has been identified by Mamadou Diouf and Momar Coumba Diop (1990) as the primary process of national cultural integration of postcolonial Senegal. It refers to the appropriation of cultural elements that are historically associated with the Wolof ethnicity by other ethnic groups. *Sabars*[8] are part of this process of Wolofization because *sabar* dances belong to the Wolof cultural complex and are appropriated and performed by women of multiple ethnicities.[9] The city women who engage in *sabar* dancing operate within Dakar's informal economy, where the line between work and nonwork is dangerously blurred and needs to be negotiated every day through creative hassling. The dance events called *sabars* facilitate the circulation of money among extensive women's networks and allow women to cultivate simultaneously expressive and economic forms of sociality. My discussion of *sabars* interrogates the degree to which ethnic, gender, and class identities are tied together and configured within the boundaries of the postcolonial nation.

The *sabar* circle introduces the subject of female eroticism, which I explore outside of the dancing circle in chapter 5. I address the relationship between class, gender, and race through a series of sexual tales that involve the figures of Black Woman, White Woman, and Black Man in an uneasy erotic triangle.[10] Through a fictional narrative, chapter 5 presents six "tales of betrayal" that engage Black Woman, White Woman, and Black Man in multiple antagonisms. These antagonisms are set off by the first fictional account, in which a young Senegalese woman recounts to an invisible listener a night of dancing in a club and a story of love that leads to rape. The location of the account forces the reader to fill in the figure of the listener and reteller of the story with the image of the white woman ethnographer—myself. My own responsibility in the making and presentation of the story sets off an interpretative crisis that does not resolve itself in the text. Rather than offering a resolution, I amplify the crisis and attribute to it ethnographic value by transforming it into a tale of collective significance. Is this story about the betrayal of Black Woman by Black Man who rapes her? Or of the betrayal of Black Woman by White Woman who makes the story public? Or both? These questions are explored in the stories that follow, which develop the antagonisms between White Woman and Black Woman as well as between different generations of women. The stories relate the theoretical antagonisms between white feminists and feminists of color to sexual antagonisms "on the ground" (of Senegal). They also allow for a reversal of the ethnographic gaze, exposing the "doings" of White Women in ethnographic narrative.

The final story in the series further explores the interdependency of the categories of class and race in the postcolonial context by presenting a heterosexual encounter between white foreign women and black Senegalese citizens. The story introduces the reader to the tourist economy in Senegal, a topic more fully explored in the final chapter.

Chapters 6, 7, and 8 offer an alternative to ethnic categorization of dances by focusing on the labor of dancing within African Ballet companies operating in Dakar, examining their relation to the larger urban milieu. Chapter 6 focuses on the *sabar* dance complex to explore the continuities between the dances performed on the stage of the theater, in tourists enclaves, in the streets of the city, and in nightclubs. I argue that dances on and off the theater stage are connected through the circulation of dancers in different social spaces and through their circulation in music videos played on the national television channels. This reality of flow defies narratives of authenticity that have been so dear to dance ethnographers intent upon locating an original site out of which other artistic forms flow as derivative. In Dakar, choreographic and musical creativity originate in different sites and feed on the whole of the *sabar* complex in an interplay of resonances and multiple validations negotiated among different sets of social agents.

Chapter 7 presents excerpts of interviews conducted with Ballet dancers to investigate their dance training and to explore the specific social spaces in which choreographic knowledge is cultivated. Contrary to romantic and racializing stereotypes of Africans as "naturally" born dancers, I argue that the relationship of social agents to dancing is mediated by their class, gender, and religious identity, as well as by the idiosyncrasies of personal life histories. Finally, chapter 8 interrogates the relationship between economic struggle and creativity through an analysis of the politics of dance production and consumption in Dakar's tourist enclaves. This discussion comes back to the topic addressed in chapter 1, the relationship between white spectators and black performers. In contrast to the first chapter, which centers on the relationship of white spectators to the spectacle on stage, chapter 8 focuses on the experiences and voices of dancers.

The conclusion reevalutes Négritude ideology in dialogue with the youth culture of Dakar and again returns to the issue of ethnicity and its theoretical formulation in the postcolonial state. I argue that Senghor's conceptualization of ethnicity fails to account for the on-the-ground workings of ethnic identification and the manipulations of ethnic-centric culture that engage the youth of Dakar in dancing and surviving in the midst of deep crisis. My reevaluation of Négritude comes at a shift in the political history of Senegal: the year 2000 marked the end of forty years of socialist hegemony, first under

Leopold Sédar Senghor's presidency (1960–80), and then under Abdou Diouf (1981–2000). In the summer of 2000, sustained by more than two decades of popular opposition, the leader of the Parti Démocratic Sénégalais, Abdoulaye Wade, won presidential elections. Wade's political ascendency was soon followed by the death of Senghor on December 20, 2001, which added physical weight to the slow death of Senghorian politics that began with Diouf and ended with his defeat in the elections of 2000. The sorrow of loss for such a towering historical figure as Senghor brings with it the need to reevaluate his ideology of Négritude from broader angles than those employed in the past. His death gives us a certain freedom as well as a deeper obligation to understand his contribution to the politics and arts of Senegal and to reevaluate idealistically (dreaming hopefully) the relationship between global culture and African art that so preoccupied his life. It is in this spirit that I write my concluding chapter.

1

The National Ballet of Senegal at a Theater in California

Ethnic Dance in the Theater: The Audience, the Performers, and the Staging of Ethnographic Research

Irvine, California, March 1995. This is the land of highways, malls, and parking lots: Southern California, the "Inland Empire." My car is my most precious asset in this empire, where the lack of adequate public transportation and a staunch belief in independence oblige us to drive everywhere, often alone. Those of us who can afford to own a car, that is. I am one of those lucky polluters, and I happily jump into the car to drive down to Irvine's Barclay Theater, where the National Ballet of Senegal is performing. It is March 7, 1995.

I arrive at the theater early, and since I am not meeting anybody I walk into the building. I have bought a ticket in the orchestra for twenty-five dollars, and I proceed to my seat. Glossy program in hand, I enter a world where shapes and colors are softened by dim lights, where the sound of steps is muffled by a thick burgundy carpet, and where I must sit among a row of cushioned chairs, each covered by the same luxurious velvet fabric of the carpet and the heavy curtains of the stage. This is a site of high-cultural production and enjoyment; purpose and status are written into the architecture of the theater.

I choose to sit in the last row of the first floor, close to the light technician, so I will be able to see the whole audience and include it in my viewing of the performance. I take out notebook and pen and begin my ethnographic project on the National Ballet of Senegal.

I observe people fill the theater. Approximately eight hundred bodies come in short waves, a couple at a time, or two, three, or four couples, like mature bunches of grapes, the women and men plump and shiny with formal attire and perfume. There are only a few African Americans—or are they Africans?—most of them dressed in African clothes. The rest of the audience, like the group of six women sitting in front of me, are Euro-Americans in their forties or older, middle and upper-middle class.[1] I write in my notebook: "The natives, dressed in their best traditional clothes, have gathered to watch the performance of the National Ballet of Senegal, a company renowned for its transnational tours and worldwide appeal." I smile, sigh, and rewrite the previous sentence: "The worldly Southern Californian audience is coming to enjoy a performance by native African dancers and musicians."

The physical separation between the white North American audience and the black African performers, engendered by the theater's architecture, provokes the ethnographer to assign the term "native" to one or the other side of the proscenium stage. The term carries deep-rooted political implications. The weight of history in the production of anthropological knowledge has traditionally configured the flux of information and cultural exchange between white and black peoples as that between ethnically unmarked white citizens and ethnically marked black "natives."[2] The colonial roots of the ethnographic enterprise have for centuries configured North American intellectuals and a wider Euro-American amateur public as the audience for ethnographic tales in which African natives perform an alien and exotic way of life. I wonder whether this configuration of identities will be hinted at and reproduced by the spectacle on the stage.

My thoughts are interrupted by that unmistakable signal to forget the outside world and focus one's attention on the stage: the lights are switched off. Comfortably seated in the darkness, I softly brush the edges of my notebook to remind myself that I am no ordinary spectator, but an ethnographer. The notebook, like a *fétiche,* gives me an empowered identity.

The velvet curtain opens to reveal a village scene. The roofs of two huts, to the left and right of the stage, emerge from behind a wooden fence. A raised platform stands at the center, and to the right a baobab tree marks a public meeting space.[3] This is the way the audience is encouraged to imagine the village in Africa: the simple comfort of the huts, the majestic and legendary beauty of baobab trees, a warm summer night. The bucolic scene shocks the spectators with its contrast to the urban landscape of the outside world.

The scenography on stage is part of a larger choreography: the First World spectators leave a complex world behind to enter into the rarefied atmosphere of the theater and confront Africa, summarized by the village scene. For eighteen to thirty-two dollars, the spectators become consumers of world culture while the performers represent a local product—their identities tied to the confines of the African village. The purchasing power of spectators qualifies them as cosmopolitan consumers even if they have never traveled outside the United States. On the other side of the proscenium, members of the National Ballet of Senegal, experienced border crossers, are presented by the scenography as natives of an African village, appealing because uncontaminated performers of a local cultural product.

The confrontation between global consumers and authentic local producers lies at the core of the concept of "world dance," which in some intellectual and artistic circles has replaced "ethnic dance" as a more politically correct terminology.[4] Both terms refer to nonwestern dance forms; one emphasizes the identity of the producers, and the other the identity of the consumers. While the term "ethnic dance" ethnically marks nonwestern cultural producers, the term "world dance" focuses on westerners as the ethnically unmarked consumers of world cultures.

Seated at the theater, I recognize the association and conflation of the ethnic with the local and, by contrast, of the nonethnic, unmarked white with the global as a fundamental premise of ethnologic.[5] Quickly, groping in the darkness, I write in my notebook, for later consideration: "The Ethnographic Mode of Representation on Stage: World Dance and Ethnic Others in Euro-American High Art Institutions." I then refocus my gaze on the stage, anxious not to miss anything.

A man is standing on the central platform of the stage. He wears red pants, and a double string of beads crosses his bare chest. He appears small against the baobab tree in the back and a huge sky above him. He takes a step down the platform, and, with a slow, sustained motion, he opens his arms from his heart into an extended welcome to the audience. He speaks/sings in Mandinka. He points to a red silhouette of the African continent floating up with the stars in the blue sky, and we understand the words "Senegal, West Africa." Women's voices resonate in the background. The man moves out of the village's square, and women enter carrying a big basket. They place it on the ground, salute each other, open the basket, and take out some scarves.

Throughout the performance the sky changes from blue to orange, yellow, green, and violet, as if to move us in time with the passing of days, from night to dawn to full day and sunset, and then along the passing of seasons or maybe the passing of years. In the sky Africa appears like a continent afloat in the vast universe—a vision or a mirage? This Africa transforms over the course of the performance. In the opening scene it appears as a homogeneous red mass that suggests a unified cultural and political territory. It then disappears from the sky only to reemerge at the end of the performance, marked by the dancers, appropriated by their feats, signed by their actions: *Ballet National du Sénégal* will be inscribed in white against the red territory of Africa.

Framing Spectatorship: The Publicity Notes

The distance between my seat and the performers is filled with expectations—thick, almost palpable, as I, with the other members of the audience, create a space of willful silence. Publicity announcements and program notes have fed our expectations, pulling us to the theater.[6] Even for those of us who came to the show motivated by our own desires and fantasies, a colorful flyer is available at the entrance—a promise of the fulfillment to come, vouched for by accredited public critics. The flyer shows on one side the picture of some company members dancing on a beach, and, on the other side, it presents us with the following newspaper excerpts (no dates or authors provided):

> [The national Ballet of Sengal] is blessed with an AMAZING ability to make spectators feel happy. Its entire works are meticulously choreographed. Yet, they are performed with such clear love of dance that the program is disarming. . . . This troupe of dancers, singers, and musicians quite literally inspires spectators to ignore decorum and join the FUN.
> —*New York Times*

> Since they embarked on their first tour 20 years ago, these ebullient dancers and musicians have dazzled thousands with their country's most visible and EXPLOSIVE art. . . . [They have] presented the traditional movement and music of their country in the most direct and heartfelt fashion imaginable.
> —*Washington Post*

Notes on the Publicity Notes

I will be helpless, disarmed, leaving behind any sense of propriety to join in the "FUN" of the dances. The theater publicity assures me that I will be watching serious art that is "meticulously choreographed," and "yet" I will have great fun. The invitation to ignore decorum seems to suggest that I will be exonerated from the critical labor usually demanded from viewers of high art. It implies that I am exonerated from thinking and instead asked to respond sensually and emotionally to the performance. I am assured of immediate communication and understanding—heart to heart—and I am thus encouraged to avoid thinking about the complexities of intercultural communication and the cultural and social origins of aesthetic judgment. The newspaper reviews suggest that the language of dance is transnational (universal?)—it speaks to thousands across the nation and across several nations.

An older program for *Pangols,* given to me by the artistic director of the National Ballet on our first encounter, presents a somewhat different framing of the performance. Written for the 1992 performance of *Pangols* at the Jean Vilar Theater (a nineteenth-century theater in Saint-Quentin, France), it presents the dances as a specific mode of representation that can be compared to other representational modes for accuracy and expressive vitality: "This troupe is a crucible that has realized and continues to realize a collection of dances, eurhythms, beats, songs, and poems. And *far from preserving them only in cold and knowledgeable books like ethnographers do, the National Ballet turns it into a lively album* in which colors merge with alternating or undulatory movements, offering these sequences to the whole world" (emphasis added).

These program notes suggest that the National Ballet of Senegal takes ethnography into its own hands to produce a representation of Senegalese culture that follows and challenges the European ethnographic tradition. Choreo-graphy becomes the writing of history and indigenous traditions, and the dances thus produced are to be read by the public of "the whole world."[7] The narrative suggests that the choreographer of the Ballet, like an ethnographer, carefully constructs an ideal village, open to the gaze of foreigners who will enjoy the display of local life. This same articulation of choreography as a representational strategy is found in Sekou Touré's celebratory description of the National Ballet of Guinea, one of the first national dance troupes to be created on the African continent:

> The National Troupe is our roving Ambassador whose mission is to encourage understanding of Africa with a view of creating the most favorable conditions for healthy and fruitful cooperation between Africa and the rest of the world. . . . The troupe is a living image of African culture. The foreign audiences that have seen the lives of our people presented on stage have seen the veil of false exoticism that envelopes the continent torn asunder and have learned better to understand our men, women, and children who are struggling to live and to be free.[8]

Touré's quote shares with the previous narratives the belief that the dances performed by African Ballets will be universally appealing and comprehensible by citizens all over the globe. Yet these narratives also differ, in so far as the American reviews define dance as pure entertainment, while the French program and Touré's introduction entrust the Ballet's performance with an educational component. The French program casts the performance as a definitive improvement over the work of ethnographers. Touré's narrative gives even more power the spectacle on stage, asserting that it will provoke spectators into recognizing exotic representations of Africa and Africans as false.

I will evaluate whether the performance of the National Ballet of Senegal at the Barclay Theater indeed entertains and/or educates in these terms. Does the Euro-American observer, seated in the dark, invited to ignore decorum and quietly yet sensually consume the spectacle, shed his or her cultural heritage to magically share with the performers the traditions of Senegal? Does the power of the dancers overwhelm the spectators with its own semantic energy? Is Senegalese tradition an obvious, transparent category? Does the National Ballet of Senegal offer an autoethnographic representation of the national cultural patrimony that is able to compete and counter (Euro-American) ethnographers' exoticizing and "cold knowledge"?

My reading of the performance will be informed by two sets of writing, the first representing the performers' perspective, the second from the audience's perspective. I have chosen written texts as dialogical voices rather than interviews with performers and audiences to establish a more equal exchange in ethnographic dialogue, matching my own criticism with that of other cultural critics.[9] Thus, the first writerly interlocutor that I engage with is Léopold Sédar Senghor, who represents perhaps the most eloquent official interpretation of the National Ballet of Senegal. The second voice I have chosen is embodied by program notes and newspaper excerpts, which represent authoritative perspectives intended to inform and influence the audience's interpretation of the performance and, more generally, of African cultures.

Take One: Analyzing the Performance with the Aid of Léopold Sédar Senghor (on Rhythm and Spirituality)

I lean back in my seat. The program tells me to relax. This is dance: fun, immediate entertainment. The lights go off. The whole audience is in front of me, barely visible, as the stage fills with dancers and musicians radiating colors and energy.

How can the spectators sit so still, not even waving their heads? The seats gently suggest passivity, immobilizing the spectator's body in soft velvet cushions. Leaning my spinal axis against the support offered by the chair I find myself tilted backward, my feet slightly off the floor. I feel trapped in this position, unable to respond, driven into passivity by the backward tilt. I move forward, with my butt resting only on the tip of the chair to root my feet solidly on the floor, ready to spring into action. But I have nowhere to go.

A group of women has come out into the onstage village square. Singing and moving their arms in flowing waves, they take different group formations. Their dresses are bright red, green, brown, yellow, blue, and violet, each with an embroidery of a different color on the chest. As the women swing their arms, the ample cloth makes rippling shapes. The rhythm is texture and color, choral songs and sustained movements, nurturing like the caresses of a female wind. A flicker of the wrists; the feet mark the beat as the head and arms swing side to side.

> What is rhythm? It is the architecture of the being, the internal dynamics that give it form, the system of waves that it emits toward Others, the pure expression of vital force. Rhythm is the vibratory shock, the force that, through the senses, strikes us to the root of our being and expresses itself in the most material, sensual ways: lines, surfaces, colors, volumes and architecture, sculpture and paintings, accents in poetry and music, movements in dance. But, in doing so, it orders all this concreteness toward the light of the spirit. Among the Negro-African, it is in the same measure that rhythm is embodied in sensuality that it illuminates the spirit. African dance abhors the physical contact of bodies. But look at the dancers. If their lower limbs are shaken by the most sensual tremor, their heads partake of the serene beauty of the masques, of the Dead. (Senghor 1956:60–61)[10]

Senghor's definition of rhythm encompasses all the different dimensions of the performance: the music, the dance, the dresses and the visual organization of colors, the pace and structure of the choreography, the spatial dynamics on the stage, the spiritual content of the dances, and the ethos of audience participation. Polyrhythms establish "unity within diversity" (Senghor 1956:61) across different expressive media—visual, kinetic, sonic, and spiritual.

At the Barclay, the polyrthythmic interplay of visual, choreographic, and musical elements is set in motion by the National Ballet of Senegal through the interaction of three groups: drummers (all male), female dancers, and male dancers. Each group is characterized by clothing of contrasting colors, as in the piece, *Yella:* the female dancers wear bright orange flowing dresses accented by a stripe of black, layered under the dress as a skirt showing at the ankles. The black stripe introduces a rhythmic break in the solid denseness of the orange. The musicians wear dark blue tunics and hats, which are accented by streaks of lighter blue. The male dancers also wear dark blue tunics, set off by lighter blue cloth that reveals itself during the movement of their arms, like wings opening in a display of colors. The contrast between the brightly dressed women and the darkly dressed men is set into motion by the drummers, who organize group interactions at an incredibly fast pace. The dance does not strictly follow the music; rather, it provides an added rhythm to the already polyrhythmic dynamism of the drum ensemble.

Throughout *Pangols,* twenty to thirty performers are often onstage simultaneously, and their actions are coordinated by a choreographic structure that designs dramatic, quick shifts between figure and ground. Unison movements connect dancers across the stage, while variations between or within groups of dancers frame actions in and out of focus. The piece *Khaware* provides a good example of this process. At the beginning of *Khaware,* only (male) drummers and female dancers are onstage. The women form a semicircle, open toward the audience with the drummers in the middle. The group of dancers shifts its weight back and forth with a swing of the arms and heads and a pulse in the feet. Suddenly, a dancer becomes the focus of attention. Her movements are faster and bigger than those of the rest of the group. She lifts her bent legs high, bouncing them in rapid sequences on the surface of the floor. All the while, she moves her arms at incredible speed, creating the impression that her limbs are flying, orbiting in small circles around her torso. She comes closer to the master drummer, who leans toward her and seems to play directly into her body as she transforms the energy of sound into high-speed pathways. Then, just as suddenly as she had erupted into motion, she reaches stillness, accenting her final pose in synchrony with the phrasing of the drumming. As the hand of the drummer powerfully strikes the end of one cycle in the rhythmic pattern, the dancer strikes a position, twisting her body into stillness, bent at the elbow and the knee. In the split of a second she has shifted from a state of intensive motion to one of total stillness. Then she merges back into the kinetic pattern of the group. Our attention is immediately drawn to another portion of the dancing circle, where motion and commotion erupt in the solo of a new dancer. Soloists alternately pull our attention toward them, with their high-energy kicks and flying arm movements, before they merge back into the group choreography. Then, with the same sudden smoothness that has shifted our focus from dancer to dancer, the choreography confronts us with a group of male dancers. They appear as by magic at the center of the stage, as the female dancers scatter in three groups at the edges of the space while remaining united by the same shifting rhythm on their bodies. The male dancers become the new center of energy, taking the rhythm into their feet and combining speed with lightness to produce intricate steps. The fluidity of their steps engages the very center of their bodies and allows them to glide to the edges of the space, as female dancers become once again the main protagonists. Finally, when we have forgotten that male dancers ever occupied the stage, we suddenly watch male-female couples shifting places left to right with great flare and speed.

The breathless shift of focus from performer to performer, group to group, and dance piece to dance piece continues throughout the show, and there is never a dull moment onstage. The performance develops for one hour, and after a break of fifteen minutes, it picks up at an even faster speed for another hour. The spectator is dazzled by the athleticism of the dancers, their incredible stamina and endurance, the eruption of energy, and the power of their performance. Lyrical pieces alternate with more dynamic ones: The soft music of string instruments precedes and follows the explosive sound of drum ensembles, moving the pace of performance from fast to slow, from dynamic to more sustained qualities. The solos of kora[11] players, of the dam[12] player, and the haunting sounds of the Peul flute[13] destabilize the pervasive Eurocentric association of African music with drums. The alternation of group choreographies and solo dance performances also counters the expectations of Eurocentric subjects, which tend to equate African dance with "tribal" dance—that is, with group dances that leave no room for individual expression and protagonism. Also, western theatrical conventions of applause are unsettled by the performers. Eurocentric conventions typically mark the ending of a dance piece with the lights off, while the audience, in the dark, applauds an empty and silent stage. A new change of lights and a new entrance by performers clearly mark the beginning of another dance piece. In contrast, at the Barclay, because the National Ballet of Senegal merges pieces into one another without interruption, the audience is forced to applaud in the midst of action, contributing to the polyphony of the performance.

The gap between the convention of passive spectatorship (engendered by the theater's architecture and by the socialization of the audience into the role of silent and immobile observers) and the ethos of active participation typical of Senegalese popular dance events remains wide. This gap is made visible by a few African members in the orchestra, who behave quite differently from the rest of the audience. During my viewing of Pangols on the first night of performance at the Barclay, my attention is repeatedly drawn to a man and a young boy who yell and voice throughout the show, at times getting up and running toward the stage. At one point the man jumps onto the stage and gives some money to one of the female dancers. Later, during a musical piece with drumming, he jumps onto the stage and dances very skillfully. I recognized him as Malang Bayo, a former member of the National Ballet of Senegal and a dance teacher in Santa Monica. On the next performance, the following night, he has come back (like myself) and is seated in the same place, strategically located next to the aisle. This night he jumps onstage during the performance of the *kora* player and places some money into the side hole of the instrument as the musician keeps playing. On the third evening, during the last drumming piece, he comes out again to dance. He is dressed in tennis shoes, a jogging suit, and a baseball hat, not to be confused with the company performers.

That same evening, three Senegalese women are seated in the audience. Throughout the performance they clap their hands, sing, and wave their bodies in their seats. When the *kora* player performs a beautiful solo, they snap their fingers, making a sound that resembles the musician's gentle plucking on the strings. These demonstrations of appreciation remind me that in an African context to appreciate is to participate: "[R]hythm . . . is the system of waves that it emits toward others" (Senghor 1956:60).

Rhythm is a movement toward the other, an encounter between people. In the circle of African dance, performer and audience are not stable roles. Each person is potentially both, choosing strategically when to shift from the role of active supporter at the edges of the circle to that of active performer at the center of the group. The rhythm produced and embodied by drummers and dancers draws into a relationship; it pulls and motivates individuals into action as a call and response between different social subjects. Furthermore, the exchange of money between Senegalese audiences and performers symbolically and materially links performers and spectators in an exchange network embedded in West African social realities. The walls of the theater bring into focus, though they cannot contain or explain, the complexity of Senegalese dance-music production and consumption. From my position in the theater I cannot understand the significance of the exchange of money on the stage, nor the kind of relationship it engenders and signifies. I will have to search for an explanation elsewhere.[14]

What about the spirit, the spiritual activation achieved through the sensual play of rhythm described by Senghor? "Among the Negro-African, it is to the degree that he incarnates himself in sensuality that rhythm illuminates the spirit" (1956:61). Senghor emphasizes that sensuality and spirituality are not opposites; the sensual engagement of bodies through music opens up the spiritual realm. The drums call the dead and the living into dialogue, giving historical depth to the choreographic and performance process. Will this dialogue be presented onstage and communicated meaningfully to the Euro-American audience?

Spirits do come alive onstage, most explicitly in the piece *Koumpo*. The program alerts me to their arrival. Under the title of the dance I read: "*Masks—Koumpo—Stilts*. The audience is invited to follow a young girl frightened by the sacred spirits." As the piece begins, four spirits appear on the village's square (or are we now in the forest?). They are dressed in white and wear white horned masks. Next them rests a big hip of hay. A group of women (maybe six) unsuspectingly encounters the spirits and tries to run away from them, screaming. The audience laughs. The hip of hay comes alive and captures one of the women.[15] She disappears beneath it. The other women run away, and the white spirits dance in unison.[16] Then the women come back. They are no longer dressed in long tunics; they now wear colorful tops and long skirts with red, yellow, and green balls attached to them. One of the women holds a staff in her hands. She steps right up to the masked spirits. She does not seem afraid of them. She dances with the masks, and then she gives her staff to one of them. A dancer on stilts enters the stage; is it another spirit?[17] It jumps vigorously from leg to leg and plays at the edge of its balance, while threatening to step on the white spirits and the women below. The audience yells appreciatively at its skillful bravery. The hip of hay becomes animated once again, swirling in energetic spirals, like a tornado, turning and turning increasingly fast, while the drums build to a crescendo. It suddenly stops and situates itself at the center of the stage to perform a series of shape-shifting moves.[18] First, it makes itself small and fat, lowering its mass to the ground and spreading it horizontally. Then, with shaking and jerking motions, it rises to a tall vertical form, thinner and thinner, taller and taller, coming to surpass the height of the masked spirits and the women. Finally, with the same jerking motions with which it ascended, it condenses its mass, descending in vertical vibrations. As it lowers itself to the floor, it distributes its mass horizontally to achieve once again the fat shape that marked the beginning of the shape-shifting sequence. The women dance energetically around it, and the one who previously held the staff takes an orange scarf from her hair and ties it on a short wooden stick that comes out of the top of the hay. A new spirit on stilts walks in as the first disappears. It has only one long leg. It menacingly travels around the stage using its leg to propel itself high, jumping and hopping vigorously in all directions.[19] As it exits the stage, the women take over the space and dance in a square group formation. They exit as a new piece begins. A musician plays the *dam* in a quiet, peaceful manner.

Take Two: Analyzing the Performance with the Aid of the Daily Paper and Program Notes (on the Recurrence of Tribalism)

I cannot interpret the symbolism of the mask dance. The details of the dance, like that of the woman tying her headscarf onto the "hay spirit" (the *koumpo*), do not yield meaning to me. Even more importantly, the narrative of group interactions and exchanges is accessible to me only at the level of spatiorhythmic interactions. The content of the images and their relationship to a mythical or social narrative remains extraneous to me, foreign and yet deceptively available in its onstage display. The program, which functions to fill the gap between my position as a foreign spectator and that of the dancers, assures me that I do not need an explanation: "The audience is invited to follow a young girl frightened by the sacred spirits." The program notes assure me of an unfolding narrative that I will be able to follow. And yet I do not follow it. As the dance piece ends, I search the program for more information that could help me interpret what I have just witnessed. I read:

LE BALLET NATIONAL DU SENEGAL
PANGOLS
The Spirit of West Africa in Music, Song, and Dance

Company of 40 Dancers
Musicians & Drummers
BOULY SONKO
Artistic Director,[20]

and on the following page:

> *Pangols. Pangols* is a West African tribal word that refers to the spiritual nature of all beings and things. Each dance in the program, whether telling a story or celebrating a movement or music form, explores the spiritual relationship of man and his environment. In traditional West African culture, the animate and inanimate alike are all possessed of spiritual aspects—good and evil spirits—which control personality and behavior, circumstances and outcomes.

As I read the text I imagine hearing the voice of a Euro-American male, enunciating each word loudly and in a monotone. I recognize his voice by the totalizing pronouncements he makes and the self-assuredness of his voice: In a short sentence he classifies each dance in the program as well as "West African culture." He provides me with the key to understanding personalities and behaviors, context and outcomes, man and his environment. His tone is categorical, leaving no trace of doubt. Later, at home, watching the video of *Pangols* available for sale at the theater, I will indeed hear his voice read this same statement as an introduction to the filmed version of the performance. His voice is loud and clear, with a distinctive Euro-American accent, and his tone is indeed impassive—the monotone of objectivity.

Who is he? I have heard his voice many times on television, recounting the deeds of great American heroes in historical documentaries or the mating habits of birds and reptiles in the famous Nature series. How did he come to read the introductory notes for *Pangols?* Did he write the text? Or, you may wonder, why am I so bothered by what he says?

"*Pangols,* a tribal word. . . ." A word of a tribal language? To which of the twenty and more languages of Senegal does the word *Pangols* belong? Are all of the indigenous languages of Senegal tribal? Or is it the meaning of the word *Pangols,* its "spiritual nature,"[21] that makes it tribal? Answering these questions will not explain nor take away the powerful associations that are conjured up by the program's narrative. It does not matter that *Pangols* is a word of the Sérér language and not some generic "tribal" language. It does not matter that there are no tribes in Senegal but rather citizens of a nation. Even before the arrival of Europeans (isn't that when real history begins?) Senegal was the home of multiethnic states and empires. This information is accessible to cultural and dance critics, and yet it is not made available to the audience at the Barclay. Why not? What can explain the seemingly contradictory association of the tribal with the transnational, postcolonial performances of the National Ballet of Senegal?

Since colonial times, "African tribalism" has become part of the dominant discourse of the West. Reading the newspaper, watching television, or browsing in the African section of a library, I am often confronted with the phantasmagoric image of the tribal. For example, when the National Ballet of Senegal began its 1995 tour of *Pangols* in the United States, I read in the *Los Angeles Times:*

> "In a Paranoid Land, Contagion of Fear Spreads: Sierra Leone, a Nation in Crisis."
> FACT SHEET:
> Population: 4.63 million
> Size: 27,699 square miles (about the size of South Carolina)
> Language: English, tribal languages

Freetown, Sierra Leone—To hear the fearful people of this nation tell it, they are cornered here on the Atlantic's edge by ruthless bandits, savage kidnappers, wayward soldiers and a shadowy guerrilla fighter whose cause has never been explained and whose face is known almost to no one. . . . Maybe the suffering of Sierra Leone is even cruder—a hellish blend of tribal revenge, opportunistic looting spilling over from the kind of tragic diversion that guns provide from the aching boredom of African poverty. (Balzar 1995:A2)

I read the paper as I drink my morning tea. I swallow the political message. The fighting in Sierra Leone is explained through the use of ethnological reason: Africa conjures up a fact as plain as the numbers that describe its size and population—tribalism. Tribal languages are opposed to the civilized languages (such as English or French) as a generic, undistinguished, and undistinguishable jumble of inferior forms of communication. This jumbled communication arises from a people governed by tribal instincts, a people for whom civil war is no more than revenge and murder a mere diversion from the boredom of poverty. The "tribal" becomes a powerful, mysterious, and incomprehensible source of negative emotions—incomprehensible to the rational mind because of its crude and instinctual nature. The irrationality of tribalism is often constructed by Euro-American experts through a clustering of themes, in particular through the association of (tribal) violence with descriptions of beliefs in (evil) spirits/powers. Balzar unfailingly proceeds to perform this pattern of associations, reporting a local newspaper's warning about the disappearance of a crocodile from a rural school: "The newspaper speculated that rebels may have killed the reptile and were planning on using the evil power of its gall bladder 'to inflict death on thousands of people'" (1995:A2). African spirituality is coded as superstition and black magic (bad magic), and the reader does not know whether to laugh at the absurdity of the rebels' beliefs or cry at the tragedy of their evil desires to kill thousands. In any case, the reader is confronted with monsters and monstrous beliefs and a naiveté that conflates the absurd and the demented (yet validated by the reporting in the local news of Sierra Leone and amplified by Balzar's article in the *Los Angeles Times*).[22]

The vertiginous associations provoked by the narrative of the program notes and echoed outside the theater by the printed media powerfully suggest that the choreography can be explained through the trope of the African village as the marker of a tribal African world. According to these narratives, *Pangols* defines a tribal world centered on a village community that dances on every social occasion: to celebrate important community figures, to showcase the talents of young men and women, and to celebrate weddings, circumcisions, harvests, and successful hunts. The National Ballet supports these narratives in its presentation of *Pangols*. The program presents the cultural patrimony of the nation and its people by performing stage versions of popular dances and music of the various ethnic groups of Senegal, which indeed are characterized by marriages and baptisms, circumcision ceremonies, rallies for political and community leaders, locally sponsored dance competitions, wrestling matches, and historical commemorations. The issue is not so much a question of truth—the dances presented are in fact the "true" dances of the people—but a question of interpretation. While the onstage village symbolically represents many different villages, inhabited by people with strikingly different sociopolitical and cultural identities, these differences remain quite vague to the white spectator, who stares at the same village setting throughout the performance and thus imagines the same social group dancing its life away (just like "tribal" people do).

What was initially presented onstage as the idiomatic and idealized locus of African tradition—the village square—takes on more specific, local identities, filled by the dances and music of the various ethnic groups of Senegal. Like the continent of Africa floating in the sky at the beginning of the performance, which took on a specifically Senegalese identity by the end of the show, the village square marks a generic rural identity that is progressively invested with more and more specificity: on the stage we will see the *yella* of the Tukulour, the *lenjengo* and the *cin* of the Manding, the *bugarabu* and the *econcon* of the Joola, the *sabar* of the Wolof, the *manoch* of the Balanta, the flute of the Peul, and the *kora* and the *balafon* of the Mande.

For the performers and for an informed audience, the dances presented onstage do not exist in a cultural and social vacuum but refer to larger sociocultural complexes. For example, the *yella* indexes a Tukulour ethnicity, associated with the Pulaar language (also shared by the Peul), a strong Muslim religiosity, and more broadly linked to the history of the northern region of Senegal. This history goes back to the multiethnic empire of Tekrour (from at least the eleventh century to the thirteenth century, Tekrour spanned a population that later produced what are today identified as the Séréér, Wolof, Tukulour, and Peul) and is associated with the first wave of Islamic conversions in the region. The *econcon* indexes the Joola ethnicity, with its associated language (Joola), rice cultivation, and a strong presence of "animist" beliefs,[23] which contrast with the strong muslimization of the Manding, who also live in the southern region of Senegal. Yet the sociocultural content embedded in the *yella* and *econcon*—as that of other dances—remains opaque to the foreign spectator. He or she interprets the shifts in dance and musical styles only as musical and choreographic variety, not as shifts in social reality. The dances performed onstage are associated by the ignorant spectator with the tribal—a homogeneous category that contrasts with the actual ethnic diversity of social groups.

Historically, the dances relate an ethnic-centric dance repertory to different sociocultural complexes in which ethnicity does not define tribal groupings but rather relates to wide economic and political processes that have shaped Senegalese history since precolonial times. If we understand the concept of tribe to encompass a political category that defines a segmentary group tracing its descent from a common ancestor and acting as a unitary cultural, political, and economic entity, tribes are not characteristic of Senegal. Since at least the fourth century, Senegal was the home of multiethnic empires that spanned a wide territory and were connected through long-distance trade to other political and economic units. Even when segmentary groups existed, they did not operate in isolation but were continually reshaped in relation to wider political entities. Continual waves of migration and processes of fission and fusion defined shifting political bodies in changing configurations that spanned from empires, to states, to dispersed segmentary groupings, with intersocietal relations running across these different social formations.[24] Yet the scenography, centered on a paradigmatic village square (*the* village square), and the rhetoric about African ethnicities promoted by the program notes and the media encourage the audience to conflate the ethnic with the tribal. This conflation depends on nineteenth-century notions of the tribe, which were later reiterated by twentieth-century anthropologists.

Nineteenth-century social evolutionism conceived of the tribe as simultaneously a biological, cultural, and political entity situated along an evolutionary line that defined a progression through history from the Primitive to the Civilized. In this context, the tribe signified a stage of human development that configured an evolutionary and hierarchical relation between Europeans and Africans. This notion was later delinked from the evolutionary narrative of the nineteenth century and suspended in an ahistorical time frame characterized by the use of the ethnographic present in anthropological literature. Yet both narratives conflated the tribal with a type of society (one situated at the beginning of human history, and the other suspended outside of historical time) that is radically extraneous to European culture and explicitly or implicitly inferior. Within the walls of the theater, these two understandings of the tribal coalesce to produce a racialized reading of ethnicity.

While contemporary notions of ethnicity refer to social and cultural differences between political groups and communities, within the walls of the theater the spectator understands the ethnic diversity presented onstage less for its differences than for its similarities. Ethnic difference is assimilated to the common trait of tribalism and comes to define a relationship between African and Euro-American societies, not the specific cultural content of the multiple Senegalese ethnicities presented onstage. The homologation of ethnic difference to the common trait of tribalism is activated by the image of the onstage village and is supported by the average white spectator's ignorance of African cultures. This ignorance is not passive; it is actively cultivated through the powerful stereotyping of African societies in the program notes and the mass media, both echoing and amplifying what Mudimbe has called the "colonial library"—the historically dominant discourse on African societies bound in thousands of volumes and stored in archives and libraries across Europe and Africa (1994:17). The spectators' conflation of the ethnic with the tribal depends on associations (village/tribe/primitive/black body) that, while acting with the rapidity of a flash, have been nurtured by a centuries-old stratum of narratives. In the contemporary context, the image of the African village acts as a synecdoche of older narratives that, while conjuring the historical memory of past racism, remain all the more effective in that they represent the unsaid. As I have argued in the introduction (a point to which I will return in the following two chapters), the concept of the tribe establishes continuities and significant ruptures in the progressive reelaboration of racist discourse. The new elaborations of the concept of tribe, rather than displacing older elaborations, sediments upon them, thus allowing for the most brutal expressions of racism to remain silent and yet implicit in the new formulations. Hence, I argue for the impossibility of an unmediated interpretation of the performance that would speak directly to the spectators in the theater, as the program notes would want us to believe. I also argue against Sekou Touré's celebratory tone when he asserts that African Ballet companies, simply by presenting onstage the dances of their country, can redress the racist stereotyping of African people. Touré's pronouncement remains to me a utopian dream. As long as the dominant narratives about African societies in the West remain racist and stereotypical, the general public in the theater (and the white public in particular) will have no recourse but to the same racist discourse in their interpretation of the performance. In the next chapter I will dwell outside the theater, to analyze the narratives that have historically been available in the West for reading and interpreting African cultures in general and African dances in particular.

2

African Dance, Africanist Discourse, and Négritude

This chapter applies the genealogical method of Michel Foucault and its appropriation by V. Y. Mudimbe to interrogate the constitution of "African Dance" as an object of study and a discursive field. Mudimbe, in *The Invention of Africa* (1988) and *The Idea of Africa* (1994), interrogates the ideological operations that have enabled the definition of Africa as a unit of meaning, as one concept, so that we can talk of *African* history, *African* politics, *African* arts, and *African* dance. Mudimbe asks: Is a truly Africanist discourse possible, and how does it come to be constituted as such? What kind of simplifications and processes of abstraction are necessary to reduce a heterogeneous space, marked by different histories, to one powerful word/world, "Africa"? Mudimbe argues that "Africa" as an intellectual space has been constructed in opposition to European civilizations, whereby local African discourses have been domesticated under western epistemological orders.

Two different but related ideological operations have defined Africa as a unitary discursive entity: one, as a space of negativity and lack (epistemological Eurocentrism); the other, as a space of saturated specificities and stubborn essences (epistemological ethnocentrism). I call these, in light of Mudimbe's analysis, the Order of the Same and the Order of the Other. These discourses about Africa have been displaced by a new order, which I call the Third Dis/Order. Epistemologically, while the Order of the Same is by and large no longer deployed, the Order of the Other is still prevalent in the western media and among the general population, while the Third Dis/Order dominates contemporary African scholarship, where it defies the homogenizing tendency of the previous two paradigms by recognizing the heterogeneities of the African world and accounting for the historical specificities of diversified societies. I have named it the Third Dis/Order because of the pluralities of perspective that it represents and the realities of crisis that it theorizes.

The following discussion will historicize narratives about African dance within these three orders while providing a historical perspective on the formation of the National Ballet of Senegal. The analysis of writings on African dance articulated within each order will provide the theoretical basis for three interpretative approaches to the work of the National Ballet of Senegal—the three layers of a polyrhythmic ensemble, as described in the introduction. These interpretative layers will be carried through and explored in subsequent chapters.

The Order of the Same: European and Euro-American Choreographers of Primitive Dance

Mudimbe, following Foucault (1973), argues that across Europe at the end of the eighteenth century and developing in full during the nineteenth century, a modernist episteme ruptured into being: Man rather than the natural world became the subject and object of knowledge, producing a concomitant paradigmatic shift from a concern with (cosmic) order to a concern with history (Mudimbe 1988:24). The consolidation of this modernist episteme in the nineteenth century coincided with the colonization of Africa. Knowledge about Africa was thus produced to aid the colonizing process and to give it ideological coherence.

Distinctions between academic disciplines, as well as the differences within them, mattered less than their epistemological unity. Historical, cultural, and biological differences were mapped along a grid established according to western imperatives and classificatory schema: geography as mapping of territories, anatomy and biology as mapping of bodies, anthropology as mapping of cultures, and theology as mapping of destinies. Each discipline configured an evolutionary schema so that the construction of western history as the apogee of human evolution was evenly distributed across all fields of knowledge, from the natural sciences to the human sciences, prescribing for the African continent a single trajectory: cultural and economic domination.

The discipline of anthropology, born in this period, was at once the intellectual side of the colonial project—concerned with the study of the cultures of colonial subjects—and the *other* of history. Anthropology replaced history in the space of the colonies: while European historians refused to engage with African history, believing Africa had none, anthropologists were assigned the task of producing a knowledge of the people of the continent. Since Africans were assumed to have no history, the anthropologists had only to look at present African societies to apprehend their past (a prehistoric past, static and immutable), but more importantly to apprehend the past of the whole of humanity (once thought to belong to archeology, it could now be reconstructed from observation of live "specimens").

History within this order was both an imperial historiography[1] and a totalizing history: "[I]t is supposed that one and the same form of historicity operates upon economic structures, social institutions, and customs, the inertia of mental attitudes, technological practice, political behavior, and subjects them all to the same type of transformation. . . . A total description draws all phenomena around a single center—a principle, a measure, a spirit, a world-view, an overall shape" (Foucault 1972:10).

Rationality—as the essential quality of the European bourgeoisie—provided the overall principle that unified and motivated the history of humanity toward a single determination: Progress replaced Providence as the motor of history. Thus, colonization was made the "burden" of the European people who had the moral obligation to bring Progress to the inhabitants of the dark corners of the earth and, by so doing, to introduce the historical process to otherwise static African societies. In the words of Jan Vansina:

> The gaze of imperial history was firmly focused on the deeds of Europeans overseas, not of any of the benighted natives. Imperial history had a pedigree as long as that of European colonization. It was in full bloom during the early nineteenth century, when it was used to justify colonies and to recruit colonials by providing them with shining examples of colonial heroes. Thus at the university of Leuvan in the 1940s one spoke only of the greatness of King Leopold II and Henry Stanley and the fight against the Arab slave traders.[2] (1994:43)

Imperial history and its contemporary anthropology constructed an order of visibility within the colonial matrix that juxtaposed the singularity of European heroes with an undefined mass of Africans. This ideology was supported well into the twentieth century, as Vansina's testimony makes clear.

Alexander Butchart (1998), following Foucault (1977), has argued that the model of sovereign power that was operative during the beginning of the colonial period structured an order of visibility/invisibility that foregrounded European subjects as grand actors in a spectacle of power.[3] The native populations were made visible not as subjects themselves but as spectators of colonial might. The visibility of natives was to accrue the visibility of Europeans and to enable the measurement of the greatness of European civilizations. Thus, a series of intellectual procedures established Europe as the center of the world and the paradigmatic referent against which all historical and cultural processes would be measured. This ensemble of procedures and discursive fields represent what I call the Order of the Same: "The African has become not only the Other who is everyone else except me, but rather the key which, in its abnormal differences, specifies the identity of the Same" (Mudimbe 1988:12). African "reality" was constructed as an imagined opposition to a European norm, not as a domain with its own ontology. The knowledge about Africa conceived under the Order of the Same was thus the product of a European monologue amplified across disciplines. Africans figured within this monologue only as refracting and amplifying signifiers of European identity.[4]

* * *

Discourses on African dance followed the theoretical imperatives of the times but also added their own specialized knowledge to aid in the ideological process that configured the Order of the Same. The import of this contribution is (sadly) still relevant today, as some contemporary scholars reproduce this ideological posture in their work. I will first analyze a canonical work on African dance of the colonization period, and then engage with a contemporary text that exemplifies how the same discourse is still operative in today's field of dance studies.

WORLD HISTORY OF THE DANCE

I have chosen Curt Sachs's *World History of the Dance,* first published in 1937 in German and English, as representative of the dance literature produced under the Order of the Same.[5] The book is considered a foundational text in the establishment of the discipline of dance ethnology in North America.

Sachs provides a second-degree interpretation of African dances, relying on the accounts of colonial officers, missionaries, and anthropologists. Yet these writers are only seldom mentioned in the text, which reminds us how much the discourse on African Primitives that Sachs drew upon was part of the common-sense knowledge of the times, a kind of public cultural patrimony. While an analysis of firsthand accounts of African dance that presumably informed Sachs's writing may be considered more informative than Sachs's derivative discourse, I have chosen his text because, unlike most writers of primary sources, he specifically positions himself as a *dance* scholar, invested therefore in constructing a specialized discourse on African dance. How did Sachs appropriate reports and descriptions of Africans dancing to construct his own specialized discourse on African dance, and what did this specialized discourse contribute to the general discussion on African Primitives under the Order of the Same?

Sachs's definition of dance at the beginning of his text addresses how dance as a domain of inquiry is specifically positioned to provide a privileged understanding of Primitive cultures:

> *The dance is the mother of the arts.* Music and poetry exist in time; painting and architecture exist in space. But the dance lives at once in time and space. The creator and the thing created, the artist and the work are still one and the same thing. Rhythmical patterns of movement, the plastic sense of space, the vivid representation of a world seen and imagined—*these things man creates in his own body in the dance before he uses substance and stone and word to give expression to his inner experience.* (Sachs 1937:3, emphasis added)

In Sachs's narrative, dance comes before words and technology out of a primordial unity that exists prior to the separation of man and nature, between the subject of creation and the object created, between the individual and the social group, and between unconscious emotions and controlled behavior.[6] Dance as a primordial and prelinguistic form of communication stands outside of culture itself, and as such exists outside of the human domain. A chronological history of dance, like the one composed by Sachs, thus starts with a description of dance in the animal realm: the dances of chickens and other birds, progressing up the evolutionary ladder to the dancing of apes. Not incidentally, in Sachs's text the Primitive makes his first appearance among a cast of dancing chimpanzees: "The psychologist Wolfgang Kohler . . . tells of a female chimpanzee, who, when he once appeared unexpectedly, began to hop first on one leg, then on the other, in a strangely excited manner. We might, indeed we must, relate this with what investigators occasionally report: that when the natives saw white men coming they danced in extreme excitement 'from one leg to the other.' In both cases the dancing is caused by a state of tension and fear" (Sachs 1937:10).

The similarity between the dancing of chimpanzees and natives is mediated by the figure of the white man, who arouses in both a state of tension and fear. The white man—Kohler, the German psychologist, or Sachs the dance historian?—wishfully makes the natives dance like apes, binding them both to a common destiny outside of history. More significantly, the narrative of dancing Primitives is tied in Sachs's writing with the narrative of white dominion over native cultures, as a perceived threat by the frightened natives or as an objective war against an African population:

> All dance is originally the motor reflex of intense excitement and increased activity. . . . Studies of animals, which we have already discussed, and experiences with primitive people confirm this statement. When the primitive man offers peace to an approaching visitor by hopping and waving his fist at the entrance to the village, or when in extreme fright at the unexpected appearance of the white man he hides his women and children in the rushes and does a war dance in the shallow water, we have examples of the simplest type of individual dance. (Sachs 1937:139)

> The pygmoid Bushmen are masters of the whole field of dance, from the purely religious standing dance to the wild and passionate one-legged jump, and convulsive dances of the young fellows drunk with love. They are so transported in the dance that in the Boer War they could be surrounded and shot down in droves while dancing. (16)

In the first passage, the Primitive reacts through a motor reflex to the sight of white Europeans, either with uncontrollable hopping and hand gestures or by engaging in a war dance. Dance establishes the animality of the Primitive because dance itself is interpreted as an instinctual reaction, springing from the body and bypassing the mind. In the second passage, the mastery of "pygmoid Bushmen" in the field of dance not only enables but justifies their conquering by the white man; their entrancement is the cause of their inability to defend themselves and a testament to their low evolutionary status. The ability to dance becomes a kind of litmus test about a people's evolutionary development:

> We must not allow ourselves to be led to the hasty conclusion that because the anthropoid apes dance, man must have been destined by nature from the very beginning to dance. What we are concerned with can hardly be regarded too seriously. If the dance, inherited from brutish ancestors, lives in all mankind as a necessary motor-rhythmic expression of excess energy and of the joy of living, then it is only of slight importance for anthropologists and social historians. *If it is established, however, that an inherited predisposition develops in many ways in the different groups of man and in its force and directions related to other phenomena of civilization, the history of the dance will then be of great importance for the study of mankind.* (Sachs 1937:12, emphasis added)

Sachs's basic procedure is to differentiate between people who have a propensity for dance and those who do not and then to establish an inverse correlation between such a propensity and cultural development. Thus he could state that "[o]n no occasion in the life of primitive people could the dance be dispensed with" (Sachs 1937:5), even if it cost them their own lives, as in the case of the Bushmen. Yet, moving forward in time, northward in direction, and upward in consciousness, "man" would leave dance behind to progress toward higher, more abstract, and more segmented forms of aesthetic communication. A certain innocence would be lost in this march forward, and the magical power of dance would be broken: it would no longer be life itself but would become spectacle; it would no longer be believed as reality but would be apprehended as a mere representation of reality.

Sachs's analysis constructs two intersecting and overlapping evolutionary narratives. On one level, his book is organized as a progression from the simplest societies to the most complex: from Primitive societies (nonwestern social systems with the exception of "the Orient"), to the Oriental civilizations (India, China, and Japan were acknowledged to have civilizations, albeit of a lesser kind than the European), to the cultures of ancient Europe, to the great monarchies of Europe, and ending with the contemporary United States. At a second level, Sachs presents an evolutionary schema within dance itself: Dance evolves from a pure movement form, in which motor activity operates below the cultural level, into "organized movement" and choreography. From this progression within the field of dance, Sachs establishes two models and interpretative frameworks that he employs in his world history of dance. The first model, applied to Primitive societies, conceives of dance as movement; the second model, applied to "civilized" societies, conceives of dance as art. Each model defines a set of analytical issues and theoretical concerns that need to be addressed by the dance scholar, which I present below in schematic form:

Paradigm 1: Dance as Movement
Theoretical preoccupations:

1. Define which specific types of movement qualify as dance.
2. Search for the origins of dance.
3. Classify and analyze dance movements.

Dance is classified into taxonomies that identify various genres and styles (like genus and species) of movement. Taxonomies are organized along an evolutionary schema, from simple to complex movements. Scholars debate, negotiate, and challenge the place that particular dance forms are to occupy within this schema.

Corollary formulations:

1. Movement belongs to the natural realm. It operates at the level of the "purely physical."
2. Dancers as the active social subjects who dance disappear, while the subject of dance becomes simply a body in movement. This body is defined by anatomical features and physiological functions as well as by emotions—the primordial voice of the body.
3. Under this paradigm, dance is defined as a prelinguistic form of communication that allows for the expression of emotions that cannot be domesticated into the linguistic system (raw instincts) because they exceed the signifying capacity of language.

Paradigm 2: Dance as Art
Theoretical Preoccupations:

1. Differentiate dance from other physical practices, such as daily movements as well as sports and physical work.
2. Differentiate dance from other arts, especially music.
3. Describe and evaluate the choreographic and aesthetic conventions of different dance genres.

Dance comes to be constituted as art in so far as it is a self-enclosed system with its own history and conventions, requiring the dance critic to develop a technical language suited for the task.

Corollary formulations:

1. Preoccupations 1, 2, and 3 serve to constitute dance as art, and more importantly as "independent art."
2. Because of paradigm 1, dance suffers an inferiority complex. Dance is the lowest of western arts, associated with a naturalized body, feminized, and primitivized, and as such, dance's place in the realm of art is continually threatened by her bodily exuberance. The dance critic must secure the boundaries that circumscribe dance as an art, upholding strict standards and policing carefully which dance forms can be allowed to claim a place within this paradigm.
3. The focus of the dance scholar is directed toward high art, which is represented by the Euro-American theatrical dance traditions. Some nonwestern aristocratic and classical traditions are also considered, such as classical Indian dance and ancient Greek dance.

4. Folklore is treated paternalistically as the only art available to lower-class social groups within high-cultural complexes (Europe and aristocratic enclaves around the world) and the only expression possible to lower cultures.

According to this schema, African dances are excluded from the realm of art but remain forever tied to the movement paradigm. For Sachs, only the refined dancing of the civilized reaches "up" to the cultural and aesthetic realms, demanding choreographic and aesthetic analysis. Yet, while he established and defined both of these paradigms in the field of dance studies, he compulsively engages in movement analysis throughout his *World History of the Dance*. Only in the following decades did dance scholars develop the paradigm of dance as art into a full analytical system (for example, Copeland and Cohen 1983; Sorell 1967).[7]

MORE OF THE SAME

The preoccupation of dance scholars operating under the Order of the Same, which obsessively focused on dance as movement, is still alive in the field of dance studies and anthropology, oddly promoted by a new set of contemporary scholars as a politically and culturally neutral operation. Such scholars argue for the need to substitute the study of "dance" in nonwestern cultures with a study of "human movement" as a less Eurocentric interpretative category (for example, Lewis 1995). This preoccupation is exemplified by the editor of a recent volume on African dance, *The Spirit's Dance in Africa: Evolution, Transformation, and Continuity in Sub-Sahara* (Dagan 1997) and by the author of the introduction to the volume (Ottenberg 1997). I will now engage with two essays by these authors that present continuities with the analytical model developed by Sachs and that exemplify the dangers that the dance-as-movement paradigm holds for a critical analysis of dance practices in Africa.

Simon Ottenberg, in his introduction to *The Spirit's Dance in Africa*, states his predilection for the dance-as-movement paradigm:

> [I]t is essential to view dance as but an aspect of all body movements in a culture, for dance is undoubtedly related in any society to these broader aspects. Dance is a specialized aspect of a culture's body movement, often associated with ritual and designated performance situations. But there are problems in distinguishing dance from other body movements in a culture. . . . Perhaps the concept of dance, a Euro/American one, like the concept of art and aesthetics, when applied to Africa adds more confusion and distortion than if

we begin with the idea of movement in a culture and try to analyze its various forms. (1997:10)

Ottenberg goes on to contradict his own recommendation to substitute the term "movement" for "dance" and combines the two to analyze "dance movement" in Africa. The result of this preoccupation is exemplified by his discussion of "sexual matters" as one of the issues worthy of notice in this general introduction to African dance:

> Sexual matters sometimes play a role in African dancing. Males who are superb dancers, in my observation, attracted females, and equally those the other way around. Dance may involve sexual-like movements and gestures which are acceptable in performance but not otherwise in public non-secular dances which serve ritual purposes. Dance situations may create an air of sexual freedom that encourages liaisons and matings, particularly if the dance is held way into the night and drinking occurs. . . . The difference in dance movements of each gender in a culture, when they occur, may relate to innate physical differences of the sexes, and quite likely to motor behavior associated with their respective work roles in society. (13–14)

It is hardly imaginable that Ottenberg would use the same interpretative framework when writing about ballet, ascribing the difference in style of dancing organized along gender lines to "innate physical differences of the sexes" (which would thus be universal and operate across cultures) or even as the result of differences in the "motor behavior" of performers—motor behavior associated with their work in the studio or outside of it. Rather, it is the African body that allows for such statements to be made and conceived, following a well-established line of thought, developed under the Order of the Same.

The disturbing resemblance between Sachs's interpretation of African dance in *World History of the Dance* and that of Ottenberg's and Dagan's, writing in *The Spirit's Dance in Africa,* is implied by the title of the latter volume. Like the writing on African dance under the Order of the Same, the title and organization of the book stress the continuities between an ancient African past and a contemporary African present, linked by an unchanging dance tradition. These continuities are conceived through the asocialization of dancers, who are denuded of social identity and reduced to anatomical bodies in motion. This procedure, typical of Sachs and the paradigm of dance analysis developed under the Order of the Same, is also deployed by Dagan in her essay, "Origin and Meaning of Dance's Essential Body Positions and Movements." Let's follow its logic in Dagan's text.

Dagan defines *the* "essential body position in African dance," a position shared not only by all dancers on the continent but, predictably, by generations of dancers from "time immemorial": "The natural bends [of all the body's joints] as the essence of the African dance [*sic*] has unquestionably existed in Africa since time immemorial. Unknown prehistoric artists throughout Africa and over the ages captured those dance bends and froze them in time by engraving them in many caves" (1997:105). "The natural dance bends" that Dagan constructs position the body of *the* African dancer bent at the joints of the ankles, knees, waist, elbows, and neck, leaning down toward the earth and forward.

Dagan proceeds to uncover the meaning of the natural bends in African dance by abstracting their significance out of her observations, filming, and recording of 252 Togolese dances during her fieldwork in 1973. She argues that these dances engage performers in "the natural dance bends as the essential body position for dance in Africa" (112–13), a position that, while always present, offers typological variations organized along nine different categories. These categories represent the narrative themes of the dances that Dagan analyzed during her fieldwork and relate the dances to "life experience," making the body bends "deeply rooted in society's needs and objectives, clearly defined by each dance theme" (119). Dagan divides the dances into two categories: those with no religious purpose, performed for entertainment, and those with a religious purpose and content. Since the nonreligious dances are always performed to entertain, she concentrates her analysis on the second set of dances and their nine themes. She relates each of the narrative themes of the dances to the natural body bends (leaving us wondering why dances performed to "entertain" require performers to bend down and forward in the essential body position). Dagan identifies the following themes: "initiation, courting, funeral, work, dry season, war, hunting, healing, black magic" (114). This list strikingly resembles Sachs's (more succinct) thematic list on Primitive dances of the "extroverted" type: initiation dances, fertility dances, funeral dances, animal dances, and weapon dances. Not only the themes considered but also the narratives produced under each theme present strong echoes and similarities between the two texts. One example will suffice to elucidate this claim:

> *The Fertility Theme: Origin and Meaning in Dance.* In reality, to ensure continuity to sustain life, one has to perform the procreation acts of *sexual intercourse, childbirth, and childcare.* The essential body position and movements, particularly of females making love and giving birth, requires *natural bends.* The natural bends are essential for the openness of the hip bones. It allows the body to be flexible, sensitive, and agile in love making (experienced

by all adults, male and female) and childbirth movements (experienced by females). . . . The different style between the hip movements in dances, of various groups, are probably derivative of the customs and techniques of each group's sexual-behavior patterns. (Dagan 1997:115)

Human fertility dances in their purest form are drawn from two different phases of sexual intercourse: the meeting and wooing, and the act itself. . . . In Negro Africa to be sure, the mimetic form of mating dances seems to have lost all religious sanctification and to have become an out and out dance of lust. As an example we shall cite the nightly dances of the Suaheli women, in which the young men look on and criticize the sexual artistry of each dancer. The whole thing is only a presentation of the functions of the female coitus. (Sachs 1937:93)

While Dagan's tone is matter-of-fact, eschewing evaluative judgments like Sachs's remark on the lust of the "Negro African," the two texts construct the dance of the African (both significantly in the singular) as an unmediated relation to the natural realm. Dagan functionally relates the bent body of the African dancer to domains of action outside of the field of dance. In fact, the nine narrative themes in her typology are related to domains of action that as a whole can be taken to constitute the way of life of the Africans, who court each other, have sex and make children, perform initiation rituals and funerals, pray for rain, perform healing and black magic, hunt, and work. The category of work includes "ploughing, seeding, harvesting, hut building, pounding, washing laundry, chopping or climbing a tree, and even loading or unloading a truck" (Dagan 1997:117). These domains resemble Sachs's characterization of the life of Primitive people intent at reproducing and working in the fields but preferably hunting, making war, and worshipping.

Dagan invites us to imagine the body of the African permanently stooped as members of "the opposite sex" court each other and mate in the typical style of "agile love making experienced by all adult male and women" and then give birth, or, in the same stooped position, climb a tree, do laundry, and "even load and unload a truck." Is the "even" supposed to remark on the extraordinary presence of a truck among the Primitive, who are considered external to and distant from anything mechanical and industrial? Is it remarkable that, confronted with a westernized machine, the African body maintains its original natural bends rather than westernizing to an erect position to unload the truck and then stooping over again as he or she goes back to hunting or working the fields?

Dagan's naturalization of the African body (generalized out of a "Togolese" dancing body) requires the naturalization of *social* activities into *physical* activities, which can then be taken out of history and geography and assigned to an essentialized, atemporal body. Yet this body, in apparent contradiction with its ahistorical and ageographical character, is African. This contradiction is only apparent if we understand that "African" in Dagan's narrative is not a marker of sociohistorical identity but of a physical type, that is, a race. The physicalization of social acts serves as the theoretical link to this construction of the African as a racial type. We can witness this operation in the passage cited above, where the eminently social act of giving birth is naturalized as a physical activity that shapes the body according to its imperatives. Dagan interprets birthing not as a social act that involves cultural agents but as a purely physical activity—"childbirth movements"—that overdetermines the functioning of the body and shapes it according to its natural imperatives. Why the courting, mating, and birthing of non-Africans do not produce a similarly stooped-over body can only be understood by recourse to racial discourse. Either those other bodies are not overdetermined by nature, because they are different bodies, or the same sexual acts are not purely physical but rather have been mediated by culture to be transformed into social acts. Both of these lines of reasoning were used by scholars of the Order of the Same, who, like Sachs, argued that the Primitive is biologically different from the Civilized, and that the "social life" of Primitives is nothing more than the motor reflex of raw instincts and primordial drives. Civilized people, in contrast, are able to mediate action through the filter of culture, and their behavior cannot be comprehended as a purely physical activity but must be accounted for through sociological and historical analysis. Dagan's insistence on defining the movements of dancers as "natural" (e.g. "natural movement vocabulary," "natural body bends," "natural physical ability of each individual dancer") turns the movements of African dancers into a purely physical category, separate from other kinds of "movement." Is *natural* movement perhaps distinct from the *social* or *cultural* movement of non-African dancers? Dagan's reductionist logic is relentlessly applied throughout her analysis and repeated for each of the nine types of dances that she discusses. In each instance "customs" are related to behavior, then behavior is interpreted as motor activity.

Is the striking similarity of Dagan's and Sachs's logic—applied fifty years apart—the result of a confrontation with an African reality that speaks to the authors and informs their concerns? Or is it rather, as Mudimbe argues, the product of stubborn western epistemes that construct the field of African dance and the kind of discourse that can be produced within it? Can *the* African dancer be salvaged from racist stereotyping when the racializing logic of colonialism is deployed to explain, describe, and make visible the subject who dances? What other discursive practices are available to the contemporary dance scholar? To begin answering this question, I will continue to follow the reconfiguration of Africanist narratives in dialogue with the shifting historical realities of the African continent. I will then analyze Leopold-Sédar Senghor's writings on African dance as emblematic of the new dance scholarship developed under the Order of the Other.

The Order of the Other and Négritude

The Order of the Same was the dominant paradigm in the scholarly engagement with Africa from the end of the nineteenth century through the first quarter of the twentieth century (Mudimbe 1988; 1994). Beginning with the 1920s and culminating with the national liberation movements sweeping across the African continent, a new paradigm—the Order of the Other— began to dominate Africanist discourses. Africans (still Primitives) became the focus of the colonial gaze not as simple refractors of colonial might but as subjects in themselves. Two fundamental currents provoked this shift. On one side, the people of the colonies organized toward the long process of decolonization, establishing international political links of rippling echoes, calls and responses, among leading intellectuals from the continents of India, Asia, and Africa. Colonial subjects disrupted the European monologue established under the Order of the Same, speaking back to the body of knowledge constructed under its regime. On the other side, many of the colonial apparatuses solidified in the years between the two world wars, and with the expansion of capitalism on the African continent came new exigencies of control and domination (Butchart 1998). The integration of the population into the capitalist mode of production, whether as miners or as cultivators of cash crops for export, required the colonizers to engage with the "customs," political structures, and "mental habits" of the colonized. Thus, the trope of the Primitive acquired new characteristics that differed from the images constructed under the Order of the Same.

The most significant shift was the reconfiguration of Primitive subjectivity away from a Eurocentric world (which forcefully denied the Primitive a subjectivity proper) into one that was ethnocentric. If scholars under the Order of the Same construed Africa as a lack, a negation, and an absence, the scholars of the Order of the Other acknowledged the existence of African culture(s) and their specificities. Yet the supposed alterity of African societies was construed from without, as a radical difference from a European norm rather than a difference articulated within Africa itself.[8] Thus, rather than making room for African pluralities (multiple social realities), the Order of the Other essentialized ethnicity as the ontological difference between Primitives and the Civilized and ascribed cultural specificities to the latter while denying them to the former. The concept of the tribe was central to this essentializing procedure and provided conceptual continuities between the two orders. While scholars of the Order of the Other rejected the social evolutionism of the scholars of the previous order, they argued for an ahistorical cultural relativism that reified the understanding of African societies as racialized "types." If under the Order of the Same the tribe was configured to index a stage of development along an evolutionary line, an intermediary between the "bands" of hunter-gathers and state formations, scholars of the Order of the Other suspended the tribe in a historical limbo, proclaiming agnosticism about past origins and future developments. The use of the ethnographic present in ethnographers' monographs produced a form of historical presentism by which the concept of tribe, inscribed on African societies by the historical realities of colonialism, was projected backward and assumed to have characterized "original" African societies untouched by contact with Europeans. This backward projection justified and silenced the policies of colonial administrators, intent upon fixing populations within discrete political and territorial boundaries.

The racialization of ethnicity was assumed and deployed not only by colonial agents but also by anticolonial intellectuals like Leopold-Sédar Senghor. Thus the Order of the Other united under the same episteme ethnophilosophy and ethnohistory, a certain brand of anthropology focused on cultural relativism and ideologies of otherness like Négritude.[9] Senghor's Négritude ideology was one of the most powerful discourses of the Order of the Other.

* * *

Négritude developed in Paris during the late 1930s and 1940s as a vocal expression of the experiences of African Diasporic intellectuals in the French colonial capital. Aimé Césaire, Léon Gontran-Damas, Leopold-Sédar Senghor, Birago Diop, Alioune Diop, Christiane Diop, and Jacques Rabemananjara are among the most notable intellectual figures associated with the movement. The term "Négritude" first appeared in print in Aimé Césaire's *Cahier d'un Retour au Pays Natale* (1939) and was then forcefully appropriated by Senghor, who elaborated the concept into a full ideology. Yet, as Bennetta Jules-Rosette (1992; 1998) and Mudimbe (1992) remind us, Négritude was foremost a political and cultural movement that did not belong to any single individual but rather was promoted and channeled through the publishing and organizing activities of *Présence Africaine*.

leged poetry and artistic expression because they believed in the interdependence of aesthetics and politics and because they understood that the very possibility of speaking particular "truths" depends on the language chosen or available. Conceiving of style *as* politics was one of Négritude's contributions to cultural activism. This connection between politics and aesthetics, established broadly to include style as a way of living (lifestyle), would characterize new social movements from the 1960s to the present.

The artists and intellectuals of the Négritude movement knew that the act of speaking (writing/singing/dancing) in an African idiom within the institutions of white culture, at the very center of Europe, was a defiant form of political protest. Paulin Joachim, one of the central figures in the formation of the early movement, expressed this point forcefully in an interview with Bennetta Jules-Rosette: "'[O]ur vocation was essentially to insert African culture into the civilization of the white man. It was to affirm our presence, pure African presence, because the colonizers had always negated our culture, as if there could be a people without a culture. . . . We wanted to create an African renaissance in Paris, to signify to the European world in which we were immersed that blacks had their own culture and could assert that culture and that presence in the white world'" (qtd. in Jules-Rosette 1998:35).

The act of self-representation by the intellectuals and artists of the Négritude movement was explicitly constructed as a retort to the anthropological knowledge produced under the Order of the Same. The Négritude intellectuals responded to the claim that Africans have no culture with a series of colloquia and festivals that performatively asserted the presence of African cultures. While the first two conferences organized by *Présence Africaine* were centered around a Pan-African literary vanguard (the First and the Second International Congress of Black Writers and Artists, held in Paris in 1956 and Rome in 1959), the First World Festival of Black Artists in Dakar in 1966 was intended to showcase and promote African arts in all their fullness, outside of the mediation of written languages.

Senghor, as the president of the host country for the festival and the fervent ideologue of Négritude, celebrated African arts as proof of the concrete achievements of African cultures and a clear sign of the greatness of past African civilizations. The contribution of Africans to the world was succinctly summed up by the Cameroonian writer Engelbert M'Veng during his opening speech to the Dakar's festival: "What does the evidence of Negro art have to tell us? That Africa, the cradle of mankind, was already the cradle of art and culture" (M'Veng 1966:xxiv). Far from being a marginal occurrence in humanity's past, African arts were proof of the African influence over contemporary world cultures: The organizers of the festival were keen to point out how African arts exerted their influence in the New World through "Blues, jazz, Negro spirituals, gospel songs, the scintillating paintings of the West Indies, and the rites of Voodoo and Candomblé" and in Europe through "painters such as Picasso, Modigliani, Braque, Picabia . . . [surrealist writers such as] Loebe, Breton, Tristan Tzara . . . [and architects such as] Le Corbusier" (xxx).

The artistic sensibility of Africans, evidenced by their contribution to world arts, was at the center of Senghor's definition of Negro-African philosophy. He conceived the dancing subject as the knowing subject par excellence and of dance as the very modality of being and knowing of the Negro-African: "[T]he act of knowledge. It is a long caress in the night, an embrace of joined bodies, the act of love. . . . 'I think, therefore I am' Descartes writes. . . . The Negro-African could say 'I feel, I dance the other, I am.' To dance is to discover and to re-create, especially when it is a dance of love. In any event it is the best way to know. Just as knowledge is at once discovery and recreation—I mean re-creation, after the model of God" (Senghor 1964a:73).

Dance becomes symbolic of the act of knowledge in so far as it embodies a process of sharing energy, that unstable, undetermined vital force that lends unity to the universe and constitutes the "surreality" of the everyday world (Senghor 1964a:74; 1956:58). Knowing is a spiritual act, realized through the "reasoning-embrace": "the reason of the touch" rather than the "reasoning eye" of the European (1964a:74). This essentialized dichotomy between the way of knowing and being in the world of African and European subjects is at the center of Senghor's Négritude and was to become the most critiqued aspect of his ideology. As his critics were keen to point out, Senghor's conceptualization of African philosophy as a dynamic ontology strongly echoed Placide Tempels's famous elaboration in *Bantu Philosophy* (1969), which in turn assumed strong continuities with Lévy-Bruhl (1910; 1922). Furthermore, Senghor's proclamation that this specifically *African* mysticism found support in the new discoveries in the field of modern physics owed much to Pierre Teilhard de Chardin's philosophy, bent as it was at reconciling the Christian faith with the new scientific "faith."

If Senghor's insertion of dance into a broader African philosophy answered racist assumptions of dance scholars produced under the Order of the Same, on another level it reified a more generalized racist ideology. We can analyze this double movement by comparing Senghor's assertions about African dance with Sachs's. Whereas Sachs stated that African dancers could not differentiate between the real and the symbolic, in so far as they use dance as means to change the world—to make the weather turn in their favor, to hunt animals, or simply to relieve their emotions—Senghor argued that Africans' "failure" to distinguish between the real and the symbolic is actually philosophical wisdom. Senghor linked the abstract qualities of African art, so admired by European modernist painters, to a search beyond the real toward the surreal. He stated that this African preoccupation with surreality contrasted with the European obsession with reality and realism, and its appropriation by surrealist and modernist painters precipitated a revolution in European art. Senghor thus inverted dance scholars' characterization of African dance as (naively) functional and mimetic, asserting that African dancers, like African artists in general, were bent toward a spiritual, metaphysical representation of reality:

> It is so that the Negro can be defined, essentially, for his *capacity to be moved*. . . . But that which moves the black is not the external aspect of an object, it is reality, or better—since "realism" has become sensualism—it is *surreality*. The water moves him, not because it washes but because it purifies; fires because of its power of destruction, not because of its heat or its color. The bush that burns and becomes green again, it is Death and Life. . . . This is to say that the Negro is a mystic. (Senghor 1964b:70–71)

Senghor associated mysticism with the artistic talents of the black subject and argued that art is the realm in which religion and morality are realized, fulfilled, and, through initiation, taught to younger generations (1972:34). By stressing the abstract qualities of African artistic sensibility, Senghor rebuked the impoverished mimetic theory of the scholars of the Order of the Same who denied creativity to African artists by asserting that they mindlessly copied the natural world.[15] We can see these opposing views expressed in conceptualization of rhythm.

Sachs, as our canonical example of the Order of the Same, argued that Africans copied the rhythms of nature, first by "slapping and stomping," then by striking the body, and finally by striking the "new noise instrument"—the drum (Sachs 1937:178). Senghor responded by asserting that rhythm was the *abstract* ordering principle of African aesthetics, unifying sculpture, dance, music, and poetry (Senghor 1956b:60):

> Once more, Africa teaches that art is not photography; if there are images they are rhythmical. I can suggest or create anything—a man, a moon, a fruit, a smile, a tear—simply by assembling shapes and colors (painting/sculpture), shapes and movement (dance), timbre and tone (music) provided that *this as-*

sembling is not aggregation, but that it *is ordered and, in short, rhythmical.* For
it is rhythm—the main virtue, in fact, of Négritude—that gives the work of art
its beauty. *Rhythm* is simply movement of attraction or repulsion that expresses
the life of the cosmic forces; symmetry and asymmetry, repetition or opposition: *in short the lines of force that link the meaningful signs that are shapes and
colors, timbre and tones.* (Senghor 1994:34, emphasis added)

According to Senghor, rhythm establishes the formal qualities of African art,
which eschews realistic representation and pursues narrative through the play
of form—"shapes and colors, timber and tones."[16] While this conceptualization of rhythm as an abstract quality stood against the racial stereotyping of
African drummers and dancers as noisy slappers and stompers, however, it remained encoded within a philosophy of alterity founded on the premise of racial difference. Similarly, while on one level the reinsertion of African dancers
into a moral field (achieved precisely through the "carnal" engagement of the
flesh—"sensualism," in Senghor's words) rebuked the racial stereotyping of
African dancers as hypersexual and lustful, on another level it canonized a new
essentialized dichotomy in the field of dance studies: theater dance (western
dance) now stood in opposition to ritual dance (African dance). Senghor thus
established the dominant narrative on African dance under the Order of the
Other, upgrading the image of African dance from one of sexual debauchery
and mindless instinctualism to religious mysticism and abstract interpretation
of the cosmos. Theatrical dance and ritual dance were the new antagonists in
a world in which race still defined the properties of subjects and their creations.
It is precisely this racialization of difference that unified Négritude with ethnographic discourses of the Order of the Other, which deployed what Mudimbe
has called "ethnological reason": "[Ethnological reason] by definition, always
extracts elements from their context, aestheticizes them, and then uses their
supposed differences for classifying types of political, economic, or religious
ensembles" (Mudimbe 1994:53).[17] Senghor deployed ethnological reason by
extracting African dances from the context in which they are produced, not
only to classify types of societies (traditional African societies) but also to define a type of man—the Negro-African—who was himself abstracted out of
history and society.

Senghor's metaphysical articulation of Négritude served the double purpose of uplifting African culture in the eyes of the colonized while avoiding a
too-threatening break with the ideals of democratic humanism so dear to
France's image of itself. Senghor's message could then be echoed by French intellectuals and be brought to political fruition, garnering support for the de-

colonization project among powerful members of French society. Senghor was quite successful in this task, presenting a Négritude that resonated favorably among different political constituencies in the French world: His approach toward African arts gained him the respect and support of the surrealists and the existentialists; his writings on African spirituality pointed toward an easy reconciliation between indigenous religious beliefs and Christianity, and were thus pleasing to Christian missionaries; his political writings on African socialism allied him with the French Left. Finally, his fervent promotion of Francophony guaranteed his acceptance in the echelons of French high culture and culminated in 1983 with his acceptance into the prestigious French Academy.

CRITIQUES OF NÉGRITUDE

The concept of race assumes that biological determinism translates into historical determinism (evolution representing the fusion of the two), and Senghor's lyrical deployment of race turned the decolonization project into a political imperative and a historical necessity. Senghor's notion of race merged cultural dimensions (languages) and biological dimensions (blood types) to produce the "Negro-African"—a new historical subject intent upon proclaiming the value of his or her culture and fighting toward national independence. Yet Négritude was caught between two utopias: It referred back to a mythical historical past (a great African civilization) and forward to an idealized future (the civilization of the universal). The assumed greatness of the African past served to guide the hopeful dreams for the future, and this forward projection of nostalgia constructed Africa as a symbol of purity and innocence standing against the evils of capitalist society.

Many African intellectuals, unlike their European counterparts, were not seduced by the poetics of Négritude but rather saw its political implications and limitations.[18] Frantz Fanon (1952; 1963), one of Négritude's earliest and most vocal critics, was able to foresee its explosive contradictions that would surface once decolonization was achieved. Fanon argued that with the coming of independence the true face of Négritude would be seen. It would echo as the empty slogan of an African bourgeoisie intent at securing for itself the spoils of the colonial state while lacking the economic power of the metropolitan bourgeoisie, and thus being unable to fulfil its historical role of economic leadership. Fanon's searing critique of the African bourgeoisie in "The Pitfalls of National Consciousness" sounds even more bitter today, now that history has proven its accuracy:

The national bourgeoisie in underdeveloped countries is not engaged in production, nor invention, nor building, nor labor. It is completely canalized into
activities of the intermediary type. . . . The national economy of the period
of independence is not set on a new footing. It is still concerned with the
groundnut harvest, with the cocoa crop and the olive yield. In the same way
there is no change in the marketing of basic products, and not a single new
industry is set up in the country. We go on sending raw materials, we go on
being Europe's small farmers, who specialize in unfinished products. (Fanon
1963:150–51)

Fanon accused leaders such as Senghor of substituting race rhetoric for
more urgently needed class analysis and of trumpeting the moment of political liberation as their only legitimate claim to power, while betraying the
political mandate given them by the African people.[19] Fanon urged the intellectual elite to face the challenges of the newly independent nation-states
by laying the basis for popular participation in politics through a decentering of the inherited colonial state apparatus away from the nation's capitals.
Fanon blamed colonialism for having created a strong internal disarticula-
tion in the colonies' economy, which, unless forcefully readdressed by the
newly independent nations, would lead to ethnic strife and the continued underdevelopment of large sectors of the nation's population (Fanon 1963:159).
These admonitions went unheeded by Senghor during his twenty years of
presidency: Senegal's agricultural policies remained narrowly centered on
peanut production, while Dakar continued to be the political, economic, and
cultural center of the nation, leaving other cities and even more the rural areas
with little state resources. Such imbalances provoked the crisis of state legitimacy openly posed by the secessionist movement in the Casamance, a rice-
cultivating region of southern Senegal.[20] Furthermore, Fanon's urgent call
to African intellectuals and political leaders to educate the mass of the rural
people also went unheeded (1963:196–205).

Fanon's critique of Négritude was echoed and amplified at the Pan-
African Festival in Algiers (1969), held at a time when enough countries on
the continent had moved beyond decolonization and were searching for new
directions as independent nations.[21] While this moment of collective reck-
oning stands as a turning point in the anti-Négritude debate, the moment
of Senegalese independence also marks a reconfiguration of Senghor's
Négritude, as it shifted from being a discourse arguing the merits of decolonization in terms appealing to the colonizers themselves to becoming the
official ideology of the new independent nation and thus addressing the
Senegalese population.

The Third Dis/Order: Africas in Crisis

While the western mass media and the general public are still caught in the logic of the Order of the Other, the anti-Négritude critique as well as the larger decolonizing movement had deep effects on Africanist discourse, challenging the most cherished assumptions of the Order of the Other. With the maturation of nationalist movements in the 1960s and 1970s, new problematics confronted African intellectuals, artists, and scholars, problematics that began to surface in the scholarly literature of the late 1970s and 1980s and are still developing today. Mudimbe (1988) was one of the intellectuals who most cogently voiced and configured the new direction taken by African studies, sifting the many threads of change into intelligible guidelines for the future. Like Edward Said had done in his seminal study on Orientalism, Mudimbe deconstructed the Otherness of Africans, showing the imbrications of Eurocentric and Afrocentrist discourses and leaving no easy refuge for proclamations of rightful difference upon which to build a politics of liberation. Like many deconstructionists' projects, Mudimbe's left little room for hope and rather bleakly assessed the future. His assessment sounds even bleaker today than it did in 1988, as the continent has sunk into deeper and more violent crises.[22]

Mudimbe argued that the dichotomizing logic of the Order of the Other trapped Africa in a marginal position, suspended between modernity and tradition and obstructed on both sides. This Africa, neither modern nor traditional, is underdeveloped:

> Marginality designates the intermediate space between the so-called African tradition and the projected modernity of colonialism. . . . [T]his intermediary space could be viewed as the major signifier of underdevelopment. It reveals the strong tension between a modernity that often is an illusion of development, and a tradition that sometimes reflects a poor image of a mythical past. It also unveils the empirical evidence of this tension by showing concrete examples of developmental failures such as demographic imbalance, extraordinarily high birth rates, progressive disintegration of the classic family structure, illiteracy, severe social and economic disparities, dictatorial regimes functioning under the cathartic name of democracy, the breakdown of religious traditions, [and] the constitution of syncretic churches. (Mudimbe 1988:5)

Mudimbe makes clear that the binary logic of the Order of the Other operated not only at the textual level but across institutions and practices, creating a social text—a whole discourse in a Foucauldian sense. Thus it appears odd that Mudimbe, in spite of such a realistic assessment of Africa's predicament, incited scholars to overcome the limiting logic of the Order of the Other by a feat of intellectual rejuvenation: He urged them to address the heterogeneity of Africa and engage with the specificities of national cultural and political landscapes in the contemporary postcolonial environment. Yet it is because social groups had already carved out social realities that exceeded the structural constraints imposed upon them by colonial and postcolonial regimes that scholars could embrace a new paradigm and see beyond the reality imposed by the Order of the Other. Tradition was revisited, historicized, and theorized as a syncretic invention, while a growing interest in urban popular culture investigated the formation of local modernities.[23]

In this context, Africanist ethnographers responded to and initiated changes in the discipline, coming from various fronts: Postcolonial studies challenged them to confront the creative agency of the popular classes, feminist studies called them to attend to the agency of subjects in the making and remaking of gender through quotidian and spectacular practices, while ethnographies of postmodernity challenged them to track flows of exchange, questioning the politics of space, place, and locality.[24]

My own research is situated within this intellectual context and stands as an example of the influence of the Third Dis/Order on narratives about African dance. A more explicit discussion of these influences on the specificities of my project can help the reader follow the shifting content of this book, which moves, hides, turns, and returns.

The choice of the National Ballet of Senegal as the explicit subject of ethnographic research defies the dichotomy of tradition and modernity, because the very existence of the Ballet puts such theoretical constructs into question. Under the spell of the Order of the Other, the National Ballet could be considered the ambassador of Senegalese tradition to the outer world (such was Senghor's mandate for the national troupe), or, alternatively, it could be shunned by researchers who do not consider it traditional enough (a stance often taken by dance ethnologists and anthropologists). The logic of the Third Dis/Order recognizes that, because the National Ballet exports a "local" (constructed as traditional) cultural product into a transnational circuit of high-art institutions, its work acquires different implications, meanings, and readings for different audiences and performers. This gap between cultural producers and consumers is mediated by the global trafficking of people, identities, and commodities across countries and continents.

Tracking one moment of flow across this divide, two sites are here juxtaposed against the figure of the National Ballet: The same program performed by the Ballet—*Pangols*—is presented to the reader/spectator in a theater in California (chapter 1) and at the national theater of Dakar (chapter 3). Yet the theoretical challenges framed by the Third Dis/Order do not let the ethnographer rest on the seat of the theater (a bit less comfortably padded in Dakar than in California) but compel her to walk into the streets, courtyards, and discotheques of Dakar to interrogate the dances represented onstage in dialogue with the popular dances of the city (chapter 4). From this urban perspective, the ethnic identity of dances foregrounded on the stage is complicated by dancers' negotiation of classed, gendered, and religious identities. Out in the urban environment, the figure of women dancers erupts powerfully into focus, suddenly imposing on the ethnographer and her ethnographing a confrontation with narratives of eroticism and desire (chapter 5). It is only through this "diversion" from the stated topic of research that the power of women comes into focus, much as it is only as a diversion from the narratives of the colonial and Senghorian state that women appear as historical subjects.

With the positive addition of *feminitude* (to echo Jules-Rosette's evocation of Calixthe Beyala's notion of African women's feminism),[25] the ethnographer returns, slowly, to the theater, weaving her analytical pathway back and forth between the space of dance sociality cultivated by dancers in the larger urban world and that cultivated by dancers on the stage (chapters 6 and 7). The presence of African Ballets in the tourist economy of the city serves to place the work of the National Ballet of Senegal in context with the work of other African Ballet companies of Dakar (chapter 8).

Having peopled the social world with dancers, the pessimism of structural analysis is tempered by the will of social subjects to ameliorate their lot and the world they live in. Squeezed, pressed, exploited, but not defeated, dancers maneuver out of their assigned lot in life in search of new options, while the urban youth of Dakar reinvent the meaning of Négritude to their own liking, defiant of or indifferent to Senghor's vision. Meanwhile, the Third Dis/Order breaks the ethnographic frame, questioning it from all sides. From this broken frame, the ethnographer can now address you directly: Readers, loop back. We have still to enter the world of Dakar . . . if you are willing to follow my lead. Then, turn the page. I know that soon, it will be your turn to lead. You will judge this writing by action or thought, and I will feel vulnerable, exposed, and dependent on your approval or disapproval.[26]

The National Ballet of Senegal at the National Theater in Dakar

The Choreographic Present and the Ethnographic Mode of Representation

Dakar, February 1996. I sit in a crowded courtyard, the neighbors' giant speakers blasting hip-hop through the air, the vibrations bouncing over the concrete wall that separates the two households. The music thunders loudly once a week, as the neighbors set up a small backyard disco to make a bit of cash. The glaring television in the living room of this compound, with bad reception and flickering images, also blasts sounds into the central courtyard. It brings us the high-pitched singing of a *marabout*.[1] The sounds of hip-hop and prayer mix in the air. I inhale these sound-aromas in one breath, recognizing in the proximity of these differences a distinct urban flavor, the flavor of this neighborhood, of this city.

Pulled by the richness of the city, I seek yet another sound-aroma, the one I have followed like a hound stubbornly seeking a stronger smell until finally reaching the aroma at its source: Tonight I am going to see the National Ballet of Senegal perform in its home theater, Daniel Sorano. Located in downtown Dakar, the Sorano was named after a famous actor of the Senegalese theatrical tradition; it opened in 1965 (Sylla 1993a).[2]

Riding a *car rapide* and walking for five minutes, I reach the theater. I buy my ticket for two thousand CFA Francs (about four dollars) and enter the auditorium. I am told that I cannot sit in the middle section, which is reserved for special guests, but I can go to either side of the space. As I take a seat on the hardwood chairs of the theater, the lights are switched off. The velvet curtain opens to reveal the same village scene I had seen at the Barclay: the huts, the baobab tree, the man and the women singing. Only, tonight, the sky no longer has the fantastic changing colors glittering above the huts. A more stable and generic yellowish light reflects against the back wall of the theater. The image of the African village shocks here, as it did in southern California, for its contrast with the outside world: the city, the tall buildings, the traffic, and the noise.

The performance onstage is the same as the one I saw a year ago in California, yet the composition of the audience is different. In the middle of the theater sits a group of two hundred African Americans who, I am told, have sponsored tonight's performance. A more sparse Senegalese audience and a few *toubaabs*[3] like me occupy both sides of the orchestra.

The spatial arrangement helps to differentiate the African American from the Senegalese public, which would otherwise be hard to distinguish by their looks. The black Americans are dressed the same as the Senegalese, sporting a mixture of predominantly Senegalese dresses of the most elegant style, complemented by carefully braided hairdos and fancy *musóór*,[4] worn by the women, and dressy Euro-American clothing preferred by men.

A rather cynical Senegalese tour-agent introduces the Americans to the side audience, in French: "These black Americans, who have an identity problem, have come here to know our culture, and support our arts, and most importantly to spend their dollars." I learn that the African American tourists have come from Baltimore and Washington, D.C., to celebrate Black History Month and to combine vacation with cultural exchange in one or two weeks of intensive activities on Senegalese soil. In spite of this trivializing introduction, the tour has great political and historical significance for the participants. The visit to the island of Gorée, just off Dakar, which was a major port of exit for slaves during the first part of the Atlantic trade, is for many the most emotional and significant part of the trip, anchoring the memory of the African Diaspora to the brutal architecture of the fort. Does the performance onstage provide another node in historical consciousness, less painful and more celebratory? What resources do the African American tourists have to interpret the onstage spectacle? The conspicuous physical presence of this African Diasporic community, so unlike the predominantly white audience at the Barclay in California, visibly reminds me of the interpretive distance that separates different constituencies of viewers. Their presence at the theater, like the presence of the Senegalese audience, provides a kind of counterpoint to my own reactions, meaningfully relativizing the point of view of white spectators, which I embody and give voice to. While I do not pursue a reading of the performance from this Afrocentric perspective, it is my hope that other scholars will, and in so doing deepen our understanding of the National Ballet's work and its significance in the international context.

The Senegalese spectators, mingling to the side with *toubaabs,* come mostly from the middle and upper-middle classes. In general, people of the underclasses, if they have two thousand CFA Francs to spend, prefer going to a disco or to hear a live concert, where they can dance and have fun, instead of going to the theater, where all they can do is sit and watch. This desire to participate, to be drawn into a relationship through rhythm, comes alive even inside the walls of theater, where the sides of the room fill with polyrhythmic clapping, singing, and loud comments, resonating with the energy and vitality of the company onstage. A few Senegalese spectators also jump onto the stage when the choreography allows for solo competitions that are typical not only of staged performances but of events held in the streets and courtyards of cities all over Senegal.[5] While I have come to expect this engaged response from the Senegalese public, I find myself surprised by their laughter in response to one scene in particular.

During a "hunter dance," I find myself laughing with the audience sitting in the wings. I remember well this dance, and my own reactions to it, from the show at the Barclay: I saw the dancer perform a dull pantomime of a lonely hunter, and I found the piece quite boring. But now the man who goes to the bush, who is frightened by strange noises and spirits and drinks a potion to fortify himself, suddenly emerges as a comic caricature that elicits ripples of laughter from the Senegalese audience. This laughter comes as a revelation, breaking through my own frame of reference. I realize that at the Barclay I was stuck in the authenticity mode of interpretation, looking at everything onstage as if it was the representation of a real tradition, a copy of what happens in "real life." The hunter must be like the hunter in the village who performs some mystical procedure to ensure a good catch, no matter how long ago that might have really happened. The business is serious, the tradition is real, yet I am bored by the narrative. My cultural referents have imposed upon me, unsuspectedly, a literal reading of the performance.

Coco Fusco (1994) has identified literalism as the main feature of racism within the walls of the theater. She argues that white audiences consistently read the work of artists of color as literal, as authentic and mimetic rather than as metaphorical, allegorical, or satirical. Senghor had argued the same point against the dance critics of the Order of the Same. Yet, without the laughter from the Senegalese audience, I would have not suspected that I had fallen into a racialized stereotyping of the performance and that the dancer onstage was making fun of "tradition." Is he, really? I think of another moment of laughter, also in the presence of spirits. The white audience at the Barclay had laughed not at the hunter's fear but at the young girl's fear of the spirits in the *koumpo* dance. I was annoyed by that laughter; I could not join in. Maybe then, too, I was too much in my role of ethnographer, concerned for the integrity of the "culture" represented onstage, feeling the duty to respect it, and thus paradoxically unable to see the satirical aspects of the performance. Do these two waves of laughter, both elicited by a person scared by the sacred spirits, carry the same meaning? Are the dancers making fun of tradition, and thus making "us" laugh, or are "we" laughing at tradition, at the dancers' representation of laughable beliefs? The Senegalese audience did not laugh at the girl's fear. Why not? Was a critical distance between what was performed onstage and what the performance represents off the stage signaled in the hunter dance that was not signaled in the *koumpo* dance? How was that distance communicated? Rather than answering these questions, I want to probe into some of the issues that they raise.

The National Ballet of Senegal assumes an ethnographic mode of representation because it is committed to bringing to the public a representation of the "tradition" of the country. Is the representation of tradition simply the re-presentation of some reality already constituted off the stage, valuable according to the standard of authenticity? Keita Fodeba, the founder of the National Ballet of Guinea, strongly objected to the fixing of value around the issue of authenticity, which he interpreted as a colonial imposition on African choreographers. Even though he was writing in 1957, his words still resonate today:

> We heard so many times the word "authenticity" employed haphazardly in relation to folkloric spectacles! Really, authentic in relation to what?! To an idea more or less false that one holds of the sensational primitiveness of Africa? No! . . . For us, authenticity is synonymous with reality . . . with living expression. . . . That is why the folklore of modern Africa is as authentic as the folklore of ancient Africa, both being the real expression of life in our country at two different moments of its history. The contemporary tendency of a folkloric company like ours [the Ballet Africaine, the national company of Guinea] must be to inform the whole world of the cultural values of those two Africas: the traditional and precolonial Africa of our ancestors, and today's Africa, which little by little is imprinted by western civilization. In fact, it would be even more absurd to fix our folklore only to the past of our country, since no folklore in this world is not partly a hybrid. (1957:205–6)

Fodeba's answer to the question of authenticity strikes us as radical even today, which is proof of the pernicious hold that the Order of the Other maintains on the representation of African cultures. Fodeba's central objection against the primitivization of African cultures is that of historicity and of social relevance. He argues that tradition needs to be dated and situated in history. Following Fodeba, we can ask: Is the tradition referred to by ethnographers and Negrologues[6] an ancient tradition, properly belonging to precolonial times, or is it a contemporary tradition, giving voice to the preoccupations of the "people"? How does the National Ballet of Senegal answer these questions?

Pangols, the show that the National Ballet of Senegal performed for close to a decade,[7] transforms the ethnographic present characteristic of the anthropological work produced under the Order of the Other into a choreographic present. The choreography of *Pangols* is not marked in time, leaving the spectator unsure where it belongs historically. The spectator is enveloped in the same uncertainty and ambiguity that he or she confronts when reading ethnographic work written in the present tense. Are the dances onstage contemporary or historical? Two dances in the program make reference to historical events: "Keme Bourama Song" is dedicated to Keme Bourama, a war leader who resisted French colonial penetration in the eighteenth century, and "Mandinkole" refers to the residents of the Gao empire (which spanned from the fifteenth to the seventeenth century). This information is given to us in the program notes (with no dates), yet nothing onstage marks these dances as significantly different from the other dances in the show. Not knowing the languages spoken in the song, or the "language" of music, dances, and costumes, the foreign spectator cannot situate the dances in time. Neither is he or she alerted to any change in time frame, which would indicate that these dances belong to, or refer to, a different historical time from any other dance in the show. Are we to think then that every dance in the repertoire belongs to the same historical period? This would suggest that the "historical" dances onstage are contemporary celebrations of history, created in the present, rather than belonging to two different historical periods.

Yet the choreographic present employed onstage suggests that the dances could belong to a time period that spans from the precolonial to the present. The ambiguity of the temporal reference is not accidental; it is consistent with the ideological premises of the Order of the Other assumed in Senghor's Négritude and his interpretation of tradition. In this symbolic economy, the onstage village stands as a marker of *African* tradition, a tradition fixed as an original state of difference, external to modernization. The binary logic of the Order of the Other, as it opposes tradition to modernity, appropriates the city as the marker of western modernity while relegating tradition to the confines of the village. To do so, scholars had to deny the presence of cities in precolonial Africa and proclaim a kind of ontological incompatibility between Africanity and urbanity. This implied that Africans in the city had to be rendered "normally abnormal" (Butchart 1998:115). Psychological science was put to the task and produced documents attesting that Africans in colonial cities tended to become violent and degenerate not because they rebelled against or suffered under white exploitation but because they could not function in the complex and disorienting urban world.[8] According to the logic of the Order of the Other, it was only through a process of westernization—acculturation into European civilization—that Africans could endure and survive the urban condition.[9]

Dialectics of Acculturation and Appropriation

To reflect on what westernization means in aesthetic terms and how this concept holds an irresistible interpretive allure for white spectators, I will analyze a photograph (see fig. 1). I imagine that the Euro-American spectators of the National Ballet of Senegal would resonate with a sense of familiarity were they to see this picture, which resembles what they may encounter in the media, browsing through a magazine or a journal. And I imagine how they would interpret it.

Encountering the photograph in the mainstream media, one might expect the caption to read: "Muslim Woman in Dakar." The "western" reader will be fascinated by the sunglasses, which may jar his or her perception of "Muslim woman" (read: traditional) with her "fashion" (a mixture of "western fashion" with "traditional dress"). Let me remark that the reader I evoke here, like myself, probably knows little about the history of sunglasses and has only a vague idea who invented them, where, and when, but he or she will assume they are western. Thus, the sunglasses will be read as a sign of westernization and may transform the caption into "Modern Muslim Woman in Dakar." This modification, precipitated by the sunglasses, will provoke all kinds of projections on the part of the white reader.

The sunglasses will not make the reader think of the weather in Dakar and the bright sun but, thanks to the caption, they will lead him or her to wonder about what kind of Muslim woman we are looking at. The glasses become a modifier of the terms "Muslim" and "woman" and acquire a quasi-

Figure 1. Photographed by Francesca Castaldi.

magical function not unlike a *fétiche*.[10] In the minds of the readers, the sunglasses may iconically mark a modified sexuality and differences in expectations, level of education, and geographical mobility between the "traditional" and "modern" Muslim woman. Like a *fétiche*—a magical object that has the power to "protect" or alter the life of the person who wears it—the sunglasses will stand in for a modification of the life-history of the wearer.

Let's imagine by contrast an American friend, dressed in a suit (let's imagine this suit as generically western, even if it may be made in Taiwan) and Italian shoes (designed by an Italian designer and made in Italy with the leather of a 100–percent-Italian cow). Nobody will think that the Italian shoes somehow modify the subjectivity of our American friend, that somehow "Italianness" will leak out of the shoes and attach to the personality of the wearer, leading her regularly to the opera house, to the incorporation of Italian cooking in her daily life, to the public display of affection and sexual desire, and to her propensity for a late marriage and a one-child family. You might respond that Italian is "western," like American is also "western," although these examples refute such homogenization.[11] But, to confront you with a more dramatic example of "difference," what about seeing this friend in the picture holding a Sony tape recorder and maybe standing next to her Honda? Is she becoming Japanized, Easternized? What about the Muslim woman in the photograph holding the Sony tape recorder? Again, the temptation will be to read the presence of the Japanese commodity in Africa as a sign of westernization, that is, of modernization.

This example serves to point out stubborn hegemonic readings of cultural difference and subjectivity that we have inherited from the Order of the Other. From this perspective, while "western" subjects can appropriate ideas, objects, aesthetics, and practices from other cultures without losing their westernness (in fact turning these items into western things themselves), Africans become less African whenever they do the same, supposedly having no power to Africanize what they appropriate. This double standard has two implications for African peoples: on one side, it binds Africans to an immutable tradition (defined as such by authority figures, usually, but not necessarily, Euro-American), and, on the other side, it precludes Africans by definition from producing anything that can be considered universal. The last point can be explained by the symbolic power relations established under the Order of the Other. Acculturation and appropriation stand as discourses marking an uneven dialectic: While "white" subjects appropriate cultural elements, erasing the traces of such appropriations, "black" subjects acculturate, losing the signs of their own identities.

Against this dialectic, the historiographic projects of Cheikh Anta Diop (1954; 1967) and more recently of Martin Bernal (1987; 1991) are the best-known examples of recuperation of African visibility within western history. These projects destabilize the core of western identity, which has appropriated the ancient culture of Greece as exclusively "white" and as the cradle of western civilization. In contrast, Diop and Bernal argue that Greek civilization was heavily influenced by ancient Egypt, which was a black African civilization. They argue that the traces of ancient Egypt have been expelled from nineteenth-century western historiography to deny black influences at the core of western civilization.[12]

The dance scholar Brenda Dixon Gottschild (1996) has undertaken a similar, albeit more limited, project of excavation in the field of modern American dance, uncovering the African influence on iconic figures such as George Balanchine, as well as the whole field of modern and postmodern dance in the United States. Gottschild and Bernal's projects are important because they radically destabilize the ideology of acculturation that was applied to African societies under the Order of the Other. As we have seen, acculturation assumed Africans' westernization as the inevitable outcome of "cultural contact" (a euphemism for the violence of colonization) with the more advanced western civilizations. These scholars, in contrast, argue that western cultures have Africanized and yet erased the signs of African influences and contributions to the West.

We can now understand how the representation of the city in the work of the National Ballet of Senegal would threaten the premises of world dance that inform the display and performance of "ethnic" art in the confines of high-art institutions in the First World. In such a context, the separation between citizens of the world—the predominantly white world-dance spectators—and ethnic performers depends on the figure of the African village. While the city is an icon of modernity and the visible sign of globalization, the village stands in for the local and reassures white spectators of their superiority, their cosmopolitanism vis-à-vis the villagers, who are supposed to be bound to a narrow and naive rural Africa. What is more, the alterity of the African performers stands in as a guarantee of their authenticity, in line with Négritude ideology. The National Ballet cashes in on these assumptions and is able to commodify "purity" at a higher price than "contaminated" representation of African dance would allow. In fact, while less-tasteful Europeans or Euro-Americans consume world culture through tourist shows in hotels and entertainment parks around the globe, the higher classes purchase better cultural products at the theater. The ethnic dance that is sold within high-art institutions costs more than the commercial and contaminated tourist performances, and it serves to distinguish crass First World consumers from more privileged ones. In this economy, the National Ballet of Senegal carries the "organic" seal of approval conferred to it by the Senegalese government and the high-cultural institutions of the West, who guarantee spectators that they are seeing "pure ethnic art." To concede to Fodeba's incitement to represent contemporary Africa onstage, the Africa of urban sprawls and *bidonvilles* that is the home of the National Ballet of Senegal would threaten these negotiated expectations.

In Dakar, right outside the door of the national theater, the urban world clamors for attention. As the performance comes to an end, the performers and spectators alike are ejected into that world.

I retrace my steps home, walking and riding the public transportation. At home, too tired to continue the ethnographic quest(ioning) into the night, I go straight to bed. Tomorrow, in the warm light of day, the city will be alive, pulsating with the rhythms of its inhabitants, and it will inevitably demand my attention.

4

Sabar Dances and a Women's Public Sphere

Dance and Urban Networks

"Dakar, Dakar, Dakaaaru! *Yeggal, bu gaw* [Get on, quickly]!" The *apprenti*—the boy who collects fares and taps on the roof of the van to signal the driver when to stop and when to move again—pushes me into the vehicle, helping the woman behind me load a bright blue bucket full of fresh fish. I squeeze into a seat, jostling for space between two passengers. The van races off at great speed, only to stop two hundred meters away to pick up more passengers. Taking advantage of the red light, two young *taalibes*[1] approach the vehicle. Reciting a prayer in Arabic and leaning into the van, they thrust an empty tomato-sauce can between the legs of passengers. The older boy chants in a loud voice, gasping for breath between long sentences, while the younger child barely moves his lips.

The man seated next to me and two women on the opposite side bends over to drop some change into the can as the van spouts clouds of dark smoke and rumbles into motion at the green light. Her voice riding over the sound of the motor, a woman to my left starts yelling at the *apprenti*: "*May ma suma wec-cit, yow! Soixante-quinze laay fay* [You, give me my change! I paid seventy-five CFA Francs]." I have seen the *apprenti* argue with customers over the price of the fare and come to physical confrontations with a few of them, if they happened to be young males of his age. Yet this time, without a word, he hands the woman her twenty-five CFA Francs as she steps off the van.

Twenty-five CFA Francs[2] in an economy of scarcity are something to argue over and for. With a twenty-five coin one can buy a thin slice of cold watermelon; a tightly packed tiny plastic bag of bright iced juice (spicy ginger or sweet *bisaap* are the most common); two small bags of cold water; a fruit-flavored lollipop or two candies; a small kola nut; a handful of peanuts, cooked or raw, sweet or salty, peeled or with shells; one Marlboro or one Camel cigarette (for thirty CFA Francs one could buy two Excellences—the national brand); a dose of Nescafé wrapped in plastic; a small square of butter to spread on bread or a spoonful of chocolate (people with a taste for the savory can ask for homemade mayonnaise or tuna paste); a small dose of pepper, salt, curry, or cayenne; five sugar squares; or a handful of dried berries.

The list could continue. A great number of products are sold in minuscule quantities by a great many people: women sitting quietly at the edges of the street, sometimes just outside their homes, displaying their meager products on cardboard boxes; young and not-so-young men in continuous motion, crowding busy bus stops and intersections to advertise in a loud voice the content of their boxes held above their heads; older men or women displaying a few kola nuts on round trays; men selling bread and mayonnaise in tiny kiosks dotting the corners of every neighborhood; or the more fortunate shopkeepers, who sell from the well-stocked walls of their own shops and market stands.

The thousands of women, men, and youth that engage in the informal economic sector crowd the streets of the city each day with their petty trading and services (pounding millet with mortars and pestles, drying fish and fruits, tanning leather and sewing *gris-gris,* shining shoes, or cutting hair). Street vendors and small-service providers are among the most vulnerable echelons of a wider informal economy. According to Meine Van Dijk (1986), more than half of the active population in Dakar works in the informal sector,[3] while unemployment reaches between 12 to 40 percent (Duruflé 1994; Bop 1995; Diop 1996).[4]

The informal sector, with its areas of commerce, production, and service, provides employment for those excluded from the formal labor market while attending to the needs of the majority of the population. Substantial earnings can be made within the informal sector, yet many within this sector earn less than the minimum legal wage and work under precarious conditions, lacking health insurance and retirement benefits (Van Djik 1986; Duruflé 1994). Thus, in the city of Dakar, the great majority of the population is excluded from access to social security[5] and is left extremely vulnerable to a steadily deteriorating economic environment.

Dakar reflects the problems facing the urban population nationwide. With a population of over two and a half million and an annual growth of 3 percent, Dakar accounts for 26 percent of the nation's inhabitants. The progressive urbanization of Senegal has been driven by an old colonial bias toward Dakar (which was the capital of French West Africa from 1902 to 1958) and by a postcolonial crisis in the rural sector.

The nation's dependence on a single crop (peanut)—established during colonial times as a typical form of exploitative integration into the international market—has left the Senegalese agricultural sector particularly vulnerable to climatic and economic changes at the regional and international level. In the late 1960s and early 1970s, the conjuncture of deteriorating climatic conditions and soil degradation, coupled with falling international prices for peanuts as well as the progressive state disengagement from this sector, produced a recession that persists today (Delgado and Jammeh 1991; Duruflé 1994).[6]

The pauperization of the rural sector has been accompanied by the underdevelopment of the industrial sector, due to low competitiveness on the international market, a limited internal market, and tense, uneasy relations with the government and the unions (Duruflé 1994). This double crisis in agriculture and industry has pushed large parts of the population into Dakar without the possibility of absorption in the formal labor market. Under these circumstances, the government has historically been the largest employer of wage earners. Yet, beginning in the 1980s, employment opportunities within the government apparatus have been shrinking as a result of Structural Adjustment Programs pursued under the influence of the International Monetary Fund and World Bank's aid packages and programs (Somerville 1997).

While this bleak economic environment has left a growing percentage of the Senegalese population outside of the formal economic circuit, the government stance toward the informal sector of the economy has drifted between negligence and repression. According to some scholars, the mid-1960s saw the progressive criminalization of poverty, culminating in the 1970s with the ideology of *encombrement humaines,* or human encumbrances (Diop 1996). As voiced by the government, this ideology defined itinerant merchants, sick people, beggars, and "alienated" individuals as undesirable and a "nuisance" to European tourists and more affluent citizens: "'Dakar is again invaded by itinerant merchants, beggars, lepers and alienated people who bother the inhabitants and are a nuisance to tourism. Echoes of complaints from tourists coming back to Europe have appeared in the media, notably in Germany. It is important to erase in a permanent way from the streets of Dakar the presence of beggars, itinerant merchants, lepers, and alienated individuals'" (qtd. in Diop 1996:64). This rhetoric makes clear that the Senegalese government held in greater consideration the complaints of tourists than the well-being of its own citizens: while tourists have a legitimate claim to the public space of city streets, the same legitimacy is denied to a large sector of the urban poor.[7] Such derogatory government rhetoric disappeared from the public discourse in the 1990s, yet the government's attitude toward the most destitute sector of its population has not significantly modified.[8]

The Feminization of Poverty and Women's Celebrations

Several scholars have argued that the informal/formal market divide is structured along gender lines, with a predominance of women in the informal sector. Codou Bop's study of women heads of household in Dakar (1995) argues that women make up two-thirds of the informal sector and are also more numerous among the unemployed.

National and international economic policies synergistically contribute to the feminization of poverty through measures that are biased in favor of the economic sectors that engage the largest number of males, while neglecting the traditionally female sectors of the economy. Thus, the Senegalese state has generally given priority to the development of "the industrial and commercial sectors of the economy where men are dominant, to the detriment of the so-called 'informal' and subsistence sectors where women are in the majority" (Ministére de la Femme 1993:7).[9] Furthermore "[T]he reduction in public expenditure, the cutbacks in jobs, the drop in food subsidies, and the devaluation of national currencies have also affected basic social services such as health, education, social security systems, of which women and their children are the main users" (9).

While women's economic contributions to family subsistence become more necessary and substantial in times of economic crisis, women's work remains at the margins of national and international development policies and economic programs.[10] In addition, high fertility rates (an average of 6.4 children per woman), the increase of children born out of wedlock, and an increase in divorce rates also put women in particularly vulnerable economic conditions (Bop 1995).

Women are not only more likely to be excluded from the formal labor market, they are most often unable to benefit from the official financial sector (Ministére de la Femme 1993:17). To finance their economic activities, women in Dakar resort to informal networks and mutual-aid associations and capitalize on reciprocal donations at family celebrations (Ministére de la Femme 1993; Bop 1995).

Marriages and baptisms are the most important family celebrations in which women act as the main choreographers, participants, and coordinators. On these occasions women hire the services of griots. "Griot" is a general term used throughout West Africa to refer to a caste of professional musicians and historians found among the ethnic groups that in precolonial times were organized under large centralized structures (kingdoms and empires).[11] Wolof griots are called *géwël* and belong to the *ñeeño* caste, one of two castes in Wolof society (Diop 1981:33–107).[12] While *géér* constitute an upper caste defined mainly in negative terms—as nonartisans—the *ñeeño* caste is subdivided into three subcastes: the *jef-lekk,* "those who eat by action" (artisans of various kinds), the *sab-lekk,* "those who eat by singing," and the *ñoole,* courtesans and buffoons (Diop 1981:34). This last group has disappeared with the disintegration of Wolof kingdoms.

The griots who mediate at family celebrations belong to the *sab-lekk* category. They act as intermediaries for the flow of money between participants: while their singing provides praise for the participants in the form of genealogies and eulogies, their drumming animates women to dance and—through their kinetic engagement—exchange great amounts of otherwise scarce cash, flowing from and to the hands, mouths, foreheads, pockets, and dress-folds of different social subjects. The cash flows to the woman holding the celebration, who receives money from other female participants. The donors and the amounts of the donations are loudly praised by the griots, and careful records of the proceedings are kept for reciprocating purposes. Friends of the woman holding the celebration contribute as much as they can afford, while the *bàjjan*—the paternal aunt—is expected to contribute a sizable amount. Fictive kinship can also be deployed to cast the net of supportive relations wider, as when the role of the *bàjjan* is fulfilled by an honorary *bàjjan*—a nonrelative who is able and willing to enter into a reciprocating relation with the holder of the event. Yet the escalation of demands toward the figure of the *bàjjan* is kept in check by the expectation that the amount of money and gifts donated by the *bàjjan* will be doubled when reciprocating the donor (now in the role of receiver) holding a comparable event. The stakes in the spiral of reciprocity can become fairly high, and women go through great trouble to meet their social obligations.[13]

In addition to kinship networks, women rely on other all-female networks of reciprocity to generate scarce capital and ensure assistance in times of need. The *túrs* and *mbootaay* are a case in point. *Túrs* (from the French *tour*—to take turns) make cash available to the participants who take turns in organizing weekly dancing sessions. In the urban milieu of Dakar, *túrs* most often involve dancing to popular *mbalax* music,[14] blasting through huge speakers rented for the occasion together with a disc jockey (always male). In this context, as in the case of family celebrations, dance facilitates the flow of money between different social subjects. The *mbootaay* further points to the strength of women's economic networks and their imbrication with dancing.

A *mbootaay* gathers women of the same age within a neighborhood for purposes of mutual assistance. *Mbootaays* resemble *túrs* in that they make money available on a rotating basis to the women who belong to the group, yet the amount of money shared is higher, and, unlike in *túrs*, women raise funds not only for each other but also for communal projects geared at improving the neighborhood. To raise money, a *mbootaay* may organize a *soirée*[15] in one of the city's nightclubs, hiring a popular *mbalax* group to entertain the crowd, or paying *géwëls* (Wolof griots) to play for a *sabar* in the streets of the neighborhood. The public will pay a fee to participate in these events, and the money earned (once costs are recuperated) will be used toward social assistance in the neighborhood. The *mbootay* may use the funds to build a neighborhood clinic, or to assist a neighbor who has become homeless, or to finance an economic enterprise that can give jobs to the unemployed youth (Faye 2000). The *sabar* events organized by the *mbootay* also serve to involve individuals in community affairs by the common practice of naming the *sabar* after a person, who is then expected to contribute money for the event. To be chosen as the name bearer of a *sabar* is an honor and an onerous responsibility, which the women use judiciously to pressure individuals toward community involvement and social assistance.

The importance of dance within these networks of female exchange suggests that dancing acts as a powerful connective space between the economic dimension of daily life and the social dimension of gender-identity formation. The urban milieu of Dakar powerfully shapes the gendered strategies of economic engagement pursued by women in the capital as well as the dance genre that engages women in the living room, courtyards, and streets of the city.

Sabars and the Wolofization of Dakarois

The majority of women's celebrations in Dakar are inscribed within the tradition of *sabar*. *Sabar* is a Wolof word that refers to a constellation of social events, drum rhythms, and dances. At *sabar* events, an ensemble of at least six *sabar* drums (each different in size and shape) plays an ever growing number of *sabar* rhythms that call for the performance of specific *sabar* dances. While the *sabar* complex historically belongs to the Wolof and Séréér ethnic groups, *sabar* dancing has become the predominant expressive idiom of Dakarois. My own research in 1996 and 1997 suggests that *sabars* are the most pervasive and popular dance events in the capital, held to celebrate births, marriages, political and sporting events, and gatherings of friends. *Sabars* may form as a tight circle of friends in a close-knit group gathered in a small room; the circle of dancers and musicians may take shape within a household court-yard filled with guests and spilling over into the street; or it may block a large intersection of the city streets with thick walls of bodies staking out the danc-ing space and protecting it from the outside world. These *sabar* events are an-imated by the live performance of drummers (*géwëls*), and *sabar* rhythms resound loudly across neighborhoods as a constant refrain in the life of the city. Furthermore, the promotion of the *sabar* musical complex at Soirées Sénégalaises in dance clubs as well as on the national radio and television channels makes it impossible for any city dweller to ignore *sabar* rhythms, if not to participate in *sabar* events.

The popularity of *sabar* music and events in the life of the city points to the Wolofization of dance: regardless of the ethnic identity of the social subjects, *sabars* are part of the expressive repertoire of Dakarois. The literature on Sene-gal has addressed the concept of Wolofization in relation to linguistic prac-tice, yet my own research on dance has led me to define it more widely as a process by which the historically Wolof cultural complex is embraced by other ethnic groups.[16] In the following pages I will introduce the reader to the lin-guistic, economic, and political processes that support Wolofization as well as the debates in the literature surrounding the interpretation of these pro-cesses. I will then come back to the circle of *sabars* to offer my own contri-bution to these debates, examining how the Wolofization of dance practices in Dakar offers insights into larger processes of Wolofization that are under way in contemporary Senegal. Finally, the *sabar* circle will allow me to in-troduce a series of questions about the relationship of Wolofization to gender-identity formation.

Wolofization in the literature on Senegal refers to a linguistic process by which non-Wolof people have come to use Wolof as their primary language (O'Brien 1998, 2002; Swigart 1992, 1994; Diouf 1994). While more than twenty languages are spoken in Senegal (six being recognized as "national" lan-guages),[17] and although French is still the official language of government and education, Wolof is the language spoken by the majority of the popu-lation. More than double the number of non-Wolof people are Wolophone, and up to 90 percent of the population has a passive understanding of the language (Swigart 1992:80; Diouf 1994:62).

The reasons for the widespread use of Wolof are multiple and are tied to the colonial history of Senegal. The Wolof were the first Senegalese people to have contact with Europeans and acted on their behalf as interpreters, facilitating the rubber trade (Diouf 1994). At the end of the nineteenth century, peanut production developed as the main export crop and became the vehicle for the progressive monetarization of the Senegalese economy. The production of peanuts was concentrated in Wolof areas, and Wolof was established as the language of commerce. The commercial centers of Saint-Louis (the first capital of French West Africa) and Dakar were also Wolof provinces, and the progressive concentration of the population in the capital, together with patterns of intermarriage between Wolof and non-Wolof, expanded the Wolof language. Finally, the central role of the Mouride brotherhood in Senegalese politics in colonial and postcolonial times and its continually growing membership (most notably among Dakar's youth in the 1980s and 1990s) have assured the prominence of Wolof in political campaigns.[18]

Leigh Swigart (1992) and Makhtar Diouf (1994) have analyzed the relationship between Wolofization, understood as a linguistic phenomenon, and the process of assimilation to Wolof culture, raising fundamental questions about the relationship of ethnic identity to language. Both have suggested that the Wolof language has become a marker of a transethnic identity, although their arguments have different implications. Diouf writes: "We will not hesitate to say that, in the majority of cases, *the Wolof are an ethnic group that is de-ethnicized. The Wolofization* of other Senegalese ethnic groups, far from being a phenomenon of acculturation, can be understood to a certain degree as a simple return to the past: when, a dozen centuries ago, ethnic differentiation was not yet clear among the Senegalese populations that lived together at Tekrour" (Diouf 1994:69).[19]

Diouf's point of view is significant in that it historicizes the process of ethnic formation and identification. He argues that ethnicity is not a stable category but rather the result of political, economic, and religious alliances that respond to and create new historical groupings. Contrary to still-pervasive stereotypes of "tribal" Africa, Diouf reminds us of a past in which ethnic differentiations were not yet marked. A "simple return" to a past centuries removed from the present, however, is not a likely sociological explanation for the continual process of Wolofization in the 1990s. Swigart, in contrast, sees the process not as a return to the past but a movement toward a new linguistic form and possibly a new transethnic identity. She identifies Urban

Wolof as "a linguistic code different from the pure Wolof (*Wolof bu xoot*—deep Wolof) spoken in the rural areas. Urban Wolof is characterized by heavy borrowing and mixing with French, a simpler grammatical structure, and a narrower lexicon than pure Wolof" (Swigart 1992:102).

According to Swigart, the growth of Urban Wolof is associated with ambiguous and contradictory processes of ethnic identification. Diouf and Swigart both propose deethnicization, ethnic homogenization, and transethnic identification as possible models for the interpretation of the process of linguistic Wolofization and its relation to ethnic identity. Beyond labeling, the interpretation of Wolofization as a form of acculturation to Wolof-centric culture (ethnic homogenization) or as a transethnic modification of this culture (transethnicization or deethnicization) has important political implications. The political stakes of this scholarly debate are made visible and explicit by Mamadou Diouf and Momar Coumba Diop in their book *Le Sénégal sous Abdou Diouf* (1990). These scholars have proposed a strong correlation between Wolofization and acculturation. They have used the term "Wolofization" not so much to mark a linguistic phenomenon but to define the political processes that have established the Wolof-Muslim model as the hegemonic cultural and political form embraced by the nation-state.

My discussion of linguistic Wolofization makes clear how linguistic homogenization has been supported by economic and political processes that are biased in favor of the Wolof ethnic group, and it is to these processes that Diouf and Diop give primary importance. They argue that the political privileging of the Wolof group was initiated under colonial times with the constitution of the four *communes* (Dakar, Saint-Louis, Rufisque, and Gorée), all of which are in Wolof areas (Diouf and Diop 1992:47).[20] The inhabitants of the four *communes* were recognized as French citizens and given political privileges (including representation in the French governmental structure) that were denied to the rest of the Senegalese population until the end of the Second World War (Crowder 1962).[21] Furthermore, the economic interests of the colonial administration in peanut production laid the base for an alliance between the Islamic brotherhoods controlling such production—in particular, the historically Wolof Mourides[22]—and the exchange of economic and political favors. The role of the Mouride brotherhood as a mediator between the indigenous population and the colonial state has continued under the postcolonial state, which has allowed the Islamic religious structure to become the only established mediator between the state and civil society. The continual spread of Islam and the continual growth of the Mourides among the capital's youth reflect the importance of Islamic brotherhood in general, and of the Mourides in particular, in the political and economic life of the population.[23] Diouf and Diop stress how Islamicization and Wolofization have tended to go hand in hand and have acted as integrative processes in the formation of the modern Senegalese nation. Yet the limits of this integration have become painfully clear with the demands for independence in the Casamance region (starting in the early 1980s) and the government's violent repression of the independence movement.[24] Diouf and Diop argue that the Joola's resistance to Islamic religion,[25] as well as the region's dependence on rice cultivation rather than peanut production, have concurred to exclude and marginalize the Casamance population from access to political power and economic resources. The clan-based political and religious organization of Joola communities has resisted for centuries the hierarchical organization of power promoted by the Muslim brotherhood as well as the centralized political authority of the colonial and postcolonial state apparatuses. Under the colonial government, the region had secured a measure of autonomy that was taken away with the coming of national independence, and the postcolonial imposition of legal regulations over land property that contrast with the customary rights of the population, together with the continual urban bias of the state, precipitated the crisis (Hesseling 1994). While demands for Casamance independence have not found much sympathy among the majority of Senegalese, the desperate cry for decentralization and the need to challenge the political hegemony of the Wolof-Muslim have been received more positively among the larger population. The prolonged political crisis between the Casamance movement and the Senegalese government has made the Senegalese population keenly aware of the responsibility of the state to embrace the whole of Senegal, culturally, politically, and economically. The victory of Abdoulaye Wade in the presidential elections of 2000 is a testament to the importance given by voters to the Casamance issue, as Wade (since the late 1980s and more prominently in the 1990s) established himself as a powerful mediating figure between the government and the separatist movement. His ascendancy to the presidency can be partly read as a popular vote of acknowledgment and support for his role in the Casamance crisis.

Sabar Rhythms and the Choreography of a Female Public Sphere

While the scholarly discussion of linguistic Wolofization has centered on evaluating the political implications of the process and its relation to ethnic identification and national integration, approaching the issue from the circle of *sabar* dancers opens up questions about the relationship between ethnicity, religiosity, and gender that unsettle commonly held assumptions. Does Wolofization go hand in hand with Islamicization, as Diouf and Dioup have asserted? Does Islamic religiosity exert an oppressive and pervasive influence on female sexuality and the expression of femininity, as much of the literature on women and Islam suggests? To begin answering these questions we need to go back to the dancing circle.

I have argued that *sabars* take place in innumerable circumstances and locations. I have also argued but not explicitly stressed that *sabars* are women's affairs. In this section I will examine the relationship between *sabar* dancing and femininity performed by women in the public space of the city. I will thus focus my analysis on street *sabars,* those that take place in the middle of streets.

Street *sabars* involve a fluid number of young women—fifty, a hundred, two hundred—who gather to enjoy the dancing competition of a *sabar* event, taking over the streets of the city. For these occasions, as for family celebrations, women patronize *géwëls*—the Wolof griots—to play for the event. *Géwëls* call with their drums for the women to gather, and as the thickness of bodies grows and participants add to the mass of the circle, so does the thickness of the drumming. The gathering of women in the shape of a circle literally opens up a space filled with their expectations and intent, protected from the outside social world. Thus women physically take over the public space of the city, and, supported by the *géwëls,* momentarily reconstitute it as a *sabar* dancing circle, with its own rules and aesthetics. In this context the idiom of *sabar* dancing defines an ethic of aesthetic presentation and public display in which an erotic femininity is vigorously performed and noisily supported. I call this relationship between ethics, aesthetics, and kinetics established through dancing *kinaesthetic.* The *sabar* kinaesthetic competes with an Islamic kinaesthetic, which defines a different ethic of aesthetic presentation and public display, linking feminine propriety to a kinetic regiment of modesty and restraint.

These two kinaesthetics compete audibly and visibly in the city landscape. Women's mobile occupation of the public urban space through *sabar* dancing is only rivaled by women's participation in religious events, most notably in Thursday-night *dahiras. Dahiras* are urban associations of *taalibes*—religious followers—who gather in a member's courtyard to pray and collect donations to be funneled to the brotherhood to which the *taalibes* belong. The gatherings on Thursday nights are staged to enter the holy day of Friday in prayer, with the singing starting in the early evening and continuing past midnight.

Dahiras are noisy affairs, as the high-pitched voices of lead singers are amplified by megaphones or microphones. The songs act as religious propaganda, while the loudness of the group advertises their power and numbers. At the same time, different *dahiras* echo each other across neighborhoods, creating a sound environment replete with religiosity, the noise seeping into one's body like smell inhaled through breathing.

Sabars are also noisy affairs that effectively compete with *dahiras* in occupying the airwaves of the city and creating a soundscape that reaches far beyond the active participants in the event. *Sabar* drum ensembles produce a galloping sound in which the high-pitched tuning of the lead drum carries *sabar* rhythms to great distances, and as with *dahiras,* it is often echoed by competing *sabars* taking place across neighborhoods.

The presence of *sabars* in the city's landscape is mobile and temporary, while intrusive and powerful. It leaves no mark on the sand of the streets nor on the structure of buildings, unlike Islamic religiosity, which is inscribed visibly and permanently in the city's architecture. The mosque, with its tall minarets, dominates the urban public space. Even in the *banlieues* (shanty towns) where the population lives in flimsy shacks and the geography of illegal housing shifts shape like slow-moving lava, the mosque stands tall and solid against the vulnerable life that surrounds it. Yet *sabars,* unlike *dahiras,* are events in which women physically take over the public space of the city, and—with the support of *géwëls*—become its sole protagonists.

Men who do not belong to the specialized professional groups of drummers—the *géwëls*—are typically excluded from active participation in *sabar* events. They only partake of the dancing as distant spectators, strategically located on the roofs of buildings that surround the *sabar* circle; but as such distant observers, they are dispensable.[26] With or without them, women dance, and the men who attempt to watch or participate in the *sabar* circle are often discouraged. One of my male friends told me that men who dance at *sabars* or that are always crowding around the circle of *sabar* dancers are called *góórjigéén* (literally "men-women," used in reference to homosexual men who take on a feminine gender identity).[27] While this opinion is not shared by other Dakarois and seems to have been an idiosyncratic comment, it points to the strong association of *sabars* with women's affairs and to the potential feminization of male participants.[28] At the same time, it calls attention to men's desire to participate in the excitement of a *sabar.*

Men find an outlet for their love of *sabar* dancing in discotheques where *sabar* music is played independently from the organization of a *sabar* event. Since *sabar* music is only one of the musical genres played at a disco—along with salsa, *funanà,*[29] rap, and reggae—men and women remain on the dance floor. Yet, when *géwëls* play live music in a club, the gender division between dancers and nondancers reappears.

Street *sabars* provide a privileged arena in which women perform as active agents and protagonists, often celebrating an explicitly sexualized feminine identity. The erotic aesthetics of *sabars* is actively cultivated at a subset of *sabar* events called *tànnebéer,* yet my own experience indicates that many *sabars* have the potential of developing in the direction of *tànnebéers* depending on the mood of the participants and the circumstances. An extra twist in the legs, a jutting forward of a quivering buttock, or eyes flapping like butterflies can transform any *sabar* step into an eroticized display, while certain dances like the *lëmbël* and the *ventilateur* (which focus on highly pulsating and rotating buttocks) properly belong to *tànnebéers.* In all *sabar* events (to which *tànnebéers* belong) women dance in solos and duets, asserting their individuality and personality by producing creative variations on a common repertory of steps.

The relationship between eroticism and dancing performed at *tànnebéers* stresses the agency of women as independent erotic subjects. Unlike western models of femininity promoted in the printed media and on the screen, where women pose seminaked as passive objects of an active (male) gaze, in the circle of *tànnebéers* women engage in spectacular kinetic stunts that both tease and resist visual objectification. The best dancers control the gaze of spectators, dramatically shifting between carefully choreographed stillness that allows the viewers to apprehend with leisure the dancer's body and extraordinary kinetic engagement that resists visual objectification by its active intensity.

The emphasis on motility establishes ideals of beauty and attractiveness that do not depend on body shape and size but on the dancing skills of the subject. Eroticism is expressed through the *sabar* dancing idiom, and dance competence defines and constrains eroticism itself. The skills of the dancers seem to correlate with the permission and appreciation of risqué bodily exposure: the more skilled a dancer, the more she will undress and expose in the dancing circle. This state of affairs suggests that poor dancers cannot be sexy not only because they cannot manage the skills to excite in their dancing but also because their inferior skills do not earn them the right to undress in the public space of the circle.

The relationship between movement, agency, and power is also affirmed by the capacity of good dancers to influence the rhythms of the drummers. While mediocre dancers confine themselves to following the rhythms provided by the drum ensemble, highly skilled dancers are able to challenge drummers to play more complex and ever-faster rhythms, earning with their skills the right to influence and even temporarily lead the drum ensemble. At *tànnebéers* the competition between drummers and dancers has an explicitly sexual content that culminates with the ability of masterful dancers to assert their power over the whole male drumming ensemble. This dynamic compels us to address the presence of male drummers at the center of the circle of female dancers and to analyze the gender play and display generated through this opposition.

Sory Camara, in *Gens de la Parole: Essai sur la Condition et le Role des Griots dans la Société Malinké* (1992), analyzes the gender dynamic between griots and their patrons and argues that Malinke griots occupy an ambiguous gender location within Malinke society. His argument can be reasonably extended to include Wolof griots.

As we have discussed, griots constitute a caste separate from the majority of the population, and rules of endogamy as well as sexual taboos separate them from the nonartisan caste. Given the gender segregation of most Malinke and Wolof family celebrations and dance events, male griots operate in women's spaces that are considered out of bounds for non-griot men. As mediators between the bride and groom's families and as agents at women's celebrations, griots routinely transgress normative gender divisions in a context generally marked by a high degree of gender segregation. For these reasons Camara interprets the male griots' gender identity itself as wavering between male and female normative gender constructions.

From my observations of *sabars*, I would argue that male drummers act as symbolic males, that is, as surrogate representatives of the male gender. Precisely because of the sexual interdictions between griots and non-griots, male *géwèls* can witness and even incite women's erotic display without conjuring the social consequences that would follow the "real" play of seduction that involves non-griot men and women. For non-griot men and women who are potential or actual partners, public flirting and displays of affection are inappropriate. Yet, given the socially established interdiction and the sanctions against relationships between male griots and female non-griots, male griots can effectively encourage women's erotic display. Thus their behavior both does not conform with male prescribed behavior toward women (because of their flirting), as Camara argues, and it does, as I argue. The fact that only male griots are drummers at *sabar* events creates a symbolic tension between drummers and dancers that firmly situates the griots within hegemonic masculine heterosexual ideals.[30] Male drummers provide the essential driving force of the dance—the rhythms—and figure as a privileged audience to women's kinetic displays within the circle, as women dancers engage face to face with the drum ensemble. Even more, the lead drummer often acts as a central catalyst to women's eroticism, detaching himself from the drum ensemble to engage in a close encounter with the dancer, as if to play his rhythms right into her body. The lead drummer and the dancer engage in a rhythmic and kinetic *tête-à-tête* that evolves into a provocative dialogue escalating to higher and higher erotic displays. The lead drummer is a master of seduction who provokes and supports with his performance women's erotic engagement.

*   *   *

The lack of male participants and spectators in the *sabar* circles and *tànnebéers* of the streets is a departure from the historically constituted relationship of *tànnebéers,* where women dancers chose male friends as invited guests to their performances. This departure from historically established patterns points to the fact that the changing relationship between men and women in the urban milieu of Dakar provokes new social patterns in the circle of dancers, while the circle of performers in turn defines new heterosexual dynamics. In this context a double process is at play: The greater and stronger penetration of Islamic sociality in the urban milieu has provoked a greater gender segregation in dance practice, while the same urban environment defines novel spaces of sociality in which young women and men mingle outside of kin supervision to an unprecedented degree, dancing the night away in clubs and discotheques. While the performance of *tànnebéers* in the clubs of the city raises considerable moral anxiety among respectable citizens, as the sociality between the sexes is regulated through the logic of public access (anybody paying the entrance fee takes part in the event), the all-female circle of dancers in the streets and at family celebrations also raises considerable anxiety because it stands as an antihegemonic social space to the dominant Islamic kinaesthetic.

Hegemonic and Subaltern Feminine Kinaesthetics

The feminine erotic aesthetic cultivated at *sabars* contrasts with the feminine aesthetic promoted by the Islamic religion, with its emphasis on physical modesty, kinetic restraint, and passivity vis-à-vis male subjects. The circle of *sabar* dancers creates a space that falls outside the hegemonic norms of Islamic religiosity,[31] and it needs the protection of the encircling audience to create a buffer to the outside social space. While the dancers' skills reflect years of socialization and training, the circle needs to be continually created and re-created for each social occasion, living as a nondominant albeit extremely popular form of sociality. An analysis of representations of femininity in the media can elucidate the relative hegemony of Islamic kinaesthetics vis-à-vis the kinaesthetics of *sabar.*

The national media officializes popular culture, legitimizing sociocultural practices by giving them airtime. Turning to the television screen at the time of my research (1996–97), I focused my observations on the *variété musical*—music videos that are eagerly watched on Saturday evenings by the Dakarois who own a TV set. I was struck by the absence of women's *sabar* dancing on the television, which contrasted with its presence in the streets and courtyards of the city.[32] This absence was marked on one side by the displacement of women performers by men, and on the other side by the representation of femininity offered by the women performers who do appear, which sharply contrasts with the aesthetics of the *sabar* circle. Music videos displace the stunning dance skills of women with those of highly skilled male dancers, and women protagonists only appear in so far as they conform to hegemonic Islamic models of femininity.[33] I will focus my analysis on the women protagonists.

A review of music videos shown on the *varieté musical* during 1996–97 shows women protagonists most often as performers of a specific style of singing that asserts its allegiance to the Islamic religion. The popular song by Dial Moussa Ale, "Jar na ko" (Well worth it), can be taken as a paradigmatic representative of this style, which falls somewhere between the praise singing that *géwëls* reserve for their secular patrons and the religious singing that praises God. In "Jar na ko," the griotte sings not the praise of a secular patron but of a *marabout,* and more specifically she sings the praise of the mother of an important *marabout.* The song is dedicated to Fadawe Welle, the mother of Alaji Maalick Sy (1855–1922), a prominent member of the Tidjaniyya order and a major proselytizer of the order among the Wolof at the turn of the twentieth century, when Islam was spreading to the majority of the Senegalese population. According to Fiona McLaughlin (1997:566), songs in praise of a *marabout* were originally motivated by a secession quarrel between two different branches of the Sy family in the 1950s. The dispute was over the position of *khalifa*[34] within the Tidjaniyya order. The followers of Ababacar Sy composed a series of praise songs to foster his nomination as *khalifa,* and since then, this genre has become well established in popular music.

The song "Soxna Diarra," performed in 1996 by Fatou Guewel, is another popular example of the genre. Soxna Diarra is the mother of Amadou Bamba Mbaké, the founder of the Mouride order—and she is praised by Fatou Gewuel for raising such an important religious figure.

In the music videos, Dial Moussa Ale and Fatou Guewel perform a specific model of femininity that asserts its allegiance to the Islamic religion not only in words but in bodily deportment: their kinesthetic expression is very contained, as the dancing is limited to the hands and the swaying of the upper body. The staticity of the body is also emphasized by its mass, as both performers embody a feminine ideal in which regal deportment is associated with impressive body size, giving weight to the subject physically and socially. According to the Islamic kinaesthetic, the relative immobility of the religious body confirms on the exterior a believer's peaceful submission to religiosity and inscribes the body into a hierarchy of beliefs that do not originate in the agency of the subject but come from above, in the religious structure that dictates the obedience of *taalibes* to *marabouts,* of *marabouts* to *khalifas,* and of all to *Yalla.* Women's proper deportment within this hierarchy serves to visibly mark on the exterior the inner balance of the spirit and their submission to male religious figures as well as male family authorities. Kinetic modesty vis-à-vis men thus marks a properly Muslim feminine kinaesthetic. For example, a woman is not supposed to walk in front of her husband or *marabout,* and she is supposed to display physical shyness in their presence (to sit with the head reclined toward the ground, to let men sit on chairs while she sits on the carpet, to cover all body parts, including the feet and the head, and to remain quiet). Women's submission to male authority then comes to define a proper Muslim ethic of respect, predicated on a more general ideology of submission to authority.[35]

The "Wolof" qualities of *sutura* and *kersa* also establish a relationship between kinetic containment and propriety. *Sutura* is the virtue of keeping quiet about difficulties and problems, problems that should not be divulged to strangers (Roberts and Roberts 2003:157), while *kersa* exemplifies a certain timidity and shyness that is welcomed as a sign of a good manners and education (Sylla 1994:85).[36] Both qualities depend on a bounded and subdued self and are especially appreciated in women, but also in members of the upper classes. These concepts suggest that the kinetics of the female subject constitute also her kinaesthetic.

I must emphasize that the contrast between the kinaesthetic of *sabar* dancing and that of Islamic religiosity lives most strongly at the level of official representation, where the aesthetic of female display is dominated by the Islamic model. In women's lives the two models coexist, and the same women strategically perform one or the other according to their place in the life cycle (young women participate in *sabars* in much greater numbers than older women) and according to the social occasion and their personal disposition. Similarly, as Mohammed Mboji has brought to my attention,[37] the same women performers that sing the praise of religious figures on television sell tapes in the local market with songs that they have composed for *tànnebéers*, with explicitly sexual lyrics. These tapes are not displayed on market stalls but need to be requested by the knowing customer. I also want to emphasize that, in spite of their differences, both aesthetics are centered on the powerful projection of femininity in the public sphere, and both underscore female agency and independence, albeit through different strategies. Fatou Guewel and Dali Moussa Ale foster women's visibility and respect in the public sphere by conforming and simultaneously subverting normative Islamic gender ideals. While the most patriarchal readings of Islamic religiosity tend to see women as spiritual children who need to follow the guidance of fathers and husbands as well as religious leaders, Guewel's "Soxna Diarra" and Ale's "Jar na ko" introduce a matricentric twist into Islamic historiography, celebrating the mothers of important *marabouts*. These songs effectively invert the infantilization of women by placing male icons of religiosity in the position of children, children of great mothers. At the same time, the lyrical deployment of motherhood establishes the singers' propriety well within the norms of Islamic religiosity, while fostering their success as performers who pursue their careers outside of the family, touring nationally and internationally. These singers are icons of success and economic independence, and they are patronized by women who can display considerable wealth.

These remarks lead us to question the triangulating relationship between Islamic religiosity, femininity, and gender identity. While even the inscriptions of femininity within Islamic religiosity offer leverage for the negotiation of gender roles in the private and public sphere, *sabar* dancing most strongly generates an alternative kinaesthetic to the dominant values promulgated by orthodox readings and embodiments of religiosity.

The eroticism expressed in *sabar* dancing unsettles the most common interpretations of the links between Islamic religiosity, Muslim women's public expression, and women's sexuality. White feminists and Islamic fundamentalists have colluded in portraying Islamic religiosity as a pervasive influence on women's lives (from the bedroom to the streets), the former deploring this state of affairs, and the latter exalting its value. Furthermore, white feminists and fundamentalists alike set up a dichotomous antagonism between Islamic and western morality, as if the two were antithetical and there was no alternative between them. Islamic religious figures have often accused African feminists of being westernized, and white feminists have tended to similarly deny the existence of a truly indigenous feminism while construing western feminism as the only path toward women's liberation from the yoke of Islam. The *sabar* dancing circle unsettles these assumptions.

The circle of women gathered to dance offers a challenge to the dominant patriarchal Islamic sexual morality, a challenge articulated in a Wolof-centric idiom that owes nothing to western feminism and at the same time is not external to the Islamic religion. While a full exploration of the relationship between women's sexuality, representation of female eroticism, and Islamic religiosity is beyond the scope of this project, in the following pages I propose my own preliminary reflections on the topic.

The circle of *sabar* dancers suggests that Islamic religiosity supports not only a wide range of political identities and agendas but also a plurality of positions with regard to women's sexuality and women's role in society. Most of the women dancing at *sabars* are Muslim, and 95 percent of the population in Senegal is Muslim. This figure points to the social and political weight of the Islamic religion in the culture and history of the country.

Islamic brotherhoods in Senegal—in particular the Mourides—have politically aligned themselves with the dominant state party, the Socialist party, while maintaining a strategic distance from the Senegalese government. While on the political level they have supported the hegemony of the Socialist party for over thirty years, at the cultural level they have been able to harness popular discontent and provide a powerful counterhegemonic cultural space that competes successfully with the western-oriented national school system and official state ideology. The Senegalese Left has decried the resurgence of Mouridism among the city youth and yet has been unable to compete with the power of Islamic brotherhoods to mediate between the state and civil society and their ability to create a network of social support that is particularly important to a population faced with a chronic economic crisis. In this context, dance provides a source of sociality, networking, and identification that is independent from Islamic religion and yet not antagonistic to it.

Dakarois women capitalize on family celebrations and *sabar* events to accumulate scarce capital and to weave a network of relations of mutual obligation and assistance that is far more reliable and effective than government social services. Government officials and male subjects often criticize the conspicuous flow of money generated at these events and have attempted, without success, to set a limit on the amount that can be exchanged (Bop 1995).

Male opposition to such practices (amplified and made official through the voice of the government) comes from the fact that males, as fathers and husbands, are expected to finance the events (in addition to the *bàjjan*'s contribution), while women reap the benefit of the flow of money. The exchange of money between female participants also celebrates an exclusively female network of exchange. This exchange is considered wasteful by male subjects who would rather see the women contribute directly to the household economy under the guidance of a male head than to an all-female network of relationships, outside of male influence and control.

Women's orchestration of family celebrations and their mutual dependence on female networks point to the pattern of economic separation of conjugal couples' budgets. While men's sponsorship of baptisms and marriage celebrations symbolically constitutes husbands and fathers as providers, materially confirming their willingness and ability to do so, the extent to which men contribute to their families in daily life is a negotiated process. In contrast to Islamic ideals, which assume the husband to be the sole breadwinner of the household, indigenous gender ideologies expect women to provide for their children by engaging in their own money-generating activities.

Studies have shown that in spite of the rhetoric concerning the role of husbands as breadwinners and heads of households, with the deepening economic crisis, women have taken over more and more of the family's financial obligations. One study by Boye (1993) suggests that in Dakar only 22 percent of fathers were fully supporting their children, versus 44 percent of mothers (with the remaining percentage being supported either by both parents or by some other relative). Other scholars, among them Bop (1995), have corroborated these figures with their own research, correlating women's economic support of their children with high rates of unofficial divorce among polygamous couples (see, for example, Antoine and Nanitelamio 1995) and with unwed mothers. These patterns suggest the presence of what Amadiume (1997) has termed a dual gender system in which a patrifocal family unit (placing emphasis on the social figures of the wife-husband-son) is competing with a matrifocal kinship unit (centered on the social figures of mother-daughter-son).

Amadiume argues that these two systems—a male-centered system and a female-centered one—are articulated within different socioeconomic processes and political organizations and also inform independent moral philosophies (continually negotiating their place in the sociopolitical sphere).[38] I would like to suggest that with Dakar's deepening economic crisis, the presence of a dual gender system has become more evident. Matrifocal kinship

structures allow women, faced with the difficulty of constituting and maintaining a male-centered family unit as the one supported by Islamic ideology, to rely on an alternative social and moral model, which dispenses with
the figure of the husband in the day-to-day activities of women.[39] This matrifocal kinship unit generates its own sexual morality, which can be seen
in the circle of *sabar* dances. This morality asserts women as active erotic
subjects who are in control of their bodies and desires, masterfully displaying their power of seduction in a public, albeit protected setting. This female-
centered sexual morality stands in juxtaposition to the dominant Islamic sexual morality, which strictly inscribes women's sexuality within marriage and
in subservience to the husband's desire.[40] At the same time, by promoting
separate male and female social spheres, Islam reinforces the strength of all-
female networks and the formation of women-centered values and desires.
The women-centered celebration of eroticism practiced at *sabars* seems to
question the primacy of a bounded, domestic heterosexual bond, if not heterosexuality itself, suggesting at least the possibility of homoerotic relations.[41]

*   *   *

These remarks are intended as the beginning of a series of questions for future
research rather than as conclusive analytical statements. Do ethnic-centric
forms of cultural production (such as *sabars*) provide an alternative to Islamic
sociality and morality, or do they interact with it in different degrees and not
homogeneously across different social spheres? What is the interactive influence of ethnicity and Islamic religion on gender roles and sexuality?[42] Do ethnic groups differ in their construction of gender, gender roles, and sexuality?
If so, why?[43] Does Wolofization, intended as a process of assimilation into
Wolof cultural practices, support processes of gender equality and women's
independence (financial as well as social) in the urban context that are progressive and beneficial to women who belong to non-Wolof ethnic groups? Or
does the urbanness of *sabar* dancing take precedence over its Wolof-centric
character, constructing a panethnic and urban sexual morality? Does it allow
for the articulation of new identities affecting conceptions of citizenship and
ethnic identification? Why has the *sabar* complex become the favorite expressive idiom of low-income city women? Does the dancing of *sabar* express desires and aspirations that cannot be articulated in other social spaces? Do *sabars*
allow for the celebration of homoerotic aesthetics and sexualities repressed
by the dominant Islamic (and Christian) morality?

I will come back to some of these questions in the next chapter. Here I will
conclude by bringing to the reader an image of the social and aesthetic con-

texts that support *sabar* performances, presenting a description of a *tànnebéer* at a *soirée* in a club in Dakar that took place during the time of my research.

Soirée Sénégalais at LT, Thursday night, March 1996, Dakar

I have been invited by Ibou's friend to join in a "Senegalese dancing night" at the club LT. Soirées Sénégalaises are held in night clubs throughout the city once or twice a week. I am told that women dressed in traditional clothing get in for free. Men pay between one to two thousand CFA Francs, depending on the club, which is a lot of money for most people.[44] At these evenings, the *mbalax* is played by the DJ and sometimes singers lip-sync to their songs. The *mbalax,* as it was explained to me by the young women in the family I live with, is the traditional modern music of Senegal: traditional because the *sabar* drums of the Wolof constitute the rhythmic ensemble onto which *sabar* rhythms are played; modern because electric guitar, synthesizer, and saxophone are part of the ensemble.[45] The fusion of modern and traditional elements is also evident in the fusion of musical styles: salsa *mbalax,* jazz *mbalax,* reggae *mbalax,* and rock *mbalax* are the most common mixtures of genres, with some groups specializing in only one genre, while other groups may play all.[46] I have been listening to *mbalax* music since the first day I arrived in Dakar, welcomed by the latest tape of Youssou N'Dour blasting loudly from so many shops and homes that it seems to define the pulse of the city.

Ibou and I are expected to join friends at Youssouf's and Fatou's house, around 11:30 P.M. Ibou advises me to wear my *grand boubou.*[47] I say I will, but then I am too cold and too tired for it (I have been out since eight in the morning). Too tired to dress up, and too tired to deal with so much cloth to fold around my body and to wear the high heels that must accompany the *grand boubou* on important events. I wear jeans and tennis shoes, a nice white shirt, a vest, a big cotton sweater, and no makeup; it will have to do. Ibou wears his usual jeans with shirt and baseball hat. At around 11:30 he calls me: it's time to go. We step out into the night. There are no street lights but stars and wind.

We are walking to Ablay's place, a friend who lives in the neighborhood; he and some of his friends will accompany us to Youssouf's house, since it is not safe to walk around alone or in couples. Ablay and two friends come along. We walk on paved roads up to the big street on Ñaari Tali and on to the sandy streets of Grand-Dakar. We are almost there; Ablay and his friends leave us. We enter a two-story building. From a courtyard we proceed up some stairs, groping in the darkness to find Youssouf's and Fatou's room.

Fatou is sleeping in bed with her kid. Her sister is there, and Thiorro, whom I meet for the first time. Ablaye and Youssouf are chatting near the window. Youssouf takes out a *grand boubou* (male version) of a light blue and shining cloth. He proceeds to undress and put it on and then tops it all with a wool hat. He does all of this slowly and meticulously. Then he adjusts all the folds of his dress and he looks at himself from the height of his head, staring down at his body at his feet and twisting around to get a glimpse of his back. He adjusts the embroidery at the bottom of his pants so that it falls right in the middle of the side of the ankles, one design on each side, and he adjusts the folds of the *boubou* again. He stands and fidgets some more with the cloth of his dress, and then he slowly undresses and puts on a pair of jeans, a jean-shirt with some ducks embroidered on it, a sweater with buttons, climbing shoes, and the wool hat he wore before. He takes out a spray can and sprays perfume on himself, passes it on to Ibou, who also sprays himself, and passes it to Ablaye, who perfumes himself, and then passes it on to me. I refuse it. I do not like the smell of it, and I think of it as a man's perfume. But they do not seem concerned about my male/female distinctions. I remember Moussa, one of the brothers of the family, asking for my perfume and insisting that he try it in spite of my vocal objections that it is a woman's perfume. I make a mental note: "Check my own assumptions about feminine and manly smells." They tell me we are ready to go.

Fatou bops her head out of bed and mumbles something. I ask her why she is not coming with us—is she sick? She says she has to stay with the kid and flops back to sleep with her child. We get up and leave, but the two women (Thiorro and her friend) do not come with us. I ask why. "They still have to dress up," Ibou says. "They will come later. You know Senegalese women, they take a lot of time to get ready."

We walk in the sand up to a big paved road. Ablaye tells us that he has a knife and shows us a thin and short baton. He tells Ibou he should be armed, that he should carry a knife, especially walking around with me. We walk in a tight group; I stay close to Ablaye and his knife. In about fifteen minutes we have arrived; I see the neon sign "LT."

We enter a dark corridor. The men at the door remark that I am not wearing traditional clothes. I tell them that this is my traditional clothing, but I still have to pay for the entrance. We step into a dark room with a bar on the side, but nobody can afford to buy drinks—I will not see people drink in the club. If one is really in the mood for alcohol, it is better to buy a bottle of beer or cheap whiskey at the corner store, out of sight of all but the most intimate friends.[48]

A few steps lead downward into a room with couches and low tables surrounding a linoleum floor. It is about 12:30, and the club is still nearly empty. Only a few men are sitting along the wall, and three men are dancing with great self-involvement and nonchalance, each in his own space and mood. We take a seat at one of the couches, and then Youssouf and Ablaye get up to dance. They call Ibou and me to join them, and we do.

We are dancing to the rhythm of the *mbalax,* with minimal effort. It is gesturing toward dance rather than "really" dancing. It is the cool kind of dancing I have seen in discotheques before, so different from the animated dancing of Ballets and *sabar* circles. *I am here, swaying to the syncopated mbalax rhythm, checking you out. Look around, walk around a little, sway side to side with an accented move of the torso, or a leg kicking up with a strong bit of the music. And, of course, I do know the music, you see. I do stop right with the last clapping of the drum. I am not sweating, I am not even close to a sweat with this.*

I remember the club I went to a month ago. They kept this kind of nonchalant dancing going for hours and got on my nerves. *Can't they be a little more animated? I am tired of this cool attitude. I will risk being too much of a toubaab and just exaggerate my efforts.* And around me a circle formed. People started to get more animated, inviting me to go into the middle of the circle, or dancing toward me, and I mean really dancing, showing me their good moves, the ones they had been saving up and not giving out—quivering at the knees, circling the hips, flapping the legs like turn-mills. But now it was obviously not worth the effort, with the club still empty and a few men moving on the dance floor.

Tonight's *soirée* has been organized by Moudu Seck. He is a young *géwël* of Grand Dakar, and he was the lead drummer for the *sabar* celebrating the one-year birthday of little Mohammed, the son of Fatou and Youssouf. That party was a great success, and Moudu's role as organizer should guarantee a good *soirée,* because Moudu knows many people and is a popular drummer.

Slowly women start to come in. In groups of four, five, and six, and in groups with men. The women are beautiful and colorful in their *boubous:* shining red with white ribbons, golden brown, black, and yellow. High heels, golden sandals. Why are they all so beautiful and so feminine *all the time?* Every day, in their homes, on the bus, on the *car-rapides,* in the market, and now here in the club, always so relentlessly beautiful.[49] I see it is an act of resistance against the squalor of poverty. I usually appreciate the beauty of the women who like flowers of the desert bloom with color and outstanding grace against the desolated landscape of the city: the decaying architecture, the bad smell of smog, urine, and garbage, the ugly face of poverty. I marvel at their courage to be beautiful, at their spirit that finds the strength to care about aesthetics even in the midst of dire circumstances. Nobody felt like me, too tired to dress up and put on feminine charm? Tonight is certainly not the time to shy away from elegance: dress to impress seems to be the rule.

The dance floor becomes animated as the groups entering the club quickly start to dance. The swaying to the *mbalax* is getting bigger, the accents more stark, all of which promise a good evening of dancing. Thiorro and her friend arrive and join us immediately on the dance floor. Thiorro is lean and tall like a supermodel, angular and round in a sensual combination highlighted by her tight-fitting dress. She is a wave of fresh energy, smoothly surging with crisp swaying movements that make the body angular. Bent knees and elbows draw semicircles and bounce at the highest point of the curve into an upward stress. We are dancing in a circle, friends joining in and responding to Thiorro's enthusiastic dancing. I do the *mu lay ce gin,* the most popular dance of the moment. I started learning it the first day I arrived in Dakar, with all the sisters of the house I live in dancing in the living room to Youssou N'Dour's latest tape, *Diapason +*. The upper body contracts in a double rhythm that sends the torso jutting forward and backward while shoulders and elbows open sideways; the backs of the hands rest on the hips; the eyes look upward and flap open and closed like big butterflies; one leg at a time pushes forward and then travels sideways with the knee bent and stops open to the side to accent the beat of the drums. I am missing that extra twist of the legs they have. Jeans are so unforgiving, every movement is visible. I cannot cover my mistakes under the cloth of a *boubou.* I feel so naked! Thiorro must think the same, because she takes one layer of cloth off her *boubou* and ties it around my waist.

We are starting to sweat and breathe heavily, but the dancing gets stronger and stronger. The DJ plays Mbaye Dièye Faye's song "Oupoukay." The whole club dances the *oupoukay*—the fan. The fanning proper does not start until the song is well established and the *sabar* drums strike the rhythm that compels us all to open and close our bent knees, once, twice—the accent on the opening movement, two beats of improvisation and then again FLAP FLAP open, while leaning the weight of the body on one leg, then the other leg, the sternum moving forward and backward, one arm supposedly holding a fan and helping to blow air onto the face, smiling, sweating, flirting with the eyes, the hips, the hands, improvising variations and being compelled back to synchrony by the strong beat of the drums.

Another favorite song, also by Mbaye Faye, is "Mustapha." The music introduces a generic Arabic theme. We all dance, swaying our hips in rhythm with the music and holding our hands up above our heads, flicking them around with a twist of the wrist while turning the whole body around on one spot of the floor. "Ya Moustapha . . . chéri je t'aime, chéri je t'adore, ya Moustapha, ya Moustapha." We all smile and sing along. The music and the dancing get progressively faster, until the music breaks into the *mbalax* rhythm, and the whole discotheque suddenly switches to dance the *mulay ceggin,* until the slap of the drums coordinates the final accent of all the bodies in the room to come to a synchronized stop. That sudden change from the Arabic style of dancing to the *mbalax* is the high point of the song, the climax that quickly leads us to end the dance.

We are all ready for a change of pace. The DJ plays the *funanà,* the sweet and dynamic music of Cape-Verde. Groups clear off the floor, and couples come swirling in, circling and swaying in tight pairs. While most couples undulate left and right, the best dancers circle around the floor in smooth centripetal turns revolving around their axes, drawn closer together as the force of their spins pulls them toward each other. They tell me Ablaye is a good dancer of *funanà,* that he performs in clubs and wins competitions. He is dancing with Thiorro, and indeed they seem the best dancers in the room. They have a greater movement range than the other couples, sometimes moving sweetly and softly in tight steps—side to side, back and forward—sometimes accelerating in large spins that send them into new areas of the dance floor, holding their heads close together, making their bodies into one and then taking some distance from each other, recovering their own boundaries of distinct selves. They sway with every beat of the music, while some couples embody only the strongest beat in their steps, losing the bouncing quality of the dance.

I exonerate myself from dancing. I explain that I do not dance couple-dances. They think I should try and I should learn: "It's easy." I do like the music of the *funanà:* it gives me a sad and sweet longing that makes me want to move and spin as they do, as the best dancers do. But last time I tried to dance I ended up upset, having to negotiate the boundaries of admissible touching more than I really had patience for, at the same time feeling too incompetent to guide the dance away from stuck and stubborn stroking and into the pleasure of synchronized movement. That is the way I feel: good dancing protects me from unwelcome overerotized bodily encounters. But as a beginner and inexperienced dancer I am too vulnerable to male manipulations and transpositions of motility from steps and floor patterns into caresses and tight holdings.

I relax in my seat. Having decided not to participate I can dedicate myself to observations. There are some same-gender couples dancing together, men with men and women with women, holding hands and waist, smiling and swaying to the music. A few people, men and women, are also dancing by themselves, shifting their upper body from side to side, one hand touching their sternum, the other raised in the air as if holding an imaginary partner, the eyes soft in an introverted dreamy look, or open in a joyful glance at their friends standing chatting to their side.

I am squeezed into my seat between my friend and strangers. There is room further down on the couch; why is this woman seated almost in my lap? I feel compressed between people like on the *car-rapides*. I spend so much time on those vehicles that take people everywhere in the city. I do love to sit, to feel, and to look at people in those colorful vans spouting dark clouds of smoke and threatening the safety of people within and without. People crowd in, pushing to get a seat on the two benches nearest to the exit, even when ample room is available on the back benches. I too have developed a preference for these seats, because they allow for greater visibility out the car's windows, and most importantly, they allow more direct communication with the *apprenti*, the young boy who collects fares and taps on the roof of the van to signal the driver to stop and to move again.

People's preferences organize the distribution of space on the couches of the discotheque and the benches of the *car-rapides* in uneven conglomerates of empty space and overlaying of bodies. I doze in a reverie of my rides in the *car-rapides*, the warmth of my neighbors on the couch supporting my digression into memory/fantasy. There are four axis along which people can sit in the *car-rapides*: two lines of benches along the tire-axis of the van, parallel to the side windows, and two more benches perpendicular to them, situated toward the driver's cabin, organizing people parallel to the driver's seat. Each of the benches fits comfortably four people, but a fifth always manages to perform the feat of sitting on the already full bench. Five people per bench in an ever-changing combination of colors, shapes, and attitudes. The task of fitting different body sizes into the same-measured bench fascinates me. The fixed length of the bench contrasts with the shifting size of passengers, and no matter how much the big and conspicuous squeeze the old and the thin, nobody grumbles.

I am pulled out of my thoughts by Ablaye and Thiorro, who take me by the hand and lead me to another couch near the back of the discotheque. The whole club is shifting arrangements as an ensemble of drummers settles at the edge of the dance floor, near the stairs. The drummers strike the rhythms of the *sabar* while people clear the dance floor and cluster at the edges. But is not time for the *sabar* yet. A young man in jeans comes out with a microphone to lip sync to his recorded song, played by the DJ. My friends tell me his name—I forget it immediately—and explain to me that he is among the rising Senegalese musical stars. The young man is singing to the rhythm of the *mbalax*. He draws a response mainly from the men in the audience, who clap their hands and jump onto the dance floor with the tempestuous appearance of *sabar* dancing. One man in particular takes the stage with his dancing: he opens and closes his bent legs, like in the *oupoukay* dance, at an incredible speed, maybe two cycles of opening and closing per second, the accent on the opening movement, the body balanced on the ball of the feet, a great smile and a sudden stop. Just as suddenly he starts again, and stops. But then he kicks up his leg and scratches his crotch. We burst into laughter. This is the *xac*, the dog dance.

The next singer comes out, and he does not provoke much audience response. A third singer takes the floor, and this time the women clap their hands and come out to dance. He is tall and lean, dressed in a light-colored linen suit. The women yell and smile at him. I recognize him from the *variété*: He is Gallo Thiello singing the popular and witty "Taxi Arrête!"

The DJ announces the dance group Kaddu gi. The drummers are playing, and three young men come out to do a dance of fishermen. Ablaye tells me that when fishermen come back to shore with a good catch, the women dance to welcome them back home. The three men perform the dance of the women welcoming back invisible fishermen, holding baskets to be filled with fishes and pulling nets. Then, without a pause, a new dance begins. A group of women enters the dance floor, while one man adorned with a cascading assemblage of strips of cloth jumps toward the drummers. One of the women falls in contortions onto the floor. The man with the exuberant dress comes toward her. *What is he doing to her, with the baton, with the water? And look: so many people, about twelve men and women flinging their bodies with uncontrollable energy. This is like a madhouse!* Yes, this must be the *ndëp*, the dance that is used to cure the mentally ill. Dancers jump and shake, throw their heads in all directions, while some of them help the people in convulsions, give them water and calm them down with embraces and caresses. The dance comes to a resolution, but I am too disoriented by the drums and the density of action to follow the choreography. The dancers leave, people applaud, and without a pause the drummers strike the strong rhythms of the *sabar*.

The *sabar* confuses me. I cannot understand the rhythm or the dance. It is so fast. I look at the legs and arms of the dancers spinning in circles, up and down, striking the earth and the sky, the jumps, the fast turns. I look for the logic that governs the sudden changes, and I am left dumbfounded.

I could have the dispassionate look of a spectator, and then I would see the dance take shape thanks to the mastery of performers. But if I look with the intent of learning, if I look as if to grasp those movements and apprehend them within my body, then I feel lost. *Like a slow woman left alone, standing on hard pavement while all her friends have run away at great speed. And, "Hei, Hei," she can't even call them back. They are GONE!* It is the speed and the energy of the dance that is astonishing and constitutes the excitement of *sabar.*

I could write calmly, like it was explained to me by a *géwël* master drummer in Saint-Louis,[50] about the drums that are used for the *sabar:* the *mbong mbong* drums, three of them distinguished by a different shape and timber (the *tukur,* the *ball,* and the *tungune*); the *nder,* played only by the master drummer because it is the drum that leads all the other drums and has a strong and particular sound that carries over great distances; the *ndënde* drums, also of three types (the *làmb,* the *talbat,* and the *gorong,* played for the wrestling matches); the *tama,* which is a complete instrument because alone it can reproduce the voices of all the other drums. I could tell you about all the sounds that the drums produce: with hands, slaps and open tones; and with sticks, striking the head and the sides of the drum, as well as the combination of the two (striking the drum with one hand and with the stick simultaneously, or in close succession). But how to understand the rhythms played during the *sabar?* I listen to a cascade of sounds, exploding downward like water-bombs striking the floor. I imagine the impact of all that water, the weight of the sound-bombs created by the hands and sticks of the drummers exploding onto the dancers' bodies, activating their limbs into four independently circling mills while the spine shoots upward and the head and the eyes wander toward the sky. The sudden stops and the sudden bursts of the dancers: I feel the weight of sound like a pulsating wall obtruding my pathway, and I imagine the dancers lifting that weight with their motions and then dropping it as they catapult themselves into stillness, and then lift that weight again with all of their four limbs, using that weight to move, to move . . . mountains? You'd think that with their energy they could indeed move a mountain, or, better, go through it, leaving a tunnel scarred into it as testimony of their whirling passage. Yet no walls or mountains are moved, only the air made dense by the sweat of dancers. The density of sounds excites the dancers to action, like water warmed to the boiling point erupting into motion.

Without a pause, the drummers strike the strong rhythms of the *sabar.* A woman gets up from her seat, runs the long empty stretch of floor that separates her from the drummers, and once situated in front of them starts to jump, striking one leg on the floor, and then the other, alternating them in an asymmetrical interplay of rhythms while her arms spin in opposing directions.

FOMP!

She falls on the floor, flat on her back. People scream in empathy with her. Water was left on the floor from the previous dance, right in front of the drummers. Water slipped her, tricked her, and took her to the ground. She lies there and then gets up, and walks back to her seat. People run to dry the floor amidst yells of indignation.

The wall of sound is again constructed by the powerful arms of the drummers. The room fills with the density of rhythms charging the air like dark clouds heavy with rain, until the women are called to the drums one by one, or in pairs, and explode into bouts of dancing, lasting between thirty seconds to three or four minutes. The women dart from their seats up to the drummers, like bullets fired toward their targets, like mothers compelled to answer the cry of their children but doing so with the fury of a desire and a joy that cannot be contained. They run, pulling up or taking off their *boubous* to show their *bééco*, that little *pañe*, a colorful shining cloth that circles their waist like a miniskirt with glittering ribbons laced across it. And they dance the *ceebu jën*—rice and fish, the meal I eat every day seated around a large bowl with the twelve women of the house. Like the dish, the dance enjoys great popularity and animates women into energetic dancing. Or they dance the *ventilateur*, with the buttocks fanning circles toward the drum ensemble, like the woman who is rushing out to the drummers and positioning herself with her butt sticking out right in front of the lead drummer's face. A stillness, a grin, relishing the expectation created by her shape. And then the fast spins of her crouched spine, circling in perfect timing with the rhythms marked by the drums.

The transition from nonchalant promenades across the stage, accompanied by radiant smiles and winks to the audience, into eruptions of exuberant dancing distinguishes the most skillful performers, who weave their movements within the embroidery of sounds constructed by the torsos, arms, hands, and sticks of the drummers. That passage from stillness into total and unforgiving motion, that switch from a focus on the audience, radiating outward smiles and plenty of charm, into a focus on movement as every inch of body and soul is dedicated to define motion—the drama of those contrasts and tensions are the marks of extraordinary performers. And the dancers taking the floor tonight are all masterful. My friends tell me they are all professional dancers, this being an evening organized by a musician of Grand-Dakar, the poor neighborhood where many *géwëls,* dancers, and drug dealers live. Most of the women entering the circle are part of the company El Mansour.[51]

I sit between Thiorro and Ablaye, their arms wrapped around me, their yells and leanings rippling through my body. Thiorro bursts forward in response to a dancer, then she holds herself back by clutching her hands onto me and the woman sitting to her other side, yelling and hooting to the dancers. Thiorro and Ablaye push me to the dance floor. I resist. "Come on, you have to dance. It is easy." They pull me to the dance floor. "It is easy. We go together." I center my weight on the couch and resist stubbornly. Only the masterful dancers are entering the ring. I will not make a fool of myself. They still push me to go, every so often, hoping I have changed my mind.

One woman comes out right in the middle of the circle. She crouches down in front of the drummers, her *boubou* pulled up to show a green *bééco* shaping her round buttocks. She rests her elbows on the floor and proceeds to move one side of her gluteus in exquisite synchrony with the drums, then the other, circling outward and inward, up and up with the accents of the drums. We yell. She turns around, now offering her butt to the drummers. She smiles, and sweat slowly descends from her forehead, while she appears perfectly still, except for that dance of one gluteus at a time. And we yell.

Another woman darts out. She lifts her *boubou* all the way to her neck, letting it rest around her shoulders like a giant scarf and exposing her torso clothed in a black bra. She sensually circles her hips and moves her sternum forward and backward. Thiorro jumps up, taking off her *boubou* and *sër* to show a very short and white *bééco,* with pink, violet, blue, and yellow ribbons across it, and a thin synthetic shirt that glues to her skin. She shakes her knees in and out while turning her hips and her sternum in opposing circles and jumping forward in a zigzagging diagonal, moving like a leaping frog toward the drummers. Arriving close to the drummers she performs the windmill-four-limbs-high-speed-rotation dance (the *ceebu jën*). FLAP—she closes into a centripetal spin, rotating inward toward her spinal axis. FLAP—she zigzags backward with the leaping-frog movements.

Women alone, women in pairs. Thiorro erupts in excitement again. In one single impulse she jumps up and rips off her *sër* (which she had properly worn again once out of the dancing circle) and crouches down next to the table, her hands and knees to the floor, her chest touching the ground while her shapely ass beats up and down at a precise and incredibly fast pace. She slowly crawls toward the dance floor while maintaining her fast pelvic contractions, and suddenly she gets up and runs back to her seat. Another woman takes the floor. Then Thiorro jumps up and strikes the floor on her four limbs, and this time she crawls to the center of the dance space, with her spine twisting her butt in the air. We yell. She moves her arms and legs slowly to advance on her four limbs while her spine contracts in fast motions, head and buttock shaking vigorously. In such a fashion she covers the ten meters that separate her seat from the center of the floor, and then she gets up and runs back to the couch. Ablaye and I welcome Thiorro back to her seat like a wrestler retiring from a fighting match. She leans exhausted in our arms while we pat her on the back and thighs in gestures of congratulation.

A few more women come out to dance, and then it is over. The DJ steps out of his booth to distribute prizes to the best dancers. There is great confusion, and I am not sure how the best are selected. Ablaye pushes Thiorro forward to get a prize. She comes back with what looks like a giant jar of condensed milk.

The recorded music blasts again, and everybody gets up to leave or to start dancing. We combine the two impulses by dancing our way out, jumping on one side of the room, a few steps, and then moving toward the exit, up the stairs into the fresh air of the night.

Thiorro and her friend have disappeared. We wait for them awhile and then decide they must have gone home with somebody else. Ibou, Ablaye, and I walk down the street while Ablaye says we should not be walking, we should be taking a taxi. We all agree, all the while continuing our walk.

Our steps make a crisp sound in the fresh air of the night as we move in a fast line down the road, marching for twenty minutes and then relaxing as we enter Ibou's neighborhood, where they have hired night guards for protection. We see them sitting around a fire; they patrol the neighborhood at intervals, armed with knives and batons. We are home. We jump over the fence of the house and say goodbye to Ablaye.

5

Tales of Betrayal

"Attaya: Three Rounds of Tea"

The first cup is sweet, even aromatic at times, with a mint leaf added to the brew. Bintu and I smile at each other. Usually the men like to prepare *attaya*, and to serve it via a young boy to all the members of the family and the guests, letting the slow process of preparing the three rounds of tea pace the visit of neighbors and friends. But today it's only the two of us. Bintu has come to my "house," a single room on the second floor of a narrow building. I let Bintu prepare the tea, pouring the liquid from glass to teapot to glass, to make a white froth at the top.

"The first cup is sweet, like he was, at first," she says, smiling. "He was a friend of my cousin. They would come together to visit. We liked each other and joked together. Soon he started to come on his own. We would sit in a corner of the yard, in the dark, whispering a few words in each other's ears. The air of his breath would tease me; his long nose would touch my cheeks as he softly spoke to me. So many desires stirred by those hands holding onto mine, squeezing pleasure out of my fingers and letting it ripple through my whole body! I would fantasize about him for days, in the noise of the room I share with my three sisters.

"We went on like this for half a year. The visits were not too frequent. He lived on the other side of Dakar and could not come often to see me. On one of those visits he asked me to go dancing. I told my sisters, and we all planned for the outing. When he came and saw the four of us together he got upset. He took me aside and told me he just wanted to go with me: what was this business of always having those sisters with me? Could we ever go out alone? He left, and we did not go dancing. I was so disappointed and sad. I talked with my sisters: 'How can I go out alone with him?' We decided that Aisatu and I would pretend to go dancing with some of her high school friends, and while she would go to visit Binette in her parents' house, I would go dancing with Pap. I told Pap on his next visit. He was very happy. He said that finally I was showing some regard for him; now he knew I cared for him. How could I ever become his wife if I did not show some independence from my family?"

*   *   *

The second glass of *attaya* is stronger, sweeter, and yet more bitter then the first, as the leaves of black tea keep boiling in the water. Bintu passed me the glass. True to form I gulped the liquid down, burning my tongue. I always wondered why, while it took so long to make the tea, people took as little time as possible to drink it. No sips, no prolongation of pleasure by rolling the warm glass in the hands, sniffing its contents, sipping the liquid at long intervals to feel how the variation of temperature brings a variation of taste. "A long process of preparation and then a gulp. That is the way it was with him," she said. "A long process, slow and steady, built of trust, and then the rupture. Wanting to taste all at once, hot, burning, too hot, too burning."

The second round of *attaya*, stronger and still sweet. Bintu poured a second wave of words into my ears. "He took me to Thiossane[1] and even bought me a Coke. I was so happy. We danced all night, leaving the floor only twice for a drink. We danced the *funanà* to the latest songs of Cabo Verde Show, my favorite group. I held him so close that my head turned sideways, rested in the concave of his shoulder. My eyes were closed to feel the stirring at the pelvis, his lead and pace, flowing like a gentle wave, then rising stronger, swirling around to create a centrifugal force that would pull me even closer to him. My breath became slower and deeper, as my life shrunk to the confines of my body, no longer projected into the past or the future, no longer connected to the many people I loved or hated, my whole life condensed in the mass of my body, thick, liquid, floating in sweetness. Like a dream. And then the music took us apart, the *sabar* drums pulled our embrace out into space and made me open my eyes and quiver at the knees. Wide awake, no longer dreaming, teasing him with my legs twisting sideways and opening at the thighs, open and closed, open and closed, the accent on the open, the torso and the pelvis twisting too, the eyes flapping like the wings of butterflies, looking up, up, until I could no longer hold the laughter on my lips. When the next round of *funanà* came on, we were sweating, our bodies sticking together like wet clothes to the skin. The sweat merged in the wave of our movements, and again I floated like in a dream.

"We went out to breathe some fresh air, and he called a taxi, to take me to another club, one I had never been to before. I was not even sure which part of the city we were in, as I got dizzy trying to follow the route taken by the taxi driver. I did not care, anyway. I was too happy, looking forward to more dancing. This club was smaller and darker than Thiossane, and the people too seemed a little darker in it. A young crowd, they seemed to know each other, or at least Pap. So many people would come around to greet him. Especially women. They came up in twos or threes and haggled around Pap for a few seconds, whispering some words into his ears while looking at me with sharp eyes. I wondered how often he went there. Maybe that was why he did not come to see me as much as I had hoped for. A pang of jealousy twisted my stomach and quickly rose to my neck, choking inside my throat like a muffled moan. Why had he never taken me dancing before?

"They played a lot of rap at this club. I do not know which groups, just American rap. They also played some slow songs and some salsa, and then of course the *mbalax* and the *funanà*. We danced, and after so much dancing I was getting tired. I wanted to go home. He said, 'Noooo, not yet, not yet.' I asked him the time. He said, 'It is only 2:30.' He must have been lying because we had been dancing for a long time, but I believed him. He wanted to go to yet another club, and we went out into the night and waved at a taxi. We rode until I could recognize the neighborhood again; it was not too far from my home. We stopped in a sandy street and stepped out. There was a long and low L-shaped building, but I could hear no music. 'Where is the club?' I asked. 'I do not see anybody here.' He smiled an uncanny smile. I told him I wanted to go home. He told me to wait and went up to the side of the building, and I noticed a man standing in a little window. They joked together, and the man handed him something. Pap came back to me. 'Come, I want to show you something,' he said. I did not want to go. He insisted: 'Come, it is a surprise.' He took my right hand into both of his hands and led me down one side of the building. He stopped in front of a door. He got out a key and opened the door to the inside of a room. He pulled me toward the inside. I resisted. He went in and turned the light on, and then smiled at me like a king. 'Come, see how beautiful this is, come in.' I stood on the threshold of the door for a long time, caught between desire and fear. He cajoled me: 'Bintu, come in. I just want to be with you in a quiet place, I just want to kiss you, Bintu. Do you want me to kiss you outside? I just want to lie quiet next to you. Come, see how nice this is.' Finally, curiosity and desire won me over. The walls of the room were freshly painted of a light blue; the whole room vibrated color like a warm sky pulsating with the fresh air of early afternoon. He took my hands and led me to the bathroom. 'See how nice this is. Do you want to take a bath?' There was a bath tub, sparkling white, beaming against light green tiles. I had never been in such a beautiful bathroom. I imagined myself in the tub full of hot water and white foam, like I had seen on TV, sitting in the warm water for hours. We went to sit on the bed. It had clean white sheets. He gently pulled me toward him, tipped me until I fell over him. As soon as I fell, his movements became harsh. Like a madman he started touching me all over, putting his hands under my clothes, grabbing at my breasts, my thighs, my buttocks, my lips, my back, rolling over me and taking my breath out with heavy kisses. I struggled to pull myself from under and sat again on the edge of the bed, pushing my hair and my clothes back into place. He took my hand again. 'What is it, sweet? Come here; where are you going?' 'Do not touch me like that.' 'Sorry, I will be sweet, like you, like your beauty,' and he pulled me again over him. But he was not sweet. His hands became hard again, pushing and pulling everywhere. His eyes too became hard like stone, like a water which does not reflect back any light. He became opaque and harsh, pushing himself on top of me, pushing his weight on my body, on my face, so I could not breathe, I could not scream, I could not move but only feel a sharp pain as he forced himself onto me. The pain erupted in my chest and in my brain like a mine exploding my thoughts and my integrity into a thousand pieces, and anger rose from my stomach like an acid wave, so strong that it seemed to choke me.

"The whole world was shaking and then coming to stillness. I felt my spirit lift off my body, looking at me from above. Then, when it was all over, it came back into me. It brought me to standing, pulling my dress together, slowly walking out the door. He followed in silence. We walked to a taxi waiting outside the building. I got off at my house, knocked at the door of my room, and met a sleepy Maryama, who opened the door for me. I slid into my bed. I cried all night, muffling the sound into the pillow."

* * *

The third cup. Bitter and strong, it wakes you up. It does not let you sleep if you drink it in the evening. It keeps you awake all night, eyes wide open in the darkness, and it forces you to think, to twist and turn thoughts in your head. "Awake, I cried all night in anger. It was not simply the outrage at his abuse but the choking anger of having my desire trashed and dismissed, my desire turned into so much pain. I had wanted him for so long, craving his body. And then having it be so bitter. Where had the sweetness gone? Had he gone crazy with desire? I should have never entered that room. It was my fault. Why did I think anything better could happen? I was ashamed. Anyone could have told me not to go into the room. Why didn't I trust those who wanted to protect me? Like my mother and my father, who do not let me go out alone. For good reasons. I did not even tell my sisters. I became silent, mute, not to let the screams and rage inside me erupt. I had already been weak enough to give in to desire. Now I could not go on with my weakness, let everybody know about it. Why did I think my family kept our meetings to the corner of the yard? To protect me. Nothing bad would have happened to me if I had stayed home."

*　*　*

"He came again with a sly smile. He was more bold with his hands. Sitting in the dark corner, instead of the words he used to whisper as caresses, he reached at me with hard gestures, grabbing at my breasts and pulling them away from me. I pushed his hands off me. We did not talk. Just sat there, the usual amount of time. I wanted to shout at him, to beat him, and yet the words choked in my throat.

"He did not come back for a long time. I was relieved. When I saw him again he was with my cousin. I looked at him with hate. He smiled a big smile and came alone the next day. I told him it was over, that I would never marry him or see him again after what he had done. He got upset with me. He said, Why did I think he wanted to marry me? That I had better not be so naive as to believe that just because a man told me he wanted to marry me he was going to do so, and he laughed in my face. I looked at him with stone eyes. He did not come back. Maybe he was ashamed too."

"Toubaab"

Let me tell you a story about a *toubaab*, a white woman: a Peace Corps worker, a researcher, an adventurer, a tourist. She is independent, she comes on her own, and we know those white women, those independent women. They wear miniskirts, when it is not appropriate here, or they dress like men and think they are men too. They fuck around like men do, that is for sure, like white women do.

We must understand. Being a white woman here is like being a rock star. All these men coming after her, pursuing her with such tenderness and sensual flirting, telling her all those things the guys at home never tell her. It goes to her head. They tell her that she is so beautiful and kind, that they want to have her child. The men at home? They just want to fuck and have fun, forget kids. The men here, they tell her that they will love her, that they want to marry her. The men at home, it takes them months to propose, that is, if they last so long. Here, she turns left, she turns right, she steps forward or backward, and there is one smiling young fellow ready to marry her and follow her back home, stay with her, adoring her. Not for long, but who thinks about the future when the present is so rich with pleasure? They make her feel like a queen, with all those compliments and attention. It goes to her head indeed. Here, there, every way she turns there is a man singing sweet words into her ears and pulling her hand, pulling her body close to his. They like her for the wrong reasons, the *toubaab* knows, but hell, people dislike her for the wrong reasons too.

She does not want to marry. Of course not. Not such a loser. She does not want to have a child. Of course not. She would have to take care of two, not one. Because these men, they are beautiful, but they are poor. And they are black and illiterate, too. They do not even know how to drive. How would she dare go back home with such a man to introduce to her family? But sometimes she does get married. It happens. Especially if she is old and has money, and he is young and handsome.

She was one of those *toubaabs*. Not old, not young, not pretty either. She was alright, but she never talked to me. She had eyes only for the guys. Mamadou, Vieux, Lamine—they were all spinning around her like flies. It was a pitiful scene, if you ask me. She could not make up her mind: she would string them all along. One time I went with my boyfriend to a reggae concert at Gorée, with lots of *toubaabs* and us all mingling together. She was there, not with Mamadou, or Lamine, or Vieux, but with somebody else. You should have seen them! Glued together. That guy would never have a black woman sit on his lap out in public like that! But with a *toubaab*. They have to show their love; you know how these whites are, with romance and kisses all over the place.

She had her own place. A nice apartment, with a private bathroom and all. We would go over for lunch sometimes, on Sundays. Mamadou, Vieux, Lamine, Omar—my boyfriend—and I. She had a cook that made a great *ceebu jën*, Saint-Louis style. It's good that she had her own apartment, because she needed the privacy! I told you that I had seen her with that guy at the concert, and I am sure he came over to visit. Mamadou too. She had finally picked him out of the three. But it did not last long. After only two weeks she told him that she did not want to be with him anymore. He insisted, but to no avail. We all stopped going over. I still saw her sometimes, and always with a different guy. Maybe what bothers me is not her, but the men. Why do they like those skinny twigs so much? Oh, yes. She buys them little gifts, and they all dream of marrying her and moving over to Europe. Even the ones who already have a wife! Take Alioune: He always says that he wants a *toubaab* as a second wife. He grins at the idea. Can you imagine a *toubaab* in a polygamous marriage? That is what excites him, to think of a *toubaab* accepting to be the second. What fools. Those women have no intention to marry.

What I hate most is all their feminist talk. They go around telling us that we need to put men in their place, that we accept too much here, that we must demand respect. Ask Coumba what she thinks. She had just given birth to little Fatou, who was only a month old. Still, she would go to the market every day to sell the dry fish she got from her sister at Mbour, to earn some cash, while he stayed at home because he had lost his job and had not found another yet. One day she felt sick. She went back home, only one hour after she had left. And she found Moudu, her husband, right there on her bed, with that woman—the Peace Corps volunteer that was teaching about nutrition to the mothers who are too poor to feed their kids properly. Can you believe that? Nutrition, my ass! She was there taking away somebody's husband when his wife was nursing his baby, her groins still sore from the delivery!

Feminist against Woman

Can a feminist listen only to those women who are worse off than she is? Does she constitute herself in that power differential, too fearful to acknowledge herself as a victim if she is to recognize that she is not freer than those she speaks for? Can she speak for herself, or must she always speak for some other woman, one darker than her?

The White woman comes to Africa to claim her independence and her voice.[2] She does so via the Black woman. She wants to measure her power against the weakness of the Black woman and feel that power differential as her own feminist achievement. She thinks she is better off, and therefore a better feminist. She takes the wounds of the Black woman and wears them like badges on her feminist uniform. She parades around with the stolen marks of her new high status. Even before coming to Africa, she used to read books about the misery of her Black sisters, written by her White sisters, to uplift her spirit.

* * *

Is the weakest the most oppressed? Or is she the strongest because she fights the most oppression to survive? Or is the weakest the one who cannot even see her own oppression because she is too busy running after the privileges marked by the color of her skin? What are we measuring, really, among ourselves, Women? Betrayals.

* * *

To come to the Black woman in Africa as an equal, the White woman from Europe or America must be betrayed by the Black man first. Without that betrayal, I figure 80 percent of the White women will be reaching to the Black women from maternalistic heights. They would reach to the Black women to help them, their poorer, more oppressed sisters. Let's think of the *toubaab*—the White woman—in the story. We saw how her head was spinning with all those Black men dancing around her. She could not see the Black women very well because her eyes were fixed on the men. Sometimes she thought there was no Black women at all, that those Black men were there only for her taking. She did not see their ties with the Black women because they did not mention them, and she did not want to see them. The wife of the Black man. His lover. His girlfriend. The woman betrayed by him for her.

We saw how the *toubaab* got dizzy with all those sweet words going to her head. Those "patriarchal" men that she so despises, that she was there to fight in the name of the Black woman—she was irresistibly seduced by them. She forgot that she held that against the Black woman, that she had reproached the Black woman for liking the Black man too much, for not being immune to his seduction, for falling in love with him. Now, gripped by her own womanly desires, she forgets.

The White woman likes the Black man because he makes her feel like a Woman. He makes her feel like a Woman more than she has ever let a White man make her feel. The White woman gets dangerously close to Woman, closer than she has ever come. She falters over the body of the Black woman in her delirious steps toward Womanhood. At that moment, if she gets betrayed by the Black man, she needs the Black woman to help and console her. Then, the White woman will go to Black women not as a feminist against Woman, but woman to woman.

If she is not betrayed by the Black lover? She will betray Black women for a Black man without notice, or maybe with just a taint of guilt. But after all, is it not the Black woman's fault to have such unfaithful men? As for the White woman who remained impervious to the Black man's seduction, bolting her sex way beyond his reach, she will take the Black woman's raped vagina and wave it like the red flag of her own feminism.

Woman against Girl

Let me tell you about another betrayal, which came first: that of the Girl who became a Woman.

The Girl discovered her sex making love to a Man. She did so with passion and abandon, giving her life to him. But not until he rejects her will she find out that she is a Woman. At that moment, when he refuses her gift, when he decides that their love was not a beautiful thing but just anything, banal, irrelevant, she will lose her virginity and step over into Womanhood. She will learn that her integrity as a Woman depends on her bond to Man, that when he rejects her she is damned as a Whore, outside of family and society at large. The same act of love and the same woman are respectable if he decides to welcome her in his reign. The same act of love and the same woman will lose respect if he rejects her. And when he does, she will be betrayed by the Women and Men who will shun her and reduce her honor to tatters. She will become Woman in that pain. Alone. Slowly she will heal, and with her scarred body she will be taken back into the family, her pride lowered, her eyes still wide with shock. If she gets pregnant in the transformation, the process will be more gruesome. She will risk physical or social death. Once again her life will depend on him. The Girl/Woman will be respected, honored, and celebrated if he accepts the child. She will conquer the high skies of Womanhood and move into the thick realm of Motherhood. If he rejects the child, the same woman will be shamed, scorned, and abused, stoned to death or symbolically buried away from sociality.

You might say that he will never betray her. Then she will remain a child, one who has never left her Father's house. You will say that she will leave him. In peace she will walk away. How many times can she do that? How many times before he decides it is one too many, and he will not let her go in peace? He will not let her break the bond that is for him to break. The counting and accounting never stops. At some point he will blow the whistle, and she will know the betrayal of Woman.

*   *   *

Woman, where are you when the Girl cries out for your hand?

Mother against Woman

Mother tells her daughter that her sex is not for pleasure but for bargaining. Mother teaches her daughter that she will have to sacrifice pleasure on the altar of marriage. Sometimes, to make it easier, Mother takes the matter into her own hands. She does not wait for the sacrifice of marriage to come. She is in a hurry. She cuts her daughter's sex. At other times she cuts her daughter's desire: she turns it into pain, she makes it feel like hell.

*   *   *

Mother wants to replace Woman. She wants to take over, suffocate Woman out of existence. Mother does it for love. She knows that Woman will be better off as Mother. She tells Woman that in the end she will be rewarded if she lets herself be eaten up by Mother.

Mother makes life, and she makes Woman too. Mother cannot believe that Woman can give birth to Mother. Mother says that *she* gives birth, to male and female. How can Woman do the same? Mother tells Woman that she is sterile.

Home, Family, Nation, and Sexual Dis-encounters

White woman begins her sojourn in Senegal as such, and as such she meets Black man. Their encounter escalates into a tight embrace, and after the entanglement of their lovemaking, the couple emerges temporarily transformed: *White* woman and *Black* man vacillate toward a new configuration: white *woman* and black *man*. How is this unstable transformation achieved, and what does it index? Even before that, what provoked the fatal attraction of White woman to Black man, and how does the glue of that attraction hold them together and structure their most intimate movements and desires?

White woman and Black man are defined by their national identities, which take on the color of race insofar as they index a location within the international world order. White woman's national identity bestows on her the pedigree of blue blood, of royalty in the kingdom of earth. She is free to roam the globe, to travel from nation to nation and cross frontiers, because her nation acts as a guarantor of her good standing. The international world order defines her position as a migrating, traveling subject, the power of the nation to which she belongs trickling down to her own personal identity. When the subject moves to the threshold of the nation, in the process of crossing national borders, her national identity stands in for class identity. The nation to which she belongs guarantees that her own finances are in order and that she will not be an economic parasite to the nation where she travels. In fact, the assumption is made that she, in so far as she belongs to a nation in good standing in the international world order, will bring riches to the country in which she travels. She will be spending "good" money and enriching the host country with foreign revenues. So she is welcomed into that little country of West Africa. The Senegalese government welcomes White foreigners as guests of honor, expecting its own citizens to give them the very best, no matter what the costs. Is she not more important than Senegalese citizens in the international order? A White guest "deserves" the treatment that only a tiny Senegalese elite experiences as its own prerogative. The Senegalese poor have not the same entitlement to luxury and well-being as the foreign guests. Rather, according to the government's rhetoric of development (of the tourist industry, for example), poor Senegalese are supposed to sacrifice to provide the rich foreigners with (cheap) service of the best quality.[3]

Black man, unlike White woman, is tied to his own nation as a prisoner. He cannot get out and roam freely into the world because his nation cannot act as guarantor of his finances. He is a suspect who must go to impossible lengths to prove that he has money, and "good" money at that. His identity as a tourist is weak and almost nonexistent. He is denied the pleasure of travel; he is denied the possibility of curiosity about other countries while being faithful to his own. He is supposed to want to desert his own nation, always, as a matter of fact. If he is able to garner enough credibility to constitute his identity as a tourist, rather than as a wanna-be immigrant, that identity will still be tenuous. As a traveling subject, leaving the borders of his nation (Senegal) and stepping into international territory, his national citizenship remains attached to him to reproduce the inequalities of the international world order in microsocial interactions. Although he will spend money in the host country, just like a White tourist, he will not be thought of as enriching the nation. Rather, his presence is considered a threat and a potential precedent to "robbery." His temporary visit is always thought of as being in danger of turning into an immigration strategy (legal or illegal matters little in this moral economy), which the developed nation configures as a strategy to rob hard-won social security, economic stability, and political democracy from its own citizens. What is more, the money of the Black tourist is not as "good" as that of the White tourist: it does not buy him as many privileges as it would for a citizen of a powerful nation. He has to continually prove that his money has value. The hosts are always suspicious: First they think he has no money to spend and avoid him as a customer, and then they suspect that the money with which he pays is not "good" (i.e. stolen, counterfeited, dirty) even if it is the currency of the host country.

Black man is a suspect in the global kingdom, relegated to the servant's quarters and not allowed to leave unless he is running an errand for the White masters. Blackness stands as a marker not of race but of class origins inscribed by the borders of the nation and by the nation's position within the international global capitalist order. Within this geography of power, Black man (and Black woman, but we are not talking about her, we do not see her) is allowed into the frontiers of wealthy nations, either at the lowest or highest end of the job market. At the lowest end, he is allowed in as an unskilled laborer to perform jobs at the very bottom of the pay scale, without the benefits that come from being a citizen of a wealthy nation (such as access to social security, political entitlements, or civil protection). At the highest end, he comes in as a highly skilled laborer, necessary fodder in the never-ending globalization process, providing specialized knowledge that will be usefully assimilated into the capitalist empire.

The family is the only other means of incorporation into a foreign national body, a means that assures greater stability than integration via labor, at least for the unskilled worker. Black man, then, seeking incorporation into the White family/nation, must seduce White woman. Back home in Senegal, he often has only two or three weeks to do so before she leaves his country and never comes back. He must do his best in a short period of time. We know that in our story he is poor, and often illiterate, while she is rich in culture and money, at least much richer than he. He cannot seduce her with power and money. He will seduce her with his body and with his love, which is great and sincere, as big as his hope. He has his family too. Since he has no money to make White woman a gift, he asks his sisters to braid her hair. He invites her to eat the delicious meals that the women of his family have cooked for the occasion. He may even go so far as to offer to take care of her laundry— that is, to have it done by his sisters. His family welcomes White woman and collaborates in the seduction. White woman is thrilled. She wants to become part of the Black family, while she is in Senegal. And so their dis-encounter takes place: he, wanting to be incorporated into the White family/nation as a marker of a permanently transformed citizenship, and she, wanting to be integrated into the Black family/nation, temporarily. Who wants to permanently trade White citizenship for Black citizenship in the global capitalist order?

Remember the *toubaab* of our story—a tourist, a researcher, an adventurer? She will know the Senegalese nation all the better through her temporary incorporation into the Black family/nation. She will feel special, forgetting the temporary status of her visit while depending on that very temporariness for her desire of integration. But there is more. I am sure the phrase did not escape your attention: "The White woman likes the Black man because he makes her feel like a Woman . . . more than she has ever let a White man make her feel." How does the Black man mediate her identity as Woman differently from a White man? We must look at the psychology of this woman and at her specific circumstances to understand the intricacies of her attraction to Black man and the ways in which he contributes to her sense of self. You will remember that according to our narrator, White woman is a feminist, independent, and acting alone. You will remember that our narrator tells us that White woman does not want to marry, but she likes the attention and the propositions of Black man, even his desire to have a child with her.

This contradiction between not wanting to marry—wanting to be independent, wanting to act alone, and to pursue her career or her "fun"—while at the same time wanting the passion and excitement that a man's expectations of marriage and procreation can generate confronts her in her homenation, precluding a happy resolution. Yet in Senegal, she is able to reconcile both pleasures: to follow the desire to engage in relationships that are not like a marriage, and yet to experience the intensity that comes from the male partner's emotional investment in the seduction of a wife-to-be and future mother of his progeny. As a temporary and foreign visitor, she can bracket out the social constraints that operate at home and live both pleasures simultaneously, like in a dream—the wildest and sweetest dream. She will feel Womanly as she has not been able to experience before. She will be seduced by this feeling of Womanhood and be inebriated by the experience. As a temporary foreigner in Senegal, she is not accountable to her home community for what she does on her visit. She can silence her love affairs: nobody will know unless she tells them. Thus she can escape the accounting and recounting of her sexual exploits, avoiding the risk of filling up her allowable quota of premarital love affairs. Once that quota is reached, she will precariously slide away from the category of proper woman (always potentially marriageable, if not married) to that of whore (with the social stigma that comes with it). In Senegal, however, she can play with the role of potential wife, because Black man insists on it, and she will simply escape the country when the visit is over, probably never to come back. Thus, she will not have to face the social consequences that "playing" around such serious matters as marriage entails in her own community. Yet, this game is not without dangers. If she stays too long, she may not be able to escape the moral codes of the local community. If she returns, her past may haunt her, and her reputation may suffer. Or she may become so inebriated by the pleasures of this fantasy made real that she may forget to use contraception and become pregnant or sick with a sexually transmitted disease, and she too suffers the risk of rape.

There is another reason for her attraction to the Black man. Sex can give her the feeling of "universal" understanding—a physical communication capable of overcoming or sidestepping linguistic and cultural barriers. The sexual relation with Black man gives her the illusion of instant intimacy not only with him, but with his family/nation. Yet, the Black man who fatally attracts her is often not a man in suit and tie holding a government job or running a successful business. To satisfy her fantasy of intimacy with the black family/nation, he must be poor, illiterate, and perform a certain kind of physicality as an artist, musician (but not a piano player, she did not come to Senegal for that—rather a drummer or a *kora* player), dancer, soccer player, or marathon runner.

White woman sometimes does want to marry and take Black man home. This desire is often configured as a struggle against racism. She wants to combat the hate and violence between Blacks and Whites with her love. The marriage will become her personal crusade, all the more so if her own family is racist. She will enter the marriage with heroic aspirations, making her love for Black man her personal fight against a mean and unjust world. She wants to be a savior. She wants to help Black man, just as she wanted to help Black woman. In the process of "helping," she will use Black man to accrue her White identity. In fact, she wants to be incorporated into the Black family/nation only as a dual citizen, without losing her status in the White family/nation. She can thus reap the benefits of a shifting identity and choose strategically when to align herself with the Black and when with the White family/nation. She may take on the Black family name—if that is advantageous to her scholarly writing, for example—to claim inside status to the Black culture and speak of it as if it were her patrimony. But when the going gets tough, she can always revert back to her White family name and identity.

In this situation of entanglement between White woman and Black man, Black woman disappears from sight. White woman takes it for granted that

Black man is there for her as a suitable partner. She assumes her privilege to legitimize her priority in access to men of a different race: Black woman does not even appear as a competitor in the pursuit of Black man. White woman assumes her class privilege in the international economic order, the privilege that comes from being a citizen of a wealthy nation where the average yearly income is at least ten times higher than that of Senegalese citizens; she assumes that class privilege as if it were the obvious consequence of her "liberated" status. That is, she makes that privilege—enforced by hundreds of years of slavery, followed by a century of colonialism, and culminating in the neocolonialism of the age of late capitalism—her own personal achievement, as if she was in fact a better woman than Black woman. For her, when it comes to sexual competition, Black woman is oppressed by patriarchy in ways that render her meek, stupid, and full of sexual complexes (remember that we are in Senegal, a nation where 95 percent of the women are Muslim). Given this vision, she takes it as a matter of course that Black man would prefer her to Black woman.

White woman is still able to maintain her self-image as a nonracist feminist because she displaces her empathy and identification with Black people onto Black man. While she cannot identify with Black woman, whom she considers too oppressed and whom she is there to help, instruct, and liberate, she does identify with Black man, whom she sees as having more mobility and power. Her attraction to Black man allows her to see herself as fighting the evil of racism and the small-minded ideology that frowns upon interracial relationships.

White woman seems oblivious to the fact that while she takes it as her prerogative to have access to Black man, Black woman cannot assume the same prerogative with respect to White man. Again, White woman tends to interpret this asymmetry not in historical terms but in personal ones, each time considering the circumstantial reasons why a marriage union between White man and Black woman could not have happened. Yet, Black woman knows that she can be a prostitute to White man, that she can be raped, that she can be married as an indentured servant, and, much less often, that she can be a proper wife. Her chances to be equal to him—to be treated with respect, to be allowed to influence the decisions of the couple and the family, and to pursue her independent work—are far slimmer than her chances to be equal to Black man. While White Woman identifies with Black man and dreams that the oppressions Black/Woman equalize each other to bring symmetry in the couple's power relations, White man and Black woman cannot hold the same illusions. The lessons of history inform White man and Black woman that such couples have been sustained by the violence of White men against Black women. In spite of this, she may want to marry White man, aspiring to social ascension like her Black brother who wants to marry White woman, wanting to upgrade their status as citizens of the world capitalist order. Living among her family/nation, she may enter into a relation with White man while being protected by her community. Yet in Senegal, religious constraints weigh much more heavily on Black woman than on Black man and limit her willingness to get involved with White man. While a male Muslim can marry a woman no matter what her religious involvement, a Muslim woman cannot marry a non-Muslim man.[4] She might escape this situation by going abroad, and yet, once away from her own community, the social constraints that mitigate the historical violence of relationships between White men and Black women will be lifted. Living in White man's country, what may at first appear as a "liberated" man—less patriarchal than others—can reveal himself to be the cruelest of dominators.

Women, Sex, and Postcolonial Feminism

These "Tales of Betrayal" are configured as the staging of a series of antagonisms intending to rupture essentialist assumptions of gender.[5] The figures of Black woman, White woman, and Black man form an uneasy erotic triangle that explodes in a series of conflicts and contradictions. The tales drift from an ethnographic fictional narrative (traditionally coded as "description") to theoretical fiction (traditionally coded as "analysis") to question the relationship between "observation" and "explanation" in ethnographic work and to reverse the flow of the ethnographic gaze.

Postcolonial critiques of feminism have brought a critical rereading of the colonial experience in relation to gender systems and ideologies and a rereading of feminism in light of decolonization struggles.[6] These rereadings have questioned the dominance of white feminist theories that have monopolized representations of women of color in the colonial centers and in the colonized nations. While more than a decade of debates in the feminist movement and academia have made it more difficult for white feminists to assume their own ideologies and agendas of liberation to be unmarked by racial and class identifications, the mainstream media has appropriated the most regressive rhetoric of neoliberal feminism to reproduce, amplify, and put to "good" political use the imperialistic impulses of the movement.[7]

In the contemporary climate, following the guidelines provided by main-

stream feminists, Third World women (those from nations that occupy a non-hegemonic position in the international world order) and Fourth World women (those from ethnic "minorities" that stand in nonhegemonic relations to the narrative of First World nation-states) have been reduced to a type, the "most oppressed woman" (Mohanty 1991:51–80).[8] Patriarchy becomes another index of backwardness in white racist narratives, another hopeless malaise of underdeveloped nations and another explanation for their very underdevelopment (Savigliano 1995:207–38; Wallerstein 1997:158–83). In other words, the extreme patriarchy of Third World nations is taken as a quotient of inefficiency that prevents economic competitiveness in the world market, and, when it matters for the regulation and control of commodities and economies in the international arena, patriarchy is also defined as inimical to democracy. Thus follows the recipe: more imperialism, that is to say, "development"—Structural Adjustment Programs, International Trade Agreements, and, when economic regulations do not suffice, intensive bombing or less spectacular "low-intensity warfare" channeled through local political antagonisms.

White feminists have until recently contributed to this racist project with narratives that depict patriarchy in Third World nations as completely divorced from the history of slavery, colonialism, and genocide that has sustained over five hundred years years of Euro-American imperialism. Rather than explaining patriarchy historically, gender is conceived as an ahistorical, universal, a priori category that defines the subjugation of one group, women, by another, men (Mohanty 1991; Amadiume 1997). Thus, white women situate themselves outside of colonial history to proclaim their solidarity (a posteriori) with women of color, while assuming the privileges of white hegemony as the achievement of their own feminist struggles.

White liberal feminists see their greater power and access to national and international resources and institutions (such as academic presses or non-profit development organizations) vis-à-vis colored "sisters" as the effect of their own feminist struggles rather than the by-product of discrimination and imperialism. They reason that if colored women have less power than white women, it is because they are more oppressed by their own (very) patriarchal men and have not yet developed a feminist consciousness that can liberate them and guide them against male domination. Given this situation, white women can, and indeed must, teach the colored ones the feminist way (a new civilizing mission) and then, only when all women become white-feminists-alike, we will be equal.

Questions of historiography become paramount for conceptualizations of feminism. White liberal feminists have monopolized the history of the feminist movement by defining the struggles of white middle-class women as "feminists," while the struggles of Andean woman peasants or Nigerian women traders, for example, are not recognized as such and are silenced in dominant white feminist histories (Amadiume 1987, 1997; Johnson-Odim 1998). This process has two interrelated repercussions: it denies nonwhite women subjectivity and historical agency, and it excludes nonwhite women's theories, modes of mobilization, and concerns from feminist platforms. Not unlike the masculine histories that feminists criticize, white women place themselves at the center of history and disguise themselves as universal subjects. The interests of white middle-class women are taken as the universal interests of "women" no matter what their class, nationality, and political identities. Thus reproductive rights and population-control measures (meaning access to contraception and abortion) may be considered more important than access to land and water resources. Whatever the specific content of these struggles, a class of white women with the power to provide money and/or access to precious resources through international organizations and institutions defines the needs of a class of nonwhite women who do not have direct access to these resources.

White liberal feminists have accepted the premise of imperialism: that capitalism is ultimately good for all, including women. Socialist and radical feminists have critiqued the conspiring nature of capitalism and patriarchy, arguing that the division between the private and public domains feeds the artificial division between production and social reproduction, appropriating women's labor without economic retribution. Yet, in general, a theorization of gender systems that have structured noncapitalist modes of production as well as peripheral economies is missing from western feminist analyses.[9] Rather, evidence of indigenous women-centric movements tends to be maternalistically dismissed or marginalized in western feminist discourses, which make ethnic (or nonwhite) women either invisible or "backward" (Mohanty 1991).[10] Discussions around matriarchy exemplify this attitude. While matriarchy is theorized as an alternative to patriarchy, this alternative is connected to a distant, primitive past. If the matricentric networks and values are acknowledged to exist in contemporary ethnic societies by mainstream feminists scholars, it is done with a sense of doom, because it is conceptualized as a function of precapitalist simplicity and thus inevitably unable to survive the complexities of the modern world. In other words, matriarchy is assumed to be the primitive child of civilization, a dream of a lifestyle forever gone or disappearing. Economic evolutionism asserts that to be grown up, with the loss of freedom and innocence that maturity entails, is to be patriarchal.[11]

Such evolutionary and Eurocentric thinking associates matrifocal kinship networks and matriarchal values with a primitive social system characterized by failure. Thus, for example, rather than viewing female-centered households as the result of women's strategic choices that reflect their strength and independence, such arrangements are depicted as resulting from a failure to understand or recognize fatherhood, itself ascribed to primitive promiscuity (Amadiume 1997:71–88). The criminalization of African American single mothers in the United States rests on these racist premises. Racist narratives tell us that African American women, like their primitive foremothers, have failed to achieve and maintain a whole family. Their kind is so uncivilized and violent that women and men of the same race cannot even get along and live together. The men are so primitive as to fail to recognize paternity and the social obligations of fatherhood. The state is thus "forced" to assume the role of surrogate father and provide with taxpayers' money the support that a breadwinner should give to his own family.

Ifi Amadiume has argued that the patriarchal and Eurocentric values of Africanist scholars have produced a "masculinization" of historical and sociological data about African societies that has failed to recognize the presence of matricentric socioeconomic and moral networks (1997:29). Amadiume states that while modern European societies are characterized by a monolithic gender system that privileges patrilineality as well as male economic, political, and religious institutions, African societies show the evidence of a dual or even a tripartite gender system. Through a rereading of classical anthropological literature (for example, Fortes 1959, on the Tallensi) and of Cheikh Anta Diop's scholarship on ancient Egypt and precolonial black African empires (Diop 1974; 1978; 1987; 1989), as well as drawing on her own research on the Igbo community of Nnobi in the Anambra state of Nigeria (Amadiume 1987), Amadiume argues that African societies are characterized by competing gender systems that balance the gendered distribution of power within a given social order and allow for matriarchal power and values to be expressed.[12] She argues that in such societies a matricentric kinship unit (mother-sons-daughters) forms the basis of economic production and consumption and provides a mode of sociality with its own political structures and affective and moral values. This matricentric unit is inserted within larger male-focused kinship networks centered on jural power and competing moral values. A gender-neutral system, in which biological sex differs from the ideological assignation of gender, mediates between the two.

While a full discussion of Amadiume's research is beyond the purview of my analysis, I have evoked her writing for the theoretical and interpretative questions it raises in the context of my own research. Her deconstruction of Eurocentrism in women's studies helps explain the jarring discrepancy that I experienced between my own perception of women is Senegal and the images of Senegalese women that I encounter in the scholarly literature. Having gone to Dakar to investigate the activities of African Ballets, I could not help being drawn to the circle of *sabar* dancers that so prominently reconfigures the streets of the city. When I came back to the United States, the public visibility of women in Dakar, coupled with the performance of power and eroticism that fuels *sabar* dancing, kept jarring with the images of Senegalese women as Muslim women that I was getting from books. These books include the feminist scholarship produced by Senegalese scholars that I used in the previous chapter (Ministére de la Femme 1993; Bop 1995), the scarce literature devoted to Senegalese Muslim women (reducible to one crucial book: Callaway and Creevey 1994),[13] and the more extensive general literature on Muslim women and Third World women written by white feminists. Senegalese women scholars (Sow 1997; M'Bow 1989) report on the complex challenges facing Senegalese women in ways that assert women's agency and creativity. Yet, as they are focused on analyzing the problems and structural features of exploitation confronted by women, they do not capture what had been my most enduring experience of women in Dakar: their beauty and their power. Women's stunning kinetic engagement through dancing materially and symbolically proclaims their power to mobilize and assert themselves as central protagonists in the street life of the city. Are we to interpret this power as a superficial manifestation of agency and freedom, which is constrained by deeper, more enduring and significant forms of oppression? Or, as Amadiume allows me to theorize, can we see in the *sabar* the expression of a competing gender system that cannot be subsumed under a monolithic interpretation of social reality? As I argue in chapter 4, the all-female networks that engage women in *sabar* dancing in the city of Dakar seem to suggest a strong correlation between economic relations, matricentric kinship units, and gender ideology. More research is needed to substantiate this initial analysis: How prevalent are matricentric kinship units in Dakar? Do they correlate with economic patterns of production and consumption? Do they generate an alternative gender system with its own ideologies and sexual morality, as the *sabar* seems to suggest?

My analysis of *sabar*, followed by the stories "Attaya" and "Toubaab," is an attempt to confront the multiple sexual codes that coexist and compete in the contemporary urban environment of Dakar. I felt the need to write the story "Attaya" to juxtapose the celebratory eroticism of the *sabar* circle with a reminder of the great dangers that women face in asserting their sexuality in a patriarchal society. Yet, how are we to interpret the story? If we are not to see the rape as an aberrant individual act but rather as an integral part of patriarchal sexuality, as feminists argue (and I myself would argue), where are we to put the ideological blame? How is the abuse justified and normalized so as to leave the woman violated in silence and without redress? Can we assert, without pausing to question our assumptions, that Islamic sexual morality is the ideological culprit? Why does this story so powerfully overwhelm the *sabar* stories, erasing the presence of women's engaged eroticism? Why do representations of Senegalese women in white feminist narratives (again I include my own) tend to exclude or trivialize feminine aesthetics and pleasures?

While pleasure and female eroticism have been important topics in white feminist writings, opening up a critique of patriarchal morality and control of female sexuality, such topics have been totally absent from white feminist writings on African women. The ways in which African women have carved out alternative sexual moralities and alternative gender values has remained largely unexplored in the literature, and it is only beginning to be addressed by a new generation of African and Africanist scholars well versed in postcolonial feminist theories (Amadiume 1997; Oyewùmí 1997). At the same time, the gap between the ways in which white women practice self-representation and their representations of the Other (woman) has generated a plethora of images and narratives on the sexuality of women of color displayed and paraded in the public domain of feminist and anthropological literature with an aesthetic of presentation that courts the pornographic (Savigliano 1995; Abrahams 1998). The moral codes that define and constrain public representation of white female sexuality have not been equally applied to the representation of black women's sexuality. Rather, the alleged sexual promiscuity of women of color has served to legitimize offensive and racist displays of "primitive customs" and abhorrent sexual features—graphic representation of genital mutilation in books and ethnographic films, the quasi-sadistic representations of museum immolation of sexual "freaks" like Sarah Bartmann, or the obscene albeit clinical depictions of African prostitutes.[14] Searching for a counternarrative, I felt the need to switch the frame of reference and produce the story of "Toubaab" and its further elaboration in "Home, Family, Nation, and Sexual Dis-encounters." These stories have the double purpose of representing white women's sexuality in an ethnographic context while exposing the antagonism between white and black women through sexual competition. A new type of white woman emerges from these accounts: the promiscuous and liberated white woman in the role of (sexual) tourist and adventurer in a Third World country.[15] This woman employs her feminist ideology to exert her racial privilege over a class of economically disenfranchised and "exotic" men, while paying little attention to the consequences of her actions for her black feminist "sisters." The exploits and high visibility of this "white liberated woman" in Senegal, coupled with the sexualization of women in Euro-American media widely accessible to Senegalese TV viewers, feeds into Islamic fundamentalist narratives about the depravity of western feminism and the evils of western culture and bolsters their arguments against locally generated feminists agendas.

Yet the antagonisms between different women's sexualities and hegemonic and subaltern narratives about them does not only involve white and black subjects; it also implicates the collective and individual struggles of women and men in the streets, courtyards, and bedrooms of Dakar. In this context, a Muslim sexual morality, which sets off the antinomies wife/whore and pure/polluted, is contested by matricentric kinship units of the kind described by Amadiume (1997). Although she does not explicitly address the issue of a sexual morality, her discussion suggests that preoccupations with virginity and the legitimacy of children, as well as the construction of filial bonds, are redefined by women in their own terms and do not depend on the mediation of men (husbands, fathers, uncles).[16] I argue that the eminently erotic and female social space created by women at *tànnebéers* supports such female-centered values and rests on the possibility of women to live their sexuality by opting to create matricentric ties and families.

6

The Circulation of Dances
on and off the Stage

Against Authenticity

In chapters 1 and 3 I have analyzed the performances of the National Ballet of Senegal as a product consumed by white foreign audiences comfortably seated at the theaters in California and Senegal. In chapter 2 I have looked at the narratives and historical relations that allow for and support the intercultural exchange between white spectators and black performers. In chapter 4 I have introduced the reader to the sociocultural landscape within which the work of Dakar's African Ballets is inserted, and I have begun to analyze dance practices from the point of view of Dakar's citizens. I have argued that within the urban context, the dominant dance idiom—the *sabar*—is articulated through a network of relations that link social subjects in a circuit of economic and affective exchange organized through the mediation of *géwëls* and supported by the Wolofization of the Senegalese population and the national media. Chapter 5 carried the reflections on eroticism aroused by the circle of *sabar* dancers outside of the dancing circle. This chapter examines once again the *sabar* complex to draw out the relationship between popular and theatrical performances and the dispersal of choreographic authority across multiple subjects and social networks. This examination recontextualizes the work of the National Ballet of Senegal in dialogue with the popular dance cultures of the country and ends with a preliminary inquiry into the relationship between dance genres and choreographic processes.

The National Ballet's performances, as presentations of traditional Senegalese dances, refer to social relations that link the space of performance to a variety of social events: marriages, baptisms, wrestling matches, circumcision coming-out ceremonies, neighborhood celebrations, political rallies, village dances, music competitions, concerts, mediatic productions, and discotheque events and performances, as well as historical commemorations. The members of the National Ballet often dance in these disparate social spaces, marking the continuity between them with the skills engraved on their bodies and exhibited in performance. The circulation of people and cultural practices on and off the stage suggests continuities between Ballet performances and the social events that occur off the stage. Each performance event constitutes the others in an interplay of references and juxtapositions. This continuity has been a central assumption in my ethnographic research. More specifically, I have posited the activities of the urban Ballets as central and coterminous with other forms of dance practice relevant to the lives of Ballet dancers. In so doing I have been critical of theoretical models that classify African dance along an authentic/inauthentic grid, valuing only "traditional" (authentic) dance practices and devaluing "modern" (inauthentic) forms. As discussed in chapter 2, such a model, common in dance studies, reproduces the dichotomy between traditional and modern societies developed under the Order of the Other by considering dances that do not belong to the traditional canon of ritual as bad copies of some originary, now-corrupted tradition, or as bad imitations of western forms. This assumption also draws from the evolutionary model developed by the dance scholars of the Order of the Other who conceptualized dance history as a movement from ritual dance (in primitive societies) to theatrical dance (in modern societies). When applied to African societies, this model conceives of the movement from ritual to theatrical dance as degenerative, as if those societies could not properly evolve out of their primitive state and produce anything but ritual dance. Both interpretations assume a one-way development and linear evolution of dance forms rather than a flux of communication between different practices and social spaces. Robert Nicholls exemplifies this assumption:

> The separation of form and function is observed in the process of artistic trivialization that is occurring throughout Africa, from Ritual-art to Folk-art to Tourist-art. Each stage represents a loss of authenticity, a loss of aesthetic quality, and a corresponding loss of historical significance and cultural relevance. . . . As if the lure of Western trappings and bright lights is not enough, the cessation of meaningful dance stimulus just when young men and women reach adolescence, may encourage them to enter bars and parties that feature modern disco and pop music. (Nicholls 1996:53, 56)

In Nicholls's analysis, African dance follows a one-way line of development from ritual, to folklore, to tourist art, paralleled by a progressive disintegration of artistic and social values.[1] This disintegration comes as a consequence of western luring, a lurid giving-up of will and agency under the pressure of western temptations: each transition signals a progressive moving away from a true African identity to a misidentification with the West and a despicable appropriation of dubiously moral western practices.

> The influence of Western thought has now limited the functions of dance to mere recreation in many African cities. . . . In Africa, the decline of traditional art means more than a loss of entertainment or a diminishing of aesthetics. Indigenous cultures are functional social instruments which have been developed over the centuries to meet practical needs. . . . Impoverishment in many rural areas in Africa can be directly attributed to the decline of traditional culture of which music and dance is an integral part. (Nicholls 1996:42)

Rather than being the effect of complex historical forces, inscribed in the history of slavery, colonialism, and neocolonial power relations, African poverty becomes the fault of weak African personalities who are lured by western thought and aspirations. This bad influence of the West acts, first, to transform ritual dance into folklore. While he does not clearly define the categories of ritual and folklore, Nicholls mentions national dance troupes as representatives of "folklore." He thus argues that national dance troupes mark a loss of "authentic" African identities and meaningful traditions and an acculturation to foreign western values. My own discussion of the National Ballet of Senegal was keen to point out that the constitution of national dance troupes, coming at the very moment in which the African population appropriated the state apparatus, can be interpreted as one of the processes of Africanization of the colonial state. Nicholls, however, interprets these troupes as unambiguously "westernized." As my discussion on Négritude should demonstrate, to do so flattens the complex political and cultural struggles that engaged African intellectuals, artists, and politicians in a redefinition of modernity to include African societies and values. This project was by its very nature ambiguous as well as hybrid, as Senghor himself often stated.[2]

Nicholls's narrative relentlessly chastises African artists for their degenerate westernization: the next phase in this devolutionary process is marked by the replacement of folklore with tourist art. Again, he does not provide a clear distinction between folklore and tourist art, a distinction that seems worth pursuing in the context of national African dance troupes, several of which, like the Ballet of Senegal, often perform almost exclusively for non-African audiences—art tourists?—abroad and in their own national theaters.

Is tourist art more degenerate than folklore because it is cheaper and thus of a less artistic quality than more expensive products? Is it less culturally relevant because it is more economically profitable? And if so, for whom? Is it less authentic because it does not take place in proper cultural institutions like theaters but is performed in explicitly commercial spaces like hotels?

I will discuss Ballet performances in Senegal's tourist enclaves at length in chapter 8, addressing the category that Nicholls defines as tourist art. Here I will follow Nicholls's devolutionary model to the end. In his model discotheque dancing (including bars and parties) stands as the most wicked of forms because it corrupts young generations of Africans away from traditional culture/dance toward western/modern culture. The description of discotheque dancing that I offer at the end of chapter 4 should make problematic the conflation of discotheques in the African urban milieu with westernized social spaces, although I am sure that Nicholls and I did go to the same clubs (he does not specify which "African" discotheque/bar on the continent he has in mind).

During my research in Dakar (1996–97), I found neither the moral and artistic degeneration assumed by Nicholls's devolutionary model nor the compartmentalization between dance practices and social spaces that his model implies. Ballet dancers may perform the same dance steps for a tourist audience in one of Dakar's five-star hotels, on a stage with a popular music group performing for a Senegalese audience, within the walls of a theater (in Senegal or abroad), or at a dance circle in the streets of the city, in a home, or in a discotheque. As dancers circulate among these different social spaces, dance steps travel from one context to the other, and a complex web of negotiations underscores the integration of new dances into "tradition." The complex interplay of improvisation, set dance vocabulary, and choreographic agency that characterizes popular Senegalese dances remains muddled by anachronistic discussions of tradition as an autocratic choreographer that imposes its will on endless generations of African dancers. I will challenge purist definitions of tradition such as Nicholls's by analyzing some relevant choreographic and performance processes typical of the contemporary and urban *sabar* complex.

Dance Citations, Variations, and Canonizations: The *Sabar* Complex

At *sabar* events, a circle of bodies constructs the performance space, a space filled with the expectations of the encircling audience and protected by their physical mass from the outside social world. The drum ensemble creates a directional pole within the circle, providing a powerful axis of directionality as performers engage face to face with the drummers. The *sabar* circle promotes competing solos in which single performers take the center of the circle to challenge each other in public displays of kinetic savoir-faire. On these occasions, *sabar* dances are defined by a core—usually embodied in one step, which gives the name to the dance—and a surrounding complex of introductory steps.[3]

Introducing steps before the dance proper is a sign of skill and poise and a creative space for performers to show their personalities and expertise. In this introductory phase, performers are allowed great freedom, which they assume constructively and inventively by creating dramatic entrances into the performance space and by gathering the audience's attention toward them. Once the eyes of the audience are glued on the body of the dancer, she or he can erupt in the dance proper, engaging in a dialogue with the drummers.

The dancers' solos are the result of complex negotiations between the dancers and the drummers. The subtlety of these choices is carefully judged by the audience, who shares in the knowledge of choreographic codes and is able to assess the dancers' creativity and the relationship between their choreographic choices and the skills necessary to embody them. The interplay between *sabar* rhythms and *sabar* dances makes the negotiations between dancers and drummers particularly complex. Although I observed many *sabars* during my research in Dakar, it was not until my consultation with Aziz Faye—an accomplished *géwël* drummer and dancer from Médina Dakar—that I came to understand more fully the relationship between choreographic and rhythmic authority and the joint authorship of drummers and dancers in the making of *sabar* performances. I will thus proceed to analyze these relationships, integrating my own interpretation with Aziz Faye's, based on our lengthy interview in Los Angeles in June 2000.[4]

Aziz Faye comes from one of the most famous *géwël* families in the country, popularly known as the Sing Sing family, named after the great Sing Sing Faye. The family, now led by Vieux Sing Sing, is a veritable institution of creativity and learning, as its members are active protagonists in the national and international music scene, performing and teaching in Dakar and abroad. The family is a testament to the aggressive creativity of griots, who are continually negotiating and redefining their relevance in a fast-changing musical and social world. This adaptive and entrepreneurial spirit is exemplified by the younger generation of Sing Sing brothers, who, in addition to playing *sabars* in social circles and events, have established themselves as central protagonists in the *mbalax* music scene.[5] Perhaps the most well-known living member of the family is Mbaye Dièye Faye, who has accompanied Youssou N'Dour as a percussionist from the start of his career, and who is the leader of his own group—the Sing Sing Rhythmes. The group Lemzo Diamono, led by brother Lamine Faye, is also one of the most appreciated *mbalax* groups of the country, while the Super Diamono of Adama Faye marked the *mbalax* scene of the 1980s, when it was at its zenith of popularity. Aziz Faye has been performing since the age of nine as a Sing Sing *gëwël*, and since the late 1990s he has settled in Los Angeles, where he has founded, with his longtime friend and collaborator Oumar Mboup, the performance group Khaley Nguewel.[6] Aziz performs regularly with Khaley Nguewel and teaches in Los Angeles and across the United States, having established himself not only as a drummer but also as a masterful dancer and dance teacher of the *sabar*. As Aziz continues to travel back and forth between the United States and Senegal, where he plays and performs with members of his family at *sabar* and *mbalax* events, he deepens and expands the tradition of *sabar* as a committed protagonist, teacher, and messenger.

Given this introduction, we can return to our discussion of the performance and choreographic processes of the urban *sabar* complex, as revealed by my own observations and consultation with Aziz.

Within the *sabar* complex, the same name is given to a dance and to the rhythm that calls for that dance, yet the two are separable units. For example, the *ceebu jën* rhythm calls for the *ceebu jën* dance, but the *kaolack* dance or the *farwu jar* dance can also be done to the *ceebu jën* rhythm, although these dances have their own rhythms as well.[7] By the same token, these three dances can be danced the same way or differently: they share the same basic step, but the ways in which the feet are lifted off the floor and placed back on the ground, the ways in which the arms circle, and the accents of the steps can create differences that mark them as unique steps/dances. It is up to the dancer to give it the inflection of a particular step/dance.

As new dances are continually created, new rhythms are also created to go with the most popular dances. Yet again, as there are varying degrees of relationships between rhythms and dances, more than one dance can be performed to the same rhythm, or the same dance can be performed to different rhythms. For example, Aziz pointed out that within the *kaolack* rhythm one could dance the *kaolack* dance, but also the *mu lay ce gin*, the *waajaru*, or the *vespa*, although each of these dances has their own special rhythm. The *mu lay ce gin*, the *waajaru*, or the *vespa* dances can also be done to the *ceebu jën* rhythm with greater ease that to the *kaolack* rhythm. To dance these dances inside the *kaolack* rhythm, one must be a very good dancer with a great sense of rhythm, because the steps and the drumming do not neatly support each other as they do within the *ceebu jën* rhythm. These intricacies are not lost on the audience, who judges the creativity and skill of dancers by the relationship the performers establish between the choreography and the rhythms played by the drummers.

The relationship between the lead drummer and the dancer brings further complexity to this exchange. During the *sabar,* while the drum ensemble remains stable on one end of the circle, the lead drummer leaps within the circle to meet the soloing dancer(s) and engage her in a rhythmic tête-à-tête.[8] This engagement is a "treat" earned by the dancer through her skills and personality, or perhaps her social standing; lousy dancers pass unnoticed by the lead drummer. In the encounter between dancer and lead drummer, often a special rhythm is generated, either by the drummer, who influences the dancer, or by the dancer, who leads the drummer to spell out her movements with his playing. This special rhythm is called a *bàkk.* The *bàkk* allows for greater choreographic variation in the solo of the dancer than what is called for by the simple performance of the dance/step. For example, the *sabar* ensemble may be playing the *kaolack* rhythm as the dancer approaches the ensemble performing the *kaolack* step in rolling repetitions. The lead drummer then plays a particular *bàkk* for the dancer. The dancer then switches from the *kaolack* to the performance of the *bàkk.* Many *bàkks* are in stock with the lead drummer, and dancers can request them before the *sabar* event begins. A dancer may call the name of the *bàkk* to the lead drummer and ask him to play it when she comes out to do her solo, or she can simply spell out with her movements one of the popular *bàkks;* the drummer will immediately recognize it and follow her lead. Master dancers can create their own *bàkk* in the midst of their solos, and because of the clarity and strength of their choreography, the drummer will be able to follow their movements, co-creating the *bàkk* on the spot. A transcription of my conversation with Aziz will clarify these dynamics:[9]

> AZIZ: You do the *kaolack* [rhythm], but you can also do a *bàkk,* many *bàkks* to it. Before I come to dance I go to the drummer and I say, "Play this *bàkk* for me [he gets up and sings]: *mbacia gin, mbacia gin,*" and so the drummer will know that when I come to do my solo he is going to play that *bàkk* for me. Not the straight rhythm, but curved and straight. The *bàkk;* it makes the rhythm curve.

FRANCESCA: Do many people ask for a *bàkk* to the drummer?

A: Yes, many do. If you are good they can see the *bàkk* that you dance, and they follow you right there. You do not need to say it in advance.

F: How do people say . . . what do they say to the drummer? They sing the rhythm, or they show him the dance?

A: They sing the rhythm, or they can just say the name of the *bàkk* and the drummer knows.

F: Can you give me an example of a *bàkk?*

A: Inside the *kaolack* or the *ceebu jën* rhythm you can have [he gets up and sings first in Wolof and then in English]: "*loo ma ndigal ndigal, loo ma ndigal ma def:*[10] whatever you told me to do, that is what I am doing; *kër gi ku fii nekk, war nga déglu tay dégg:* this house, if you stay here, you have to understand today, you have to listen." That is the whole *bàkk.*

F: It's like a *taasu.*

A: Yes, like a *taasu.* You can just go to the drummer and say, "Play the *looma ndigal ndigal,*" and they know.

The *taasu* is a song, or a refrain, a proverb, a call to the audience that is accompanied by a (*sabar*) dance. This definition of *taasu* as a song accompanied by a dance is highly contextual and stems from my own encounter with *taasu* from within women's performances in Ballets or *mbalax* musical groups. *Taasu* is more commonly defined in the literature as a form of poetry associated with women, constituting one of the genres of praise singing and oral poetry of the Wolof and Lebou. Lisa McNee's study (2000), the first book-length treatment of the subject, defines the genre by its orality, while failing to account for the dance performances that often accompany *taasu* poetry.[11] McNee argues that *taasu* is a female autobiographical genre and uses it to destabilize canonical definitions of literature, exploring the continuities and discontinuities between *taasu* and written autobiographical narratives. Unfortunately, while stressing that *taasu* must be understood in context, McNee ignores dancing completely in accounting for its performance. This is a serious shortcoming in an otherwise excellent book. My own engagement with dance acquainted me with *taasu* as a total performance that includes dancing and singing, to the extent that it took me months before I realized that *taasu* is properly defined as oral poetry. In a similar manner, I came to learn of *bàkks* from a dancer's point of view, within the *sabar* circle, and thus my own discussion reflects the dancers' and drummers' biases.

These biases are an important addition to the academic literature, which, with the notable exception of Tang (2000), has defined *bàkks* much like *taasu*—as oral poetry.[12] In fact, while *taasu* is a female genre, *bàkk* is a male genre, associated with the praise singing of wrestlers.[13] Yet because of the close interrelation of singing, drumming, and dancing, *taasu* and *bàkks* come to mark not only sung poetry but also danced and drummed phrases. A further engagement with Aziz Faye's narrative will better elucidate these complex interrelationships:

> FRANCESCA: How do you create a *bàkk?*
>
> AZIZ: Sometimes we create the *bàkk* from a *taasu;* sometimes we just create the *bàkk.* Sometimes we create the *bàkk* from Youssou N'Dour's song, or Baaba Maal's. For example, from N'Dour's song "Diamono" [The Town], he sings the song, and we pick up a verse from the song, and we make a *bàkk* for it. Sometimes we play the rhythm that is in the song, we take the *bàkk* from the drums; sometimes we take the *bàkk* just from the words of the singer. The drummer [of the original group, the one from which they take the *bàkk*] may be playing something while the singer sings, so we may just take the *bàkk* from the song and do our drum rhythm from the song. Or we may take the *bàkk* from the guitar, or the drum set. If you are a talented musician you can get the *bàkk* from any instrument. You can get it from this fan here [we are sitting in front of a fan], or you can get it from people clapping hands, or from the guitar, or the drum set. All you have to do is to make it sound fine.

It is clear that in Aziz's comments the *bàkk* refers to a drum phrase. This drum phrase can be created in response to a song—be it a *taasu* sung at a women's event, or a *bàkk* sung at a wrestling match, or the refrain of a widely popular singer, such as Yossou N'Dour or Baaba Maal. Picking up a verse from a song and making a *bàkk* to it points to the historical relation of speech to music and the directionality of that communication—from speech to music. This directionality explains how drums as well as other musical instruments "talk."[14] For example, in the *sabar* complex the *tama*—the Wolof "talking drum"—talks by close association between a Wolof sentence and a rhythm.[15] That is, a formulaic verbal expression is spelled out on the drum, and once this association is established in the more or less public realm of performance, the mere playing of the rhythm will elicit the listeners to supplement in their minds the associated words, even when those words are no longer performed. Some of this "talking" will only be intelligible to the initiated, while other rhythms can be decoded by a wider audience, yet association between rhythm and speech is arbitrary and socially determined, much like the relation between signifier and signified. Without proper socialization the rhythms remain inert, unable to speak to an audience. Specific social and performance contexts as well as specific musical instruments are privileged for this kind of communication. In the *sabar* complex, for example, the talking drum is the instrument of choice for this kind of codified communication, but other drums talk as well. I want to stress that this kind of drum talking is done in the local community language(s) and is associated with specific linguistic meanings of a formulaic nature: drums can call or ward off spirits, bless someone, or announce the arrival of important people or upcoming events. Yet drums also talk because their rhythms are consistently sung by drummers and dancers. In this case a stock of phonemes is conventionally used for one drum family and not for another; each family in a sense "speaks" its own language. Thus for the *sabar* one could hear *ragia gin tas tas mbatas,* while if hearing *cra cra cu cu cra cu cu cra cra* one would know that this is a dance and a rhythm for the *jembe.* This talking differs from the codified talking referred to above: if in the case of the "talking drum" the drum is thought to replicate human speech, here it is people who replicate the "speaking" of the drum. The singing provides a precise replication of drum sounds, with each phoneme corresponding to a specific drum stroke. I call this talking "singing the rhythms." Rhythm becomes the language common to dancers and drummers, and singing the rhythms is a form of orality that allows for communication between them. Thus, it is not uncommon for masterful dancers to be able to teach new rhythms to drummers without ever touching a drum. They play with their tongues, singing in the language of the drums. Similarly, masterful drummers can instruct a dancer to perform specific movement sequences simply by singing the rhythmic text of the dance. The transfer of information between drummers and dancers is mediated by the verbalization of rhythm, which provides a common language across musical and dance practices. The translation of dancing into drumming and drumming into dancing assumes fluency in singing rhythms and the capacity to translate this form of orality into either dance or music. While dance can be sung, drum sounds are songs that can be danced.

The centrality of rhythm in dancing, orality, and drumming explains how *bàkks* can be defined as rhythmic, danced, or sung phrases, depending on the speaker's biases. Yet the centrality of rhythm in linking the domains of speech and action points to the importance of understanding *bàkks* from a drummer's point of view. Significantly, Aziz, who as a *géwël* is an expert orator, dancer, and drummer, defines a *bàkk* from the location of drummers. This definition clarifies my initial confusion between *taasus* and *bàkks*. If the drummed *bàkk* (understood as a complex drummed phrase or string of phrases) is accompanied by women's singing in a specifically women's gathering, then the sung phrase will be called a *taasu*. Yet if the drum rhythm marks the performance of a wrestler and his own laudatory boasting, this singing will be called a *bàkk*. Moreover, a *taasu* event may feature singing and dancing without drumming, or a *bàkk* may be performed solely as a musical phrase by a *sabar* ensemble performing in a theater or playing a for a *mbalax* group, with no dancing or singing accompanying the drumming.

The independence of *bàkks* from oral narrative is underscored in Aziz's account, which asserts that *bàkks* can be created not only in response to verbal utterances but also in response to other musical instruments, like the refrain of a guitar or a drum set. The more creative the drummer, the greater the inspiring stimuli for his *bàkks*. This creativity and the associated capacity to create *bàkks* is the prerogative and the test of good drummers. In fact, much as *bàkks* allow for greater choreographic variation in the dancers' solos, so they also allow for virtuosity in the drummers' playing. Coming back to the *sabar* dancing circle, we can once again follow these subtleties.

We have addressed how the *sabar* complex is composed of many dances, each based upon a (core) step, repeated over and over by the performer. Similarly to the dance, the *sabar* rhythm that accompanies a dance is performed in rolling repetitions by the *sabar* ensemble. The *bàkk,* however, allows for rhythmic complexities paralleled by complex choreographic variations: it twists and turns the dance rhythm, bringing accents, sudden stops, and dramatic shifts of weight and tempo into the dance.

Improvisation by either the dancer or the drummer determines the switch from *sabar* rhythm (associated with a specific *sabar* dance) to *bàkk* (associated with a choreographer or improvised complex dance phrase, also called *bàkk*). The switch from *sabar* dance step to *bàkk* allows the dancer to show her virtuosity and personality, just as the lead drummer can showcase his talent through the *bàkks* he plays. Furthermore, although many *bàkks* are in stock for drummers and dancers alike, great dancers create their own dance phrases in the midst of a performance and lead the drummers to simultaneously create a *bàkk* for them. These improvised creations are predicated on the mastery of the established—if always growing—repertory of *sabar* dances and *bàkks* by dancers and drummers who cultivate their skills in their own separate but interdependent arenas.

I will now address the dialogue between canonized dances and new creations by analyzing the establishment of two new dances in the *sabar* repertory. I will also continue to explore the relationship between the aural and kinetic elements of performance, as well as the interplay of improvisation and set dance vocabulary.

*   *   *

At the time of my research, two dances were among the most popular at *sabar* events: the *mu lay ce gin* and the *Tink's daye bondé*. Their popularity was partly due to their novelty, which gave Dakarois dancers the opportunity to show their coolness by demonstrating how "in" on the latest development of the *sabar* complex they were. In fact, while some old-time favorites are appreciated precisely for their longevity and continued popularity, other dances are popular because they are "in fashion": they represent the edge of the expanding *sabar* complex. The national television station, with the presentation of music videos, often acts as the launching platform for new dances, which enter the living rooms and courtyards of Dakarois through the airwaves. This was the case for the *mu lay ce gin* and the *tank daye bondé*, which were the signature dances of two popular songs created and performed by two of the Fayes' *mbalax* bands: the Lemzo Diamono and the Sing Sing Rhythm, respectively.

The Lemzo Diamono of Lamine Faye presented the dance *mu lay ce gin* in their song and music video "Simb." The *simb* is a popular game in the low-income quarters of Dakar and is related to an old celebration in honor of hunters who have survived the attack of a lion or killed a lion. These hunters are thought to have become part lion, having assimilated the spirit of the animal. In the game, the hunter performs the lion dance while running to attack children, who scatter in great excitement. The Lemzo Diamono capitalized on the popularity of the game to promote their album *Simb* with the music video of the same name. As wrestlers dressed in lion costumes perform the dance of the lion, men in military camouflage perform the *mu lay ce gin*. Thus the *gaynde* ("lion" in Wolof) dance, which is old, is performed side by side with the *mu lay ce gin*, which was created to make the video popular and readily caught viewers' attention. Like many popular dances, the *mu lay ce gin* is accompanied by a short refrain, originally performed by the Lemzo Diamono in their video but often replicated by dancers to spice up their own performance. True to this pattern, when Aziz got up to demonstrate the *mu lay ce gin* during our interview, he also sang the refrain:

We sing:[16]

> *Mu lay ce gin*
> *dama dawal vélo*
> *rege gin tac! rege gin tac!*
> *mu lay ce gin*
> I drive the bike
> *rege gin tac! rege gin tac!*

By analyzing the meaning of the refrain we can better appreciate the relationship between the aural elements of the song and the kinetic elements of the dance. I asked Aziz the meaning of the refrain:

FRANCESCA: What does *mu lay* mean? *Ce gin,* that is just the sound for the movement?

AZIZ: Yes, *ce gin* is the movement. *Mu lay,* it's just a name. *Mu* means "do something." *Lay* is just a name, because there are many men named Lay. Often the dances are named after somebody.

Wolof differentiates between action verbs and stative verbs, and *mu* is a pronoun attached to action verbs to indicate that the action is performed by the third-person singular[17] (for example, *mu ngiy dem* [he or she is going]; *mu ngiy nelaw* [he or she is sleeping]). Thus Aziz translates it as "do something." *Lay,* he does something, he *ce gins?* Was the dance created by a certain *Lay?* Aziz could not tell me. At any rate, the first line of the refrain promotes loose associations because of the ambiguity of the language, which articulates sounds that are a mixture of Wolof and of the language of the drums. The second line of the refrain is sung in Urban Wolof,[18] which is a mixture of Wolof (*dama dawal*) and French (*vélo*), and it aids in the interpretation of the dance by suggesting that the movement refers to a person riding a bike. The last line of the refrain is solely sung in the language of the drums, bringing the emphasis back to the rhythmic aspect of the dance and its relation to the music. By focusing on the purely rhythmic section of the refrain we can understand how singing the rhythms not only allows communication between dancers and drummers but represents a form of movement analysis that aids dancers in learning and remembering the dance. I will explore this analytical proposition through a cumulative writing and rewriting of the refrain, juxtaposed with a description of dance movements. The sung phrase under analysis is:

> *Mu lay cegin*
> *re ge gin tac!*
> *re ge gin tac!*

The first two phonemes—*mu lay*—mark a shift of weight to the right achieved by moving one leg in the direction in which the movement travels, followed by the other (for example, the right leg first, and then the left leg). This shift of weight is accompanied by a closing in and out of the knees while the dancer leans the weight of the torso over the leg that started the sequence and juts the sternum forward and back, while holding the hands as in driving a bike, shifting the handles forward and back in rhythm with the leg twist. On the two following phonemes—*cegin*—the whole sequence is repeated to the left. The second line of the phrase is a variation of the first: on the *re ge gin,* the same shifting of weight, twisting of legs, and jutting of the torso is repeated. The *tac!* registers a pelvic thrust forward, followed by a silent (still) beat constituting what I call a (pelvic) exclamation mark. This pelvic contraction is interpolated before the repetition of the *re ge gin* sequence to the left. A reordering of the text that can visually account for the relationship between phonemes and movement units—the sung and danced phrase—would visually reconfigure the written phrase as follows:

> *Mulay cegin*
> *regegin tac!*
> *regegin tac!*

This scripting helps further clarify the relationship between different body parts and the rhythm of the movement phrase. In fact, while the first line of the text "sings" the shifts in the feet (*mu-lay* = right foot/left foot, traveling to the right; *ce-gin* = left foot/right foot, traveling to the left), the second and third lines register the movement of different body parts. Thus *regegin* registers the shuffling of the feet as well as the opening and closing of the knees, sounding the same movement that begins the sequence with three phonemes rather than two: *re-ge-gin* = step with the right foot/step with the left foot while closing and opening the knees. The *tac!* draws attention to the pelvic interpolation between the side shifts of the dancer while maintaining the spatial symmetry of the steps, achieved by repeating the sequence to the left (the third line above). A rewriting of the phrase to visually organize phonemes to parallel the spatial relations in the danced phrase would read as follows:

> *mulay* (travel right)   *cegin* (travel left)
> *regegin tac!* (travel right)   *regegin tac!* (travel left)

This printing of the phrase follows the delivery of the sung lines as performed by the dancers and clarifies spatial and rhythmic relations as well as the the performer's emphasis on different body parts—feet, knees, and pelvis. The sung phrase effectively embodies movement analysis and performs a pedagogical function that helps practitioners learn and remember the dance. The continuity between singing and dancing suggests that choreography in the *sabar* complex should be defined as the *relationship* established by dancers between the aural elements of the *sabar* (the drumming) and the danced elements. I will return to this definition and its relevance for understanding choreographic agency below. Here I want to follow the choreographic process that canonized the establishment of the *mu lay ce gin* as a dance in the *sabar* repertory.

The Lemzo Diamono, as an ensemble of charismatic players and performers who have confirmed their public authority by gaining access to the national media, were able to popularize the *mu lay ce gin* and foster it as a new choreographic invention that spread like wildfire in the living rooms of the viewers. By associating the dance with a rhythm and a refrain, as well as giving it a name, the Lemzo Diamono made the *mu lay ce gin* a crowd favorite: every *sabar* circle I went to in 1996 featured it. The dance was so popular that it was always played at the end of *sabar* events, as everybody would come out to dance it. Because of its success, the dance produced choreographic derivatives, which in turn became dances in their own right. This was the case for the *vespa* dance. Vespa is the name of a small Italian motorbike frequently used by the most fortunate youth of Dakar who can afford a private means of motorized transportation. As a derivative of the "bike dance" *mu lay ce gin,* the *vespa* is another bike dance, so similar to the first that in my interview with Aziz I thought they were the same.

> FRANCESCA: Wait, wait [Aziz is performing the steps of the *mu lay ce gin* and singing the refrain]. Is that like the *vespa?*
> AZIZ: The *vespa* is not the same. That was done by Alioune Kasse. When he was getting ready to have a new album, for the promotion of the album, he was going on TV and on the radio. He made the *vespa* dance. He saw the *mu lay ce gin* first, that was so popular, and he made a new dance, the *vespa.* A new dance for the *mu lay ce gin.* He made it different, he created his own.

The Senegalese public appreciates the slightest choreographic variations and confers choreographic authorship to the performer of successful variations, which then become dances in their own right. After talking to Aziz I went over my collection of music videos that I recorded while in Senegal in 1996–97 to compare the *mu lay ce gin* to the *vespa* dance. The *vespa* dance, as performed by Alioune Kasse, is more static than the *mu lay ce gin:* Kasse, rather than shifting his weight side to side, keeps the legs grounded and the torso still, while putting the movement into his hands and feet, as if pushing down on the gas pedal and accelerating by turning the handle of the bike. The *vespa* dance, as it acquired status in the social circle, was performed to its own rhythm (created by Kasse). Yet, as a derivative of the *mu lay ce gin,* it could also be danced to the *mu lay ce gin* rhythm (created by the Lemzo Diamono).

When I came back to Dakar in 1997, a few months after my first visit in 1996, the *mu lay ce gin* was still one of the most popular dances, but those in the know were already performing a new dance, the *Tink's daye bondé.* Similarly to the *mu lay ce gin,* the *Tink's daye bondé* was launched through a song of the same name, created and performed by the charismatic Sing Sing Rhythme of Mbaye Dièye Faye. The popularity of the group, as well as their access to the national media, assured that the *Tink's daye bondé* was popular among TV viewers who were eager to perform it in the *sabar* circle. The refrain that accompanies the dance was sung by Aziz as he demonstrated the *Tink's daye bondé* in the course of our interview:

> We sing:
>> *Tank*[19] *daye bondé*
>> *bien sure daye bondé*
>> *ler na, wor na, daye bondé*
>> (The Tennis ball bounces,
>> yes, it bounces
>> clear, it's sure, it bounces).

The dancer bends forward, keeping the torso parallel to the ground and one leg bent while straightening and bending the other leg to the rhythm of the drums, so as to visually foreground one side of the butt bouncing and re-bounding. The round butt, oh yes, like a Tennis ball it bounces!

The centrality of dance in the social life of Dakarois explains why many *mbalax* groups hire dancers to perform for their music videos and concerts: Having a choreographed dance launched with a song increases the popular-ity of the song and the charisma of the musical group. The music tape be-comes a favorite in the homes of people who feverishly practice the dance step to the music until they master it. TV viewers then bring (back) to the social circle the new dance, as performers gain prestige for keeping up to date and for being able to embody the latest dance nonchalantly, as if it had always been in their own personal repertoire. Thus in the *sabar* complex, old and new dances stand side by side, and a novice to the *sabar* will not know the difference. Some dances, like the *ceebu jën,* the *farwu jar,* or the *kaolack,* go back many generations, and it is the pride of *géwël* families to have acted as mediating link between generations of performers. I asked Aziz how old these dances are:

> FRANCESCA: How old are they?
>
> AZIZ: Old, old. They were there before I was born.
>
> F: And before your father was born?
>
> A: Yes, before my father was born.
>
> F: And before his father?
>
> A: Yes, before his father.
>
> F: How many generations? How many generations does it go back? Three: you, your father, your grandfather, your great-grandfather?
>
> A: Yes.
>
> F: Before then?
>
> A: That I cannot say. Because that is how we know, from our father.

Rather than thinking about age in terms of years, the history of a dance is measured in terms of successive generations of dancers, who teach the dance to younger generations.[20] The intergenerational communication within *géwël* families allows for the preservation as well as the creative expansion of the *sabar* repertory, yet no dance is assured a permanent status within the repertory. Instead, dances need the active support of performers in the dancing circle, who continually choose through reenactment which dances are memorable and literally worth re-membering, and which are destined to oblivion.

* * *

We can now come back to Nicholls's schema and evaluate its validity for the urban *sabar.* If I were to use Nicholls's terminology I would say that commercial dance (such as music videos) informs the creation of new dances for rituals (such as baptisms and marriages in which women perform within a *sabar* circle) through the mediation of *géwëls.* In the case above, a "traditional" griot (Aziz Faye or Mbaye Dièye Faye) creates a commercial product for the national media (either on their own or inspired by the performance of a dancer in the social circle or in a club), which then circulates in nontraditional spaces like discotheques as well as in traditional *sabar* events. The fact that the mass media plays no role in Nicholls's schema suggests that for some scholars the presence of the mass media in Africa is still unthinkable when one is discussing tradition.[21]

By identifying the ritual context as the originary site of truly African creation and discrediting the commercial context as westernized, Nicholls's schema reifies "African tradition" as a static and immutable category. I have argued that this reification of tradition muddles dance scholars' understanding of the choreographic process by reinscribing the modernity/tradition dichotomy of the Order of the Other in the field of dance: tradition becomes a collective form of artistic production from which individual agency is absent, while modernity is the marker of individual choreographic innovations. Yet, the dichotomy between individual creativity and group stasis does not help us understand choreographic agency in social dances like the *sabar*. The *sabar* complex engages individuals and groups in the choreographic process through the interplay of improvisation and the canonizing of successful inventions into the group repertory. Individual and group choreographic agency are thus not mutually exclusive processes that belong to different dance genres (for example, theatrical art and ritual dance) but rather operate dialectically, embedded in complex social negotiations. In other words, choreographic authorship is relational.

The relationality of choreographic choices is apparent in the *sabar* circle and operates at different levels. At one level, dancing is a social intervention within the assembled group, and to decide to enter the circle is much like making a public statement at a social gathering. Solo dances acquire meaning and value in context: they can be striking or not, depending on what precedes and follows them. Who follows whom is also evaluated, as it takes daring to enter the circle after a spectacular intervention. Thus the timing by which dancers enter the circle is crucial, as is the relation they establish with the previous performance, either by contrast or by rippling echoes.

At another level, relationality is also a crucial component of the choreographic process, engaging the dancer in dialogue with the drummers. In this context choreography is much more than the organization of movement; rather, "movement" acquires meaning through its juxtaposition to rhythm. As several of my dance teachers were fond of saying, "If you cannot dance to the drums, you cannot dance!"[22] This relationality often articulates the choreographed interventions of dancers, who use improvisation to assert their own skills and character, as I have underscored in the previous discussion of *bàkks*. Another example of improvisation as a dialogue between dancers and drummers is the habit of master dancers to perform dramatic shifts from action to stillness in the center of the *sabar* circle.[23] These shifts assert the volition of the dancer, who is able to hold her ground in stillness against the great rolling force of the drumming. The capacity to stop the dance and pick it up on the right beat and at the proper speed requires skills that only good dancers can master. Riselia Duarte Bezerra, discussing what she calls "stepping into samba," captures eloquently the skills necessary to step into the samba dance that are also necessary in entering the *sabar* circle:

> To step into samba is like jumping on a horse that is taking off at a fast run. The fast running horse can be thought of as a metaphor for the different time and space that the samba dancer jumps onto. The jumping alludes to the lack of a formal "warm up" or gradual preparatory exercising of muscle groups as practiced in dance studio tradition. In samba, the dancer's whole body immediately enters into muscular contractions and releases, the heartbeat quickly progresses into a fast pace, pumping blood saturated by readily made adrenaline. . . . Stepping into samba operates an *implosion,* the use of a dancer's precision and skills irrupting at full energy into the rhythm, conveying full presence. (Bezerra 2000:100)

A *sabar* dancer, similarly, has to "irrupt at full energy into the rhythm" played by the *sabar* ensemble. At a *sabar* event, the drummers are the first to arrive, calling people to the event with their playing. As the *géwëls'* drumming gathers more and more people into the circle, adding mass to its outer edges, the thickness of the sound increases, with the drumming getting sharper, louder, and faster. By the time people start dancing, the rhythm may have been rolling on for more than an hour, which means that dancers do not step into an empty and inert circle but approach a pulsating entity. They have to catch the rhythm of the drummers, like a rider jumping on a fast-running horse. This operation is risky, and less-skilled dancers do not dare attempt it more than once: they simply run up to the drummers and deliver their dance to them.

Stopping the dance is also a risky operation, because the dancer has to jump off the rhythm at the right time. Often this operation is supported by the lead drummer: while the drum ensemble rolls on, the lead drummer plays a closing drum call, at times effectively putting an end to a solo he may not enjoy. The dancer may ignore the cue and continue dancing until another stopping point is provided. But to stop anywhere but the ending of the closing call is a disgrace, like falling off a horse. Beginning dancers dutifully follow the lead of the drummer and welcome his guiding call, while skilled dancers enjoy jumping on and off the rhythms at their will, without the guidance or support of the lead drummer. These dancers insert their own punctuation into the performance, knowing when a "comma" (a short pose), a "period" (a longer pose), or a "parenthesis" (an improvised dance phrase) can be inserted into the dance without disturbing the syntax of rhythm. Jumping off the rhythm is most dramatically achieved by entering stillness by striking a pose, which is held for a second or two before the dancer delivers a joking gesture, or a call to the audience, and suddenly resumes dancing again. The dancers and the encircling audience treasure the tension created by these dramatic shifts between absolute motion, achieved in a split second, and absolute stillness, also achieved in a split second, as well as the sudden implosion into another bout of dancing.

Similarly, to interject improvisation within the established choreography of a dance requires a command of rhythmic complexities and dynamic play with the drummers that is dared only by good dancers. While established dances are the result of tested relations between the dancers' choreography and the rhythms played by the drummers, improvisers are effectively testing their musical ear in front of a crowd of spectators. For this reason unskilled dancers do not dare improvise. They are afraid to ruin their performance by failing to intersect with the drums in an intelligible manner. This skill is not only technical but a test of power and poise. An improviser asserts her freedom against the drum ensemble: by doing so she asserts herself as an author, as an author-ity.

Choreographic Authority, Social Contexts, and Dance Genres

The above discussion on *sabars* and choreographic authority calls for important qualifications that limit the application of hasty generalizations about this model to other Senegalese dance complexes. The first qualification has to do with the mediating role of television for its ability to connect dancers on and off the screen in rippling corporeal echoes. The second qualification points to further connections between choreographic authority and the specific social contexts in which choreographic and performance knowledges are articulated.

The Wolofization of TV and radio programs has allowed Wolof dances and rhythms to circulate more widely across different social spaces than other ethnic-centric dance forms. While scholars (notable O'Brien and Swigart) have emphasized the linguistic component of Wolofization, I argue that Wolofization can be understood more broadly as the sharing of Wolof-centric culture by other ethnicities. Both processes are at work in the national media, which reflect and affect Wolofization. In particular, radio and TV programming (unlike newspapers and journals, in which French greatly predominates) have made room for the transmission of programs in the Wolof language and have privileged the Wolof cultural complex in the diffusion of music and dance videos.[24] Non-Wolof dances, being less represented on national television, are therefore more dependent on body-to-body transmission and need to be passed on from actors sharing the same physical space with one another. Thus, they circulate among tighter social networks and follow different pathways of choreographic negotiations, which would need to be carefully studied.

The second qualification has to do with the relationship between choreographic authority and dance genres/social contexts. We need to make clear that different rules about choreographic intervention apply, depending on the social space to which the dances belong. For example, while individual and collective creativity is fostered in the circle of social dance, more sacred occasions call for historical continuity in choreographic forms. The more sacred a performance, the more important it becomes to respect the choreographic authority of the elders, extending back to nonliving generations of ancestors. Severe sanctions may occur if one is to sidestep, ignore, or oppose the authority of the elders and the specialists. While sacred dances are generally choreographed by specialists (such as families who inherit the guardianship of certain masks or spirits), social dances are open to anybody's choreographic intervention. In these less restrictive forms, it is often the younger generation who takes the lead, engaging with youthful enthusiasm in the creation of new dances. Thus, generationality tends to mediate the relationship to choreographic authority, as the more "serious" a dance, the more choreographic authority falls on the shoulders of the older generations, including nonliving spirits. This is an important point for understanding the work of Ballet choreographers and their relationship to ethnic communities outside of the stage. An anecdote will help elucidate some of the issues at play in relation to Ballet performances and the choreographic authority possessed by Ballet choreographers.

During my discussions with Bouly Sonko, one of the artistic directors of the National Ballet of Senegal and the choreographer who oversees the Ballet's daily rehearsals, I asked him if some dances are forbidden from stage presentation. He replied flatly that any dance that belongs to the people can be performed. His reply was technical and at the same time evasive. Interpreting it demands that we understand and define which dances "belong to the people." I inquired further: Are there not mask dances that should not be performed on stage? Again he replied that the Ballet represents the culture of the country, and as such, any dance of the people can be performed. Frustrated,

I decided to let the issue rest. Another conversation provided the occasion for some important clarifications on the subject. I asked Sonko about the difference between the *kankuran* and the *fambondy,* two important masks/spirits that are performed in Manding villages. In the course of our conversation, I mistakenly associated the mask of the *kankuran* with the *koumpo* mask, because they are both made of hay, and (I am ashamed to confess my mistake) they both have names that start with *k.* I stated that I had seen the *kankuran* performed by the National Ballet. Sonko replied that it was impossible, since they do not perform the *kankuran.* He then told me the following story. Many years before, there was "a Tukulour" at the Sorano Theatre who was getting ready to present a show entitled *Kankuran.* Sonko was called by the elders in the Casamance, who sent an emissary to the theater to find out what was going on. As a choreographer at Sorano, and because he is Manding, they thought he was the one putting on the show. They told him that the *kankuran* was not to be performed in the theater and that they were ready to sanction him if he disobeyed. Sonko told me that the elders will make people sick (by working with spiritual powers) if they disobey their authority. Sonko passed on the information to the Tukulour, and it became clear that he had prepared the performance of the *koumpo,* but (like me) he had gotten confused and called it *kankuran.*

Even though he is a grown man in a position of authority, Sonko would have suffered the social sanctions imposed by the council of elders if he had attempted to choreograph a powerful spirit. The elders effectively guard the performance of important spirits, preventing their appropriation and consumption by community outsiders who are likely neither to respect the spirits nor to be accountable to them. This anecdote points to the fact that while some dances are deemed universally appealing and appropriate, those with a specific social function other than celebration or entertainment are restricted from circulation. Powerful spirits/masks are deemed dangerous, and their dances are guarded with secrecy. Even community members are forbidden from participating in and watching such dances, which are reserved for a specific sector of the population. This is the case with the *kankuran,* a mask/spirit that is associated with Manding male initiation. The mask comes out to the secluded site where the initiated live to protect the young men from the evil spirits that lurk around them as they are made vulnerable by circumcision. The *kankuran* also comes into the town when the circumcised return home, and women and uninitiated boys try to get a glimpse of the mask while hiding from it, lest they get too close and receive a small beating. Bouly Sonko and other men also told me that the *kankuran* beats up unruly boys who have misbehaved in the course of the year. The mask effectively delivers social sanctions to a section of the community, "like the police."[25] Yet many spirits are losing their power, which decreases their capacity to enforce respect, making their performance less restrictive. For example, I was told that the *fambondy* used to be a spirit similar to the *kankuran,* although much more powerful (it could fly faster and be in more than one place at the same time), yet it lost much of its power with colonization. This decreased power corresponds with more laxity over performance, as the spirit can now be represented in Ballet performances outside of its ritual context.[26]

The dance scholar Alphonse Tiérou has developed a theoretical model that accounts for different levels of restriction in the learning and performance of dances that also points to the relevance of social context for defining rules of choreographic intervention. In *Dooplé: Loi Éternelle de la Danse Africaine,* Tiérou discusses three concentric circles that refer to different spheres of inclusion in dance performance (1989:57–62). These spheres in turn connect pedagogical relations to the sacred/secret content of dances. A discussion of Tiérou's model will clarify these assertions and their relevance for the Senegalese context.

Tiérou establishes the first circle as a social circle in which dances are performed by a community (a "village" in Tiérou's words) on festive occasions. In these circumstances, anybody can dance in the circle, and dances are learned through a process of socialization that begins in childhood and carries on through the years. In the Senegalese context, the ethnic-centric dances that are performed by the city Ballets belong mostly to this first circle. These dances are part of the regional milieu in which people grow up—both village and city traditions—and each ethnic group has its own specific dances. Thus the National Ballet of Senegal presents the *seruba* dance complex of the southern Casamance, in which the *lenjengo* (a Manding dance) and the *econcon* (a Joola dance) are often performed together to the rhythms played on the three *seruba* drums: the *sabaro* (lead drum), the *kutiriba* (big *kutiro*), and the *kutirindingo* (small *kutiro*). These dances, like the dances of the *sabar* complex, are performed on festive occasions like marriages and baptisms or gatherings of friends or political figures. The Ballet also presents the *bugarabu,* a Joola dance performed on festive occasions and accompanied by the *bugara,* a set of four drums played by one man. The *yella* of the Tukulour—from the Fouta in northern Senegal—and the Peul acrobatic dances also belong to this category. As with the *sabar,* these dances encourage choreographic variations and improvisations, a characteristic that Tiérou associates with the first circle.[27]

The second circle is more restrictive, and it requires formal learning outside of the flux of socialization that distinguishes the first circle. Initiation dances fall under this category. In the repertory of the National Ballet, the *cin* (for men) and *ñaka* (for women) are Manding initiation dances performed at the time of the coming-out ceremony, when the initiated return home and perform in the town square. As public dances performed by a socially restricted group of people, they are considered appropriate for presentation onstage. These dances are performed in the piece that I have described as the *koumpo* (see chapter 1). The *koumpo* itself is a mask that embodies a benevolent spirit that comes out to play with young people. Other masks are present onstage and also represent benevolent spirits associated with fertility. These dances are more codified and less amenable to change and improvisation than the dances that belong to the first circle. In the case of the *cin* and *ñaka,* initiates must learn obedience, among other things, and if they do not follow the strict choreography of the dances while in training, they are beaten.[28] The correct performance of the dances is thus necessary to assure obedience to the older generations, and it cannot be changed at an individual's whim.

The *manoch* is another dance performed by the Ballet that falls within Tiérou's second circle. This dance comes from the village of Ndam at the border of Guinea and Senegal, where once a year a competition is organized to select the best male dancer. When the winner is crowned, he shows off his skills to the audience. Lore has it that women irremediably fall in love with him and compete for his attention. The *manoch* can only be performed by the best dancers, and even in the Ballet it is an honor to get to dance the leading role of the winner. Because of the skills required to perform it, the dance of the winner falls within Tiérou's second circle. Yet Tiérou argues that dances belong to this circle not only because of the level of skills necessary to embody them but also because of the process of learning that accompanies them. Specifically, he argues that the dances that belong to the first circle are learned through a process of socialization spread over years of participation in frequent social events, while the dances that belong to the second circle are learned through formal training that distinguishes clearly between teachers and students, master dancers and amateurs. On this account, too, the role of lead dancer of the *manoch* belongs to the second circle.

Tiérou's last circle embraces dances that customarily belong to experts such as ritual specialists or families of griots. These dances are transmitted within a professional stratum that guards the knowledge of the dances from outside appropriation and consumption. Strict rules guide the pedagogical process as well as the performance of these dances. A breach of these rules carries severe sanctions in the social and spiritual realms. Thus, dances belonging to this circle are not generally performed by Ballets and, as my (failed) conversation with Bouly Sonko shows, even talking about these matters with a foreigner is frowned upon.

Tiérou's model is helpful in framing the activities of the National Ballet of Senegal and other Ballets within a larger context. Although performances for foreigners and tourists are a relatively recent phenomenon, the differentiation between dances appropriate for unrestricted circulation and dances that are to be guarded from "outsiders"—however defined—is much older.[29] Tiérou's model allows us to read the performances of Ballets for tourists as continuous practices within an evolving tradition rather than as a radical break with tradition. His model also points to the existence of processes that protect certain dances from foreign consumption and appropriation, with the clear purpose of avoiding "trivialization" of sacred matters in contexts where accountability between performers, and between performers and audiences, is not enforceable. Yet protection also depends on the individual responsibility of choreographers, and their own judgment of appropriateness. Sonko's story about the *kankuran* points to the responsibility of individual choreographers in respecting the sacredness of performance. Another example can elucidate Ballet choreographers' responsibilities in mediating the circulation of dances between entertainment and ritual circles.

The *ndëp* is a ritual associated with the Lébou (an ethic group historically related to the Wolof), marking the relationship of the living with different classes of spirits—the *rab* (genies) and the *tuur* (ancestors). These spirits can cause sickness (often in retaliation for some breach in social conduct) and also heal it. A *ndëp* can be organized for a person who belongs to a family in which the cult of the spirits is observed who is afflicted by mental disorders, sterility, or impotence. The ceremony is public and can last three, six, or even twelve days (Ndiaye 1986:63–69).[30] Although witnesses are necessary to the healing, attending the ritual is not a matter to be taken lightly, as the spirits can befall a person witnessing the ritual or even a curious passerby unaware of the power of the *rabs*.[31] This would be especially true if the ritual were not properly performed under the guidance of a qualified priestess. Given these circumstances, several of the Ballet dancers that I interviewed expressed the opinion that the *ndëp*, as a healing ritual, should not be performed by Ballets. As my description of a *soirée* at the club LT indicates, however, the *ndëp* was indeed staged as a choreographed performance by the Ballet Kaddu gi. I reported this in an interview with a dancer of another Ballet in an effort to provoke his reaction and find out how dances are deemed appropriate (or not) for theatrical presentations. An excerpt from our interview follows. I have given the dancer the pseudonym of Souleymane.[32]

SOULEYMANE: The *ndëp* is not for sale. It is something that one re-spects. Among us one does not sell it on the market, for show biz.

FRANCESCA: But I have seen it performed by a Ballet, in a club, right here in Dakar.

S: Really?

F: Yes, yes.

S: Yes, but those people choreographed it on an academic level. In Senegal one does not sell that.

F: It will not get out of Senegal?

S: It will not get out. Because if it gets out of Senegal, one cannot show the ballet *ndëp,* and you, you the whites, will not know what it is for. . . . Then it is something one does not sell. Because if you want to simply have fun, OP! there is a guy that comes out PAFFS! [makes a gesture that shows the guy falls to the ground]

F: I am telling you, I saw it performed at a club, the Ballet did the *ndëp* in a discotheque.

S: You know, here in Senegal, people in Senegal they all want money. You see, he, he does not know what to do, PAFF, he does the *ndëp.* But it is dangerous, because one can play the *ndëp,* and there is a guy passing by, he looks and PAFFS! he falls. He starts AHH AHHH! [he mimics a person running around holding his head and screaming] because that music there, it is mystic . . . it is dangerous to have fun with that.

Souleymane's conclusion that the *ndëp* I witnessed must have been cho-reographed "on an academic level" was confirmed by my interview with one of the choreographers of the Ballet Kaddu gi, Ndiuwar Thiam. He stressed that the presentation was not the "real" *ndëp* (and thus it was not dangerous) and that it had been performed for educational purposes only. Yet the dif-ference between the performance of a ritual and its representation is tenuous, and as Souleymane stressed in his narrative, it can be crossed inadvertently. The fact that Ballets dare perform for a wide audience dances that historically have been restricted to target communities points again to the weakening of "spirits." More appropriately, it underscores how communities of ritual and dance specialists are losing the power to instill respect for and fear of their specialized knowledges, if not losing social relevance altogether. It further points to the relatively new importance of Ballets as mediators between his-torically recognized dance authorities and a wider public. The role of Ballets in the education and dissemination of dance knowledge and choreographic authority is the subject of the next chapter.

7

Urban Ballets and the Professionalization of Dance

The Work of Dancers

Ballet troupes animate most of the popular neighborhoods of Dakar, rehearsing in schoolyards, classrooms, youth centers, football fields, and other open spaces. Every late afternoon, when the heat of the day is more bearable, a fluctuating membership of ten, twenty, and up to thirty youths gathers under the direction of an older dancer/choreographer to dance intensely for two or three hours. Ballets share in common a commitment to represent the ethnic repertory of dances of the country and to provide a unique opportunity for the youth of the city to learn and practice these dances. Furthermore, Ballets share an interest in capitalizing on performance as a money-making activity, yet the degree to which they succeed varies greatly.

While the biggest and most established Ballets regularly perform in hotels and at organized dance events throughout the city, smaller Ballets have little chance of performing and may spend years practicing without an audience. For this reason, while Ballet dancers perform basically the same kind of work no matter which Ballet they belong to, only a few dancers receive a wage for dancing. The majority precariously gamble on dancing as an economic-generating activity, jostling for a position in the few Ballets that provide economic rewards. Ballet troupes can thus be distinguished by their relationship to the economy and divided into two categories: 1) the small number of Ballets that are part of the formal economy of the city, performing regularly at hotels and theaters; 2) the greater number of Ballets that are part of the informal economy, since they perform only sporadically and have no assured income.

During my sojourn in Dakar, rather than surveying the innumerable Ballets of the city, I opted for an intensive study of two from each category. I examined the National Ballet of Senegal and the Ballet Mansour[1] from the first category: being the oldest and incontestably the most well-known and respected Ballets of Dakar, they are part of the formal economy of the city. No other Ballet in the capital replicates the artistic and economic success of these two prominent dance troupes, and dancers from all over the city and country vie to become members of either of them.

The two other Ballets that I chose for my study differ significantly from the National Ballet and the Ballet Mansour: the means at their disposal, such as performance space, instruments, and costumes, as well as their access to performance venues, are much more meager. These are the Ballet Fambondy, operating in the popular neighborhood of Parcelle Assenis Unitè III, founded and directed by Djibril Sane since 1990, and the Ballet Kaddu gi, founded by Adama Diallo and Ndiuwar Thiam in 1995 and drawing dancers from the neighborhood of Ñaari Tali. As essentially neighborhood Ballets, they are typical representatives of the majority of Dakar's Ballets, precariously situated at the margins of the informal economy.

Rather than presenting the work of each of these four Ballets separately, I will draw on my research to address a more general question: What are the claims to professionalism that Ballet dancers and choreographers assert through their work? This is a particularly relevant question because Ballets compete on one side with griots (Mande and Wolof in particular), who have historically occupied the position of professional musicians and choreographers, and on the other side with the dancing skill of the general population, which is well versed in entertainment dances (those belonging to Tiérou's first circle, as discussed in chapter 6). This last point is especially relevant because, as with the National Ballet, a troupe's repertory often includes the very dances that are performed by the general population at social celebrations. The ways in which the skills cultivated by Ballet dancers and choreographers differ from those cultivated by dancers in the social circle constitute the ground on which Ballet dancers and directors lay claim to economic retribution. I will thus address the question of professionalism by once again returning to the *sabar* complex to contrast the skills of Ballet dancers and choreographers with those cultivated in the social circle of dancers. While this discussion is focused on the *sabar,* many of the same observations can be reasonably extended to include Ballets' relationships to the other ethnic repertories of the country. In the second section of the chapter, I will continue to interrogate the position of Ballets in the larger social world through the presentation of interviews with Ballet dancers and choreographers. The interviews center on the question of "vocation" and learning so as to map which social practices and institutions are the training grounds for contemporary choreographers and dancers.

*   *   *

How do the dancers' skills in the social circle of *sabar* performance compare to what is required for the performance of *sabar* within a Ballet? And what is the role of choreographers in this context?

I have argued that in the social circle the roles of dancer and choreographer are united as successive performers take the center of the circle for a brief intervention. In Ballets, however, the roles are separated. Furthermore, in contrast to the soloing dancers in the *sabar* circle, Ballets feature ensemble work with eight, ten, fifteen, or twenty dancers sharing the stage with drummers and other musicians.[2]

In this context choreographers use polyrhythms to garnish the steps of individual dancers, as well as to coordinate interactions between groups of dancers.[3] At the level of single performers, the same dance steps can be performed at different levels of rhythmic complexity, and Ballets often display the most sophisticated version of steps. For example, while less-skilled performers in the circle of social dancers can deliver a step with a two-beat rhythm, more-skilled dancers can double the time to a four-beat rhythm. Since dancers activate multiple rhythmic centers in the body, a slower beat can be maintained in the feet, while the doubling of the beat can take place in the pelvis, the chest, the shoulder, or the head. Also, dancers can add accents to their dance in different parts of the body so as to mark or complement the rhythm of more than one drum. An extra sway of the hip, a jump, a flick of the wrists, a double shake in the shoulders, a twist of the legs, or an extra step can mark the polyrhythmic structure of the music with kinetic subtlety. The capacity to embody polyrhythmic complexity requires dancers to articulate different body parts following the rhythmic line of more than one drum, and at times to make manifest the implied synergistic effect of multiple rhythms. At the level of the dance ensemble, choreographers like to organize groups of dancers in polyrhythmic interplay, requiring the ensemble to perform as a dynamic whole composed of independent yet interrelated smaller groups. Choreographers configure and translate polyrhythmic relations spatially, distributing rhythmic lines among separate and interlacing groups of dancers. Most often, one group of dancers embodies the rhythmic base of the drum ensemble with a simple and repetitive step that visually frames a more dynamic group, or a successive stream of dancers, performing complex dance steps in shifting geometrical patterns. Dramatic transitions between background and foreground, which suddenly shift spectators' attention from one group to the other, are the mark of good choreographers and a well-rehearsed Ballet. The continual formation and disintegration of geometrical patterns in the course of performance distinguishes Ballets' dances from the stable frame of the circle that is characteristic of the arena of social dance.

Precisely because the ability to coordinate group work is the mark of Ballets' performances, choreographers like to exploit ensemble work to maximum effect and consequently limit the amount of improvisational freedom they allow to single dancers. Thus, if in the circle of *sabar* dancing it is one of the prerogatives of good dancers to initiate the performance of a *bàkk,* in Ballets it is the choreographer who decides when a *bàkk* should be performed. Furthermore, rather than being performed by the soloing dancer with the support of the lead drummer, the *bàak* is most often performed by the whole dance ensemble with the support of the whole drum ensemble. Just as the *bàkks* of soloing dancers introduce complexity into the more routinized performance of *sabar* dances, in Ballet performances *bàkks* showcase the skills of dancers as well as the sophistication of choreographers.

With the creation of *bàkks* for the whole dancing ensemble, choreographers make strategic use of group unison to showcase dancers' command of rhythmic complexity amidst the velocity of execution of highly dynamic steps. In turn, the multiplication of kinetic patterns among the body of dancers performing in unison foregrounds the choreographed aspect of the dance. The stunning speed, complexity of steps, and sudden shifts in phrasing of dancers in perfect synchrony with the drum ensemble make these ensemble *bàkks* a relished spectacle. As is the case with drummers, *bàkks* allow choreographers to distinguish themselves for their creativity and virtuosity, and in fact *bàkks* are the markers of each choreographer's originality and the distinguishing features of their Ballet's *sabar* performances.[4] Yet, as my discussion with Aziz Faye brought to the fore, *bàkks* are first and foremost complex drummed phrases, and thus the creation of choreographers closely follows that of the master drummer(s), who compose the musical *bàkk* for the company. The choreographer follows the musical creation closely, at times even making suggestions, yet the authority of musical authorship remains with the drummer(s). Only highly successful *géwëls* can master the role of musical composer and choreographer at the same time, creating a *bàkk* as both a musical and dance phrase. This last point highlights the issue of competition between choreographers and *géwëls,* and indeed griots of other traditions, like the Mande *jàlís.*

As the historical guardians and creators of the dance traditions of the Mande and the Wolof/Séréér ethnicities, griots have a professional advantage over the general population in becoming Ballet choreographers and directors. Yet the institution of Ballets gives non-griots a chance to become choreographers and professional dancers, a chance that was previously unavailable to them because of caste interdictions. This opportunity is treasured by many Ballet choreographers and dancers.

Ballets specialize in the presentation of ethnic dances, and many opt for a multiethnic repertory. In this context, knowledge of a multiethnic repertory becomes a distinctive requirement for aspiring Ballet choreographers. Unless they become Ballet choreographers themselves, however, griots master only their own ethnic repertory. The depth of griots' knowledge compensates for the Ballet choreographers' familiarity with various ethnic genres, since choreographers who have not extensively studied with griots or with ritual specialists only know the most common entertainment dances typical of the circle of social dancers. For this reason it is not unusual for Ballet choreographers to consult with griots, if not to engage in formal learning with a griot's family.

Two patterns emerge from the sociological dynamics that characterize Dakar's Ballets in their relationship to Senegalese ethnic repertories. On one side, Ballets exhibit a tendency for multiethnic representation of dances. On the other side, several Ballets tend to privilege exclusively the Mande dance complex—I will call this pattern the Mandification of Ballets.[5] Both patterns counter the Wolofization of dance practice that has been under way in postcolonial Senegal and the diffusion of the Wolof-centric cultural complex as the privileged national music and dance idiom.

The Mandification of Ballets can be attributed to the strength of the *jàlí* tradition in the cultural area of which Senegal is part. Mande griots are among the most famous in West Africa, and their musical and dance traditions cut across the regions of contemporary Mauritania, Mali, Niger, Senegal, Gambia, Guinea-Bissay, Guinea Conakry, Sierra Leone, Burkina Faso, and the Ivory Coast.[6] The Mandification of Ballets, at least in the context of Dakar, can be interpreted as a conscious strategy against Wolofization. Similarly to language associations that have been formed in the last twenty years as a reaction to the Wolofization of language, a Ballet's choreographer may choose to privilege those ethnic traditions that have been marginalized in the cultural life of the nation. Yet, given the strength and vitality of Wolof griots, why do Ballets not also exhibit a Wolofization of repertory? The prevalence of the *sabar* tradition in the social life of city dwellers accounts for the fact that Wolof griots can profitably make a living by fulfilling their historical role as intermediaries and entertainers at social celebrations or by occupying the new commercial niche offered by *mbalax* bands, which play regularly at Dakar's clubs and can also tour internationally. In fact, the growing importance of *mbalax* bands in the world music scene has challenged the previously uncontested dominance of *jalis* in the international marketing of Francophone West African musical traditions. Given the commercial success of *mbalax* bands, as well as the widespread demand for the services of *géwëls,* Wolof griots have less incentive than their Mande counterparts to establish and direct Ballets that specialize in the Wolof repertory.

However, the majority of Ballets, rather than presenting only one ethnic repertory, opt to represent the dance repertoire of the ethnic groups that make up the majority of the Senegalese population, featuring the most common social dances of each ethnicity. In these circumstances, what is the work of Ballet choreographers?

Ballet choreographers, like dancers in the social circle, establish their authority by successfully negotiating the tension between "quoting" a common dance repertory and introducing their own innovations. This means that Ballet performances are judged at one level for their ability to give a "truthful" representation of the ethnic traditions of the country, while at another level each Ballet choreographer competes with other choreographers in defining his or her own style and producing original dance pieces. As within each "tradition" itself, too much conformity to the established repertory produces boredom, while too much diversion from it is considered an unwelcome distortion. Just how much is "too much" is continually negotiated in the social arena and is partly dependent on popularity and the ability to win social approval. Thus, some choreographers privately commented unfavorably about their colleagues mixing dance styles or the proliferation of new steps, while others downgraded their colleagues for their lack of creativity and their simple staging of common dances. Yet, all Ballets have in common the rule of adhering to the ethnic repertory of dances; if mixing occurs, it is produced by blending different ethnic styles and not by mixing ethnic dances with nonethnic styles like disco dancing or modern dance. I will return to the importance of this practice in the conclusion. Here I want to consider the skills of Ballet dancers vis-à-vis those of dancers in the social arena.

*   *   *

Unlike soloing dancers in the social circle, Ballet dancers must integrate their performance with the whole ensemble. This requires that they cultivate the

ability to perform flaring individual movements while negotiating the performance space so as to compose geometrical figures without running into
other dancers. They must also be able to move across space so as to arrive at
the new geometrical configuration together with other dancers and in precise synchrony with the drumming. The challenge lies in commanding precise
geometrical floor patterns while performing highly explosive movement sequences that demand the activation of weight centers (head, pelvis, arms, and
legs) along kinetic pathways characterized by a high degree of momentum.
Dancers must be able to keep track of precise spatial coordinates while combining the exuberance of individual movements with controlled group formations negotiated according to the rhythms of the drums. The juxtaposition between the geometrical design of two or more groups of dancers in
ever-shifting compositions and the flaring energy of individual performers
provides a visually stunning contrast and a kinetic challenge cultivated by Ballet dancers and choreographers.

Stamina is another characteristic that distinguishes professional from social dancers. Unlike the social circle, in which interventions of single dancers
last from a few seconds to a few minutes, Ballet dancers must have command
of a full-length repertory spanning from half an hour to two hours. Ballet
directors often train their dancers by enforcing grueling rehearsals to prepare
them for the most arduous touring conditions. Also, they look for the aesthetic qualities cultivated in the social circle of the popular dances they present, which require a tremendous dynamism of delivery, speed, and force.
Thus, once Ballet members have mastered the choreographies of the repertory, they train to increase the output of energy and the speed of delivery of
their dances. For these reasons, the typical two-hour rehearsal of Ballets is a
form of physical labor so intense that only the strongest athletes are able to
sustain it over the years. Most dancers are very young, even though the best
dancers may be in their thirties, forties, and even fifties.[7] In spite of their
strength, dancers and drummers at times get sick with exhaustion.[8]

The dancers' stamina parallels their capacity for memorization, as Ballet
members must remember a full repertory, comprised of complex movement
sequences as well as complex rhythmic patterns. Finally, unlike dancers in the
social arena, Ballet dancers often have to master more than one ethnic style.
This feat can be considered equivalent to learning to speak different languages.
In fact, different ethnic complexes require competence in their own kinetic
"grammars," which in turn requires different kinds of skills and kinetic fluen-
cies. For example, while the *sabar* complex is characterized by the complexity of rhythms and erect posturing, the Mande complex marks mastery by the

ability to perform steps with grounded elasticity and the graceful articulation of arms and wrists. Peul dances, however, demand many level changes as well as acrobatic stunts by men. Ballets are often attractive to dancers precisely because they offer the unique opportunity to train and come to know the different ethnic dances of the country, and mastering successfully these different styles is a mark of experienced dancers. We can now turn to my interviews with Ballet dancers and choreographers.

How Did You Learn How to Dance?
Interviews with Ballet Dancers

In this section I present excerpts from interviews with members of the Ballets that I followed in my research. These are not quantitatively significant "samples" nor exhaustive representations of dancers' experiences. I have chosen these excerpts because they open up areas of inquiry that have not been previously addressed in the academic literature and that I hope will be picked up by other researchers. The interviews were structured around one simple question: How did you learn how to dance? This question seemed particularly relevant in light of pernicious stereotypes shared by scholars of the Order of the Same as well as the Order of the Other, like Senghor, who romanticized Africans as "naturally" born dancers. The question also addresses the more specific concern of my research, interrogating the continuities between dancing in the social arena and dancing as a professional activity.

The first excerpt is from my interview with Bouly Sonko, artistic director of the National Ballet of Senegal. The interview was conducted in French; it took place in February 1997 at Sonko's office at the Thèâtre Daniel Sorano.

> FRANCESCA: How did you learn how to dance?
> BOULY SONKO: I learned how to dance when I was young. You know, in all the villages, the young people are often artists. And I was part of those youngsters who danced a lot, and finally it became a virus, a disease, and *voilà*, today it has become a profession, a way to earn a living.

Sonko calls his passion for dancing a disease, a virus. I found his deployment of medical discourse quite telling. Western medicine objectifies diseases as biological facts that operate outside of the social world. Viruses do not belong to a cultural world amenable to social rules but are biological entities that attack a person at the cellular level. The biomedical conceptualization of disease contrasts with indigenous conceptualizations, which tend to stress the somatic element in any sickness and the links between the physical body and the social body. The idioms of spirit possession and witchcraft are often employed to address sickness as a physical and moral phenomenon that is symptomatic of a breach in the social fabric in which the "patient" is inserted. While the biological model exempts the patient from responsibility for his or her sickness, the indigenous model stresses the responsibility of the sick person as well as his or her community. Sonko, by resorting to a biological metaphor to describe his passion for dancing, seems to argue that he had no choice but to follow his passion. Much like a sick person in the western biological model, he cannot be faulted for this "disease." At the same time, Sonko refers to indigenous conceptualizations of sickness by a reversal of logic: he metaphorically pathologizes as a physical disease a social breach in class/caste relations. By becoming a professional dancer and choreographer, Sonko, who is Manding, has taken a role that has historically been reserved for the griots and that has been interdicted to his caste—the *hóró*. As pointed out in chapter 4, *hórós* and *jàlís* are separated not only by their professional prerogatives but also by codes of behavior that inscribe the two groups within a hierarchical moral and status system. More precisely, for a *hóró* to behave like a *jàlí*, outside of specific circumstances and circumscribed social roles, is to fall below his status.[9] Thus, for a *hóró* to dance outside of prescribed social occasions (such as circumcision ceremonies or warrior dances) and to make a spectacle of himself on a daily basis has been historically considered a disgrace. Because it implies a loss of status and moral standing, the permanent engagement in the art of dancing has been eschewed by "healthy" *hóró* members of society, to return to Sonko's metaphor. By calling his passion for dancing a disease, Sonko implicitly refers to his professional dancing as a breach of tradition. A more explicit discussion of this breach was prompted by my further questioning:

> FRANCESCA: And you told me that at first your father was not happy that you were a dancer. Why?
>
> BOULY: My parents did not want me to dance because, you know, in the ethnic groups there are what are called warriors. I am from a family of warriors, of nobles, so people had to dance for us, and not us for them. That is really the tradition. But I had finally understood that my vocation was dance, and in spite of the interdiction of my parents I became a dancer and now a dancer-director. And *voilà*, now my parents are happy because I help them a lot.

F: They accepted you when you started to earn money, or to be known?

B: Yes, be known and earn a little money. I went to see them, and they understood that, well, the tradition cannot always go on. One sometimes has to follow his vocation. That is what I have done.

For a *hóró* like Sonko to take on the role of professional dancer is a breach in social roles that confounds historically defined caste relations. He refers to the loss of status implied in permanently entertaining an audience when he says that "people had to dance for us [the nobles], and not us for them." This loss of status involves not only the single subject, in our case Bouly Sonko, but his entire family—thus the interdiction of his parents. Yet, Sonko was part of a generation that rejected the social restrictions of tradition and pursued art as a career. At the same time, he did not reject his role as the good son who must provide for his aging parents and share resources with an extended family. Significantly, his parents, after their initial opposition, "are happy" because he "helps them a lot." His success, and the fact that he is willing to share his success with his family, as tradition imposes, pardons him for the breach in another aspect of tradition. Furthermore, his position as director of the National Ballet of Senegal provides a new context in which his role brings prestige, rather than a loss in status.

Sonko's rejection of caste restrictions to pursue dance as a career was not an individual act of rebellion but a decision inserted into a larger social context, which he describes as nothing less than a "revolution."

FRANCESCA: Coming back to [our discussion of] tradition, musicians and drummers come from *géwël/jàlí* families, but do dancers also?

BOULY: Yes, now, now that does not exist anymore. You must have noticed that now everybody dances, everybody drums. It's not a question of being a griot or not being a griot. Now dance has become a revolution. You have seen it, you have noticed that people now dedicate themselves to traditional dance, or to modern dance, or to rap. You have seen it; it has become a revolution.

The relationship between griots and dancing has been silenced in the literature on griots, which has focused instead on orature and the playing of musical instruments.[10] Given this scarcity of information, it is difficult to evaluate to what extent dancing has been an exclusive prerogative of griots, and in what respects griots' dancing has differed from non-griots' practices.

Sonko's assertion that the contemporary expansion of dancing is a revolution makes clear that we are witnessing a profound change. Aziz Faye, a Wolof
griot, echoed Sonko's assessment of the "dancing revolution" by remarking on the magnitude of the widespread practice of dancing beyond the griot
caste. He added a sociological explanation for the phenomenon:

FRANCESCA: You are a géwël?

AZIZ: Yes.

F: Anybody can dance; but only you can drum?

A: No. Not anybody can dance. For some people, it is not for them
   [to dance]. Only the géwël can dance.

F: But you, do you get money to dance? You get money to play; but
   do you get money to dance?

A: They give me money to play. Sometimes they ask me for a special
   dance, and they give me money just to dance. At a ngente [bap-
   tism], or a takk [marriage], or if they open a new hospital.

F: Because in the books, when they write about the griots, they say
   that you sing, that you play, but they do not say that you dance.
   And I see people who dance, while they cannot play the drums.

A: Most of the dances, they cannot do [them]. They do not know
   how.

F: And they should not do them? It is bad if they dance; they say it is
   bad to dance.

A: No. They do not say that it is bad. But it is not for them. They say
   that it is only for the griots. A long time ago, we did everything.
   We drummed and we danced, and people just sat there and
   watched us. They were not supposed to dance. But now everybody dances, because it is power. Because they can make money
   from it, and they can take it far away [to other countries].

F: Really, they just sat there and watched? They did not dance?

A: They just watched. But maybe ten years ago, [that is when] you
   have half of the Senegalese population that is an artist: painters,
   drummers, singers, dancers.

F: It started ten years ago?

A: Or before.

F: Yes. Now everybody is an artist, but some people do not know
   how, and they go away with it [abroad].

A: Yes. Some cannot even hold a stick [of the drum], and they go
   and play.

F: But you, do you get paid by Senegalese to teach them how to
drum and how to dance?

A: Yes.

F: Senegalese? Senegalese pay you?

A: Yes.

F: You get paid to go to a Ballet and teach?

A: Yes. But individuals come to me too and pay me to teach them to
play.

F: And to dance?

A: Yes, to dance too.

F: Senegalese pay you.

A: Yes, they pay me to teach them to drum and to dance.

Aziz Faye echoes Sonko's assertion that dancing has historically been reserved for the griot caste when he says that "not anybody can dance. . . . Only
géwëls can dance." Rather than drawing attention to the moral and social implications of such a division of labor, however, he emphasizes the skills necessary to perform, skills that are lacking among the general population:
"Most of the dances, they cannot do [them]. They do not know how." When
I explicitly, if rather simplistically, addressed the stigmatization of dancing
(paralleling the stigmatization of griots) as a morally dubious activity, Aziz
replied by drawing attention to the social fact that what is appropriate for a
griot is not so for a non-griot. It is not so much that dance is "bad," and thus
by extension griots are morally reprehensible, but that dancing historically
belongs to the griots. As a *géwël,* Aziz is offered money to dance, a point that
I insisted on clarifying given the paucity of discussion in the literature. Yet,
while the retribution of griots' dance performances falls within the tradition
as a practice that conforms to the historically defined separation between the
castes, to be paid to teach dancing and music to other Senegalese coincides
with the breakup of such caste divisions. It is precisely because dancing has
become a monetarized activity outside of the client-patron relations between
griots and nobles that the latter are willing to pay griots—the experts and
professional dancers in Senegalese society—to teach them how to dance. The
extent to which the general population actually pays griots to teach them
how to dance remains to be determined. What is certain is that those who
intend to pursue dance professionally recognize griot families as institutions
of learning, and foreigners and Senegalese turn to them for dance training.
Yet the rule of endogamy that binds the griots as a separate caste from the
exogamous nobles is broken considerably less frequently and carries much

more severe social consequences than the venturing of non-griots into the professional territory of griots.

Within the four Ballets I examined, only the Ballet Mansour had *jàlí* choreographers. Those choreographers who were not griots themselves sought out the knowledge cultivated by griots, either by entering a Ballet directed by a griot or through their social contacts with the griots. This was the case for Sonko:

> FRANCESCA: Before coming to the National Ballet, did you dance in other Ballets?
>
> BOULY: Yes. I was an *animateur* in my village first, when I was very young. I was interested in dance, I followed the griots in their travels. So after my studies at Zinquinchor I came first to Tambacounda to learn about the Malinke culture, and then I came to Dakar to be able to have access to the Thèâtre Daniel Sorano. So since 1972 I entered at Sorano as a singer and a dancer in the Troupe National Dramatique. In 1974, with the creation of Sira Badral, the second Ballet [of the state], I was assigned there as a dancer, and later, in 1979, I became adjunct director of that Ballet, and in 1980 I became the director of Sira Badral. In 1983 I was again moved to the first Ballet [La Linguère], which I directed as adjunct since 1985, when I became the director. And since then it's okay, I am still the director of the National Ballet.

Sonko followed the griots and carried out his own research in different regions of the country until he moved to Dakar specifically to enter the National Ballet of Senegal. Similarly, Djibril Sane, the choreographer of the Ballet Fambondy, stressed his consistent exposure to dance specialists. Sane emphasized his noble heritage to make the point that many griots entered and performed in his household, giving him the chance to learn by watching them. Furthermore, he pointed to the importance of his mother who, because she was infertile for many years, was a *dimba*. A *dimba* is someone who belongs to a group of women in a similar situation who appeal to spirits to be cured. As the son of a *dimba*, Sane found himself surrounded by music and dance and developed a great passion for it.

The capacity to learn by watching the dance experts was stressed by several of the interviewees, who emphasized self-learning as a way to overcome the social resistance and barriers between them and their passion for dancing. This was the case for Ndiuwar Thiam, one of the directors of the Ballet Kaddu gi. He had this to say of his training:

FRANCESCA: What pushed you to create the Ballet?

NDIUWAR THIAM: That is a long story, eh eh [we laugh]. It's a long
story because I have always loved art, and I have always loved
dance. Because, you know, I had an uncle who was a member of
a Ballet—he was in the National Ballet. I was too young, too
young. It was 1961, 1962. He would take me often to *Sorano* to see
his performances. As a nephew watching his uncle dance, that
was really a pleasure, and it inspired me to tell him: "Uncle, I
want to do like you." "Ah, really?" "Yes, I want to do like you." I
was not even seven. I was four years old, six years old. . . .

F: So he taught you how to dance?

N: No, no. After, after. . . . It was him who gave me the passion. I saw
a *grand,* an old person, he also had been in the sacred forest. He
had created a Ballet, here [at Ñaari Tali, the neighborhood where
we conducted the interview].

F: How old were you?

N: I was twelve, because I was in the third [grade]. He told me, "You
little one," because, well, he believed, he thought that one day he
would have a contract to leave with his group, and I was a minor,
I would not be able to go, participate in his group. He told me:
"You are young, really, wait until you are sixteen, seventeen." I
said, "No, I really want to dance." He refused me. I spent two
months going there looking. I would go and stay to the side to
watch the artists dance, the drums, the *jembe,* the *sabar.* Really,
that excited me the most. The day, and the day after, I went. It became stronger, stronger. I could not stand it anymore. One day I
came with my jumpsuit, and I said, "Well, *grand,* I am going to
dance." He said, "No, wait." I said, "No, I am going to dance no
matter what." So he said, "Okay. Get up, dance." So I just started.
He taught me how to dance. He taught me how to dance. Because he was a *grand,* and I owe him a lot.

The "grand" who taught Ndiuwar Thiam how to dance was Abdou Ba, who
now teaches at the National Conservatory. Thiam brings our attention to Ba's
expertise by telling us that "he had been in the sacred forest" (unlike Thiam)
and thus possessed the knowledge required to lead a Ballet. Yet Thiam, like
Sonko and Sane, emphasizes his own persistence and initiative, nurtured by
a great passion for dance that enables him to overcome the obstacle in his way.
In Thiam's narrative we learn that he was inspired to dance by a member of

his family, and the fact that he was not the first in his family to enter the profession made it easier for him to pursue such a career. Yet, he had to prove his determination against a skeptical Ballet director and win his way into the company. The next interlocutor—Ismael—also stresses his love for dancing and his independent learning process, which led him from dancing in nightclubs to performing as a member of the Ballet Mansour.

FRANCESCA: Can you tell me how you learned how to dance? How did you get into dance?

ISMAEL: By chance, by chance, because it is my sister who brought me to a club. When she took me I was young, I did not know the club, I did not know the environment for dancing. We went and left, and it was good for me. There was good music, people were dancing. I was very young.

F: How old?

I: I was sixteen. After that I started going by myself. I started to go to clubs to dance funk. I really like funk, and when I dance funk I listen, well, to the music; I go with the music. I would go to dance, the entrance was five hundred CFA, I would go and pay, and I danced, I danced. I wanted most of all to dance. I was not there for women or for drinking. I was there to listen to the good music and to dance. Little by little people started to notice me. Since I have a bit of white color, in that milieu I am easily noticeable. So, rapidly, I integrated in the environment, and there were many people who saw me and told me: "You dance well, little one, you dance well, little one." There were competitions, demonstrations. I would see the dancers; it was good. But I trained by myself before coming to do a demonstration. It is after that that a great M.C. saw me, and said: "You have to dance, because you dance well. You have to do a dance show." Well, I did a demonstration, and *hoplà*, people applauded, and I started to do competitions. I won, and I won prizes.

F: Competition in clubs?

I: Yes. I won prizes. I won a television; I won a Sony tape recorder, to listen to music; I won an airplane ticket Dakar–New York–Dakar, but they gave me money for it; I won an airplane ticket Dakar–Las Palmas–Dakar, that was a real ticket. I was eighteen years old. I was young, I was going to school, so I gave that to my mother. She went. Then little by little I had small contracts. With

Marlboro, I had some dance shows like the Grand Gala for Miss Europe. In nightclubs also we would often perform choreographies with two, three friends. And clips too, I have done two clips. One with Super Diamono—"Sai Sai"—and another clip with Kine Lam. For Kine Lam, I danced for her for three years. Now she is in the United States. She has a contract there.

F: You danced at her concerts.

I: *Voilà*, at the concerts.

F: And there, you danced the *sabar?*

I: No, I did not dance the *sabar.* I danced modern, some steps of modern and some steps of Ballet; it was Afro-modern, yes Afro-modern. I would take the *mbalax* music, and now the *mbalax* music, people can dance it modern style, because it has the tempo: "tac, tac" [he snaps his fingers as he sings the rhythm]. You can take the Ballet steps, and you dance within the *mbalax,* and you take the modern steps, and you dance within the *mbalax,* you see.

Ismael started to dance "by chance" as he discovered that he loved dancing by going to a club with his sister. As he became a regular at discotheques, he drew attention to himself and was encouraged to perform and compete in the clubs.[11] These competitions allowed him to slowly get contracts for commercial ads and entertainment, and finally to gain a long-term contract with a musical group, led by Kine Lam, a respected and popular singer of the *mbalax* genre. As a dancer in her group, Ismael could use the skills he had honed through dancing at clubs to perform "Afro-modern." Just as *mbalax* music fuses *sabar* drumming and singing styles with influences from funk, jazz, rock, and salsa, so Ismael was called to perform a dance fusion of styles that allowed him a freedom of expression and creativity similar to that he had cultivated on discotheque floors. In this context, the Ballet steps that he mentions comprise the African side of his "Afro-modern" classification, while his own steps developed from dancing funk in discotheques comprise the "modern" element. Although I did not pursue this line of inquiry in the interview, it is reasonable to assume that just as he had taught himself to dance funk, he picked up steps from the *sabar* or from other ethnic complexes of the country and was able to perform them in his choreographies. His experience with Kine Lam provided an intermediary step between discotheque dancing and Ballet dancing: After dancing with her group, Ismael entered the Ballet Mansour, and at the time of our interview he had been with the Ballet for more than three years. Joining the Ballet Mansour, Ismael was exposed to many ethnic dance genres.

Prompted by my questioning, Ismael reiterates the familiar narrative of his parents' initial opposition to dancing. As his father had been working abroad for many years, the opposition to his engagement with dance came from his mother:

> FRANCESCA: Then, you are the first in the family who dances?
>
> ISMAEL: Yes. I am the only artist.
>
> F: And your parents, did they approve?
>
> I: At first my mother did not approve, because I was going to school and I danced too. I could not do both at the same time; it was too hard. But the latter was easier for me, because dancing was a pleasure. But I was a good student. Little by little it was a bit hard, with French, that is a bit hard. And mathematics, physics, chemistry, I was not that strong with those. I decided to continue dancing, and now I know that dance can be a real job, it is something really practical.
>
> F: Then your mother . . .
>
> I: Yes, my mother now has accepted, because she has seen that I am a great dancer. She has seen me on TV. She has seen me dance with the musicians, and I have also given her gifts, like the ticket Dakar–Las Palmas–Dakar. First she thought it was a fake ticket, but then she said it was real. She left on vacation, and she said: "My son is a great artist."

Parents' opposition to their offspring's involvement in dance is assuaged when they achieve a certain measure of success. Exposure to the media, association with widely popular music groups, and performances at prestigious cultural institutions like the National Theatre provide a degree of celebrity status that can counter the negative association of dancing with the griot caste. Furthermore, in Ismael's case dance proved to be a "real" job capable of bringing an income that does not depend on the mediation of scholastic knowledge and the credentials conferred by French literacy. Dancing could be pleasurable and remunerative. The symbolic value of money and gift exchange in these negotiations should not be overlooked: it reflects a commitment to affective relations and the acceptance of obligations of mutual support and assistance that links individuals to their families and establishes historical continuities from generation to generation. Thus, through the redistribution of resources and the circulation of gifts to their families, dancers are able to assuage their parents' social antipathy for dancing.

The next interview echoes these themes and, like Ismael's narrative, points to discotheque dancing as the space in which the subject's love for dance was developed. Rather than stressing the smooth continuity between discotheque dancing and dancing in a Ballet, however, the interlocutor stresses the radical discontinuity between the two. Souleymane exposes the complex negotiations of identity that each social space required of him. Again I asked how he had learned to dance.

> SOULEYMANE: How have I learned how to dance? *Voilà,* I told myself: "I am a dancer in night clubs. I believe . . . [he searches for words] . . . John Travolta. I believe in that man. John Travolta, Michael Jackson. But one day I told myself that, *voilà* . . .
>
> F: [overlap] . . . So you would go into night clubs; you would do your own steps, your own routines?
>
> S: Yes, I danced. *Voilà.* I listened to jazz, thanks to my father. I listened to jazz, but I always loved funk. Funk, disco. But one day I asked myself. "But we, what do we have?" Because John Travolta is Italian, he lives in the States, he is a movie actor, he dances funk and disco or modern or jazz. So I told myself, "Travolta, he has that," and there is also Michael Jackson and other dancers too, classical dancers, the Russians, so I told myself, "How will I know to my own advantage that I am black?" I will search for something, do research like you. . . . I was an oil electrician; I would put electricity at gas stations. One day I left all of that, and I converted to dance. I did some research on dance, but my parents did not want me to, because my parents told me, "You have left your studies very soon. Now you have left your work, and now you dance. Dance is for homosexuals." Yes. If you dance one says you are not a man.
>
> F: Traditional dance, or the dances you were doing before at the disco?
>
> S: Yes. At the beginning. But when you are inside, they will know you are a man.
>
> F: When you were doing jazz, things like that?
>
> S: Yes. They would say, "What do you do like that? That is for homosexuals. Leave it." So I left it. I was practicing basketball, and one day a friend came and said, "I would like you to go to Blaize

Senghor [a cultural center]. I would like you to go there. There
are some Ballets there. You are a dancer. You go there and you
dance, you are going to dance." So that guy, he saw me dance. I
am a dancer. He saw me dance. So one day I went there, and
when I looked I . . . [he laughs] . . . I did not believe it. "We have
all of that!" There was the *jembe,* the *cium* [another drum], and
there were some girls who *danced.* I cried, I yelled. I even was
afraid. I told myself, "I cannot dance like that." And before leaving I asked a woman, and she said, "If you want to enroll, you enroll and you come." So I enrolled.

Souleymane speaks of his entrance into a Ballet in terms of a conscious
search for a black African identity. At the same time, his rejection of discotheque dancing was precipitated by contradictory negotiations over his sexual identity. While his parents associated dancing with homosexuality, his own
involvement with club life provoked a crisis in his heterosexual relations. He
states that while his parents anxiously questioned his heterosexuality because
of his involvement with dance, on the "inside," within the club's milieu, his
sexual orientation was evident: "When you are inside, they will know you
are a man." This statement was further clarified in our following discussion:

FRANCESCA: When you were there in the nightclubs, you had style
when you danced there.
SOULEYMANE: Yes. Oooh. But after, I knew that . . . [he laughs] . . .
After, I had many girlfriends, and that made me suffer. I loved
women a lot. But outside dance women did not love me. Women
loved me because I danced well. And one day I told myself, "But
me, if I were not a dancer, women would not love me." People
told me that, "Yes, it is like that." "Ah, it's like that? Then I leave
it." And I no longer had women, I no longer had women. I wondered why when I danced women loved me, and when I stopped
dancing, when I came into the house . . . they do not even look
at me [I laugh]. It is only in the discotheques that I can have a
girl. So I cried, and I asked God that I would no longer have girlfriends. So then he did that, but then I cried and I said, "But God
help me [we laugh]. It is too much." Yes [we laugh]. Because you
know what is dangerous in life? One should not say "I am famous, I am beautiful," because there are some women—"fans"
[in English]—do you know "fans"?
F: Ah yes, "fans." They follow you, they adore you.

s: Yes, but you know that is not good, that is not good for an artist—the fans.

f: You had a lot of fans.

s: A lot. And that is evil. Do you know why it is evil? Because if you can no longer dance, they walk by and tell you "bye bye" [in English]. Now there are other dancers more precocious, more beautiful, faster than you, and now they no longer look at you. Or they are married, or they are looking for a husband, and their parents tell them, "You should not believe in dance. Because that guy is a dancer he cannot give you anything." Then I told myself, "I am not going to let myself be manipulated. I have to look at the truth in the face, to leave dance." So I stopped. But I danced alone. But one day traditional dance woke me up. It told me: "Hey, wake up!" [he claps his hands]. I woke up with the *jembe.* It told me: "You are here. You are an African, you should not quit." So I ran to discover.

Souleymane describes how his nocturnal forays into Dakar's discotheques provided him with a constant pool of women fans. Women loved him because he was a good dancer, yet they seemed to not even notice him outside of a club. He became uneasy about the discrepancy between women's desire for him as a dancer and women's indifference toward him as a person. He began to question his power to attract women through dancing, and he concluded that "it is only in the discotheques that I can have a girl." This observation suggests a strong relationship between kinetics and aesthetics, a relation that I remarked upon during my description of *sabars.* Dance, as an aesthetized kinetic activity, has the power to transform the subject into a beautiful person. Beauty is constituted in action rather than being an aesthetic property of the subject. Souleymane was disturbed by the contextual power of seduction that he possessed, which seemed to be extinguished the moment he stopped dancing. He may also have been disturbed by his parents' association of discotheque dancing with homosexuality. This association may have been provoked by the fact that, in the contemporary urban environment, dancing is foremost a social activity pursued within women's networks, while professional dancing is a prerogative of griots, both male and female. Because a male griot's identity does not depend on the norms of behavior proscribed to the general population, a griot's sexual identity is not threatened by his dancing. In contrast, the same engagement in dancing on the part of male non-griots threatens normative constructions of masculinity. Historically, the advent of Islam and the fall of precolonial political and social structures diminished the social context in which non-griot male dancing is appropriate. Male dances considered fit for the general population were linked to men's roles in war and hunting, male initiation societies, and wrestling. Significantly, these dances are performed by Ballets which then offer the opportunity for men to engage in unambiguously masculine dancing. In this context, the gender identity allowed for by discotheque dancing remains ambiguous and seems to support a fluid and negotiated construction of gender, not yet marked by historically normatized social roles. Traditional dance, however, affords dancers the opportunity to display a normative and unambiguously masculine subjectivity. Thus Souylemane's engagement with a Ballet may have assuaged his parents' fear about his homosexuality. Likewise, the performance of accepted and stable gender roles afforded by Ballet dancing allowed him (and his social milieu) to put to rest the question of sexual orientation and to foreground the relationship of dancing to ethnic and racialized identities.

Souleymane interpreted the foregrounding of his ethnic identity through his membership in a Ballet as a "conversion" precipitated by a series of questions: "But we, what do we have? . . . Travolta, he has that . . . How will I know to my own advantage that I am black?" Through the encouragement of a friend, Souleymane was directed to the youth cultural center Blaize Senghor. The center provides free space for Ballet troupes to rehearse and an opportunity for the youth to enroll in a Ballet. Souleymane's witnessing of Ballet dancing at the center, after he had quit dance and kept his passion alive as a solitary activity, was dramatic: "I cried, I yelled, I even was afraid." The *jembe,* a powerful drum of the Mande complex, woke him up and precipitated a series of life-changing events. Soon after he was enrolled in a Ballet he was able to direct his passion for dancing toward fulfilling his quest for a meaningful identity. Significantly, Souleymane's "conversion" to traditional dance also precipitated his conversion to Islam. He came from a Christian family and was ostracized by his parents for many years because of his change of faith.

If for Souleymane a conversion to traditional dance meant also a realignment of his faith toward a more African religion, interviews with women dancers instead stressed the incongruity between their religious identities as Muslim women and their professional engagement with dancing. This incongruity was not so much experienced by the dancers themselves as voiced by their families, who opposed their daughters' choice of dance as a career.

Oumi, a dancer who has spent more than ten years with the National Ballet of Senegal, like her male counterparts talked about her parents' opposition to her dancing, yet she underscored the gendered aspect of their opposition:

> FRANCESCA: How have you learned how to dance?
> OUMI: I have learned how to dance with the Ballet Mansour. It was hard at first. My parents did not want me to dance. I was their only daughter.
> F: Why do parents not want their kids to dance?
> O: Because they do not know. They think it is not good for a girl. Dance has a bad reputation. But as I was here with my mother, I could do it. Mothers are more understanding. My father was not here in Dakar.

While in the social circle women dance more than men, they encounter fiercer opposition within their family than their male counterparts when they decide to take up the profession of dancing. Significantly, Oumi suggests that her parents' hostility to dance is determined by ignorance—"because they do not know"—as a way to express her disagreement with their opinion and with the notion that dancing is morally reprehensible. Furthermore, the fact that she stressed how her parents specifically say that it is not good for a *girl* to dance suggests that religious rather than caste considerations play a role in their judgment. This interpretation is supported by the following excerpt, taken from an interview with another seasoned performer of the National Ballet of Senegal, Ramatou.

> FRANCESCA: Were you the first one in your family to dance?
> RAMATOU: Yes. I am the only one. I am not the only one. I am not the only one. For example, in my paternal family I am the only one, but in my maternal family we are two: the woman with whom I danced for the anniversary of Senghor, she is my cousin. Our two mothers have the same mother and father. . . . But on our paternal side I am the only one who dances, and I had all the problems in the world to dance. Because my family did not want me to do this job, you see.
> F: I hear that all the time. Why do the parents not want their children to dance?
> R: Because, as you know, Senegal is a very religious country that believes a lot in Islam, you see. And well, like our parents say, Islam does not accept dance. I do not know [why], but it does not want it. I belong to a very religious family, very religious, you see, and

that is why my father did not want me to do such a job. Well, after, well, he died. It is after that that I started to persevere. It was when I was a student that he died, and he really did not want me to dance. But I, it is something that I have always loved in my life, since childhood, since I was in school I always loved to dance.

When asked about her family, Ramatou thinks first of her patrilineage and thus answers that she is the only one in the family to dance. She immediately corrects herself, claiming double descent and thus including her matrilineage in her family history. Her maternal cousin, with whom she performed at the National Theatre for the ninetieth birthday celebration of Leopold Sédhar Senghor, is also a dancer. She goes on to say that it was her father who most vehemently opposed her dancing; it was only with his death that she found the strength to realize her love for dance and pursue a professional career.

Ramatou was introduced to me by Bouly Sonko as the only one in the Ballet who had received an academic education in dance, as opposed to the training of the "streets" and the "forest" that was common to all other members. Ramatou studied for three years at Mudra Afrique.[12] She then spent two years at the National Conservatory before joining the National Ballet of Senegal. The fact that she attended what many consider an elite institution, Mudra Afrique, and a government center of learning like the National Conservatory must have helped assuage her family's concern over the respectability of her career choice.

Echoing Oumi's remark about her parents, who did not know better than to condemn dance, Ramatou claims that she does not know why the Islamic religion condemns dancing as a morally dubious activity. By claiming ignorance, she signals her distance from such an ideology as well as her "innocence": as a professional dancer and a Muslim herself, she leads a respectable and morally righteous life. Also similarly to Oumi, she implies that "mothers are more understanding than fathers" and suggests not only that Islam proscribes different rules of conduct for men and women but that gender also plays a role in the way in which those rules are interpreted. As other scholars have remarked (Boddy 1989; Masquelier 2001), women's interpretations of Islam are generally more lax than men's and make more room for ethnic practices such as dance or spirit possession to coexist peacefully within a coherent religious subjectivity.

My interviews with dancers and choreographers bring into focus four social clusters in which dance knowledge is cultivated: 1) the griot caste; 2) Ballet companies; 3) academic institutions of the arts;[13] 4) discotheques. While my research has only begun to investigate Ballet companies, I hope that as more scholars focus on dance, the differences and interconnections between these arenas of dance training will be interrogated. Such interrogations would bring to the fore important aspects of popular culture and the changing intergenerational relationships that define negotiations over choosing dance as a career and a way of living.

The next chapter will explore some aspects of the relationship between the politics of underdevelopment and the politics of dance production and consumption in Dakar's tourist enclaves. The chapter focuses on the activities of the Ballet Mansour, which is the second most important African Ballet in the country after the National Ballet of Senegal, and which maintains a virtual monopoly over dance performances in Dakar's hotels and the surrounding area. Through an in-depth analysis of a series of interviews with a member of the Ballet, I will explore the relationship between choreographic creativity and economic exploitation. The concept of *terànga* will guide our exploration into the moral economy that sustains the exchange between Senegalese performers and foreign tourists.

8

Exploiting *Terànga*

Hospitality and Ballet Performances in Tourist Enclaves.

The hospitality of this country, this is how we're praised.
The singer's singing the hospitality of Senegal,
the rapper is telling about the hospitality of Senegal,
the writer is writing about the hospitality of Senegal.

Since hospitality is what we are known for,
we should never prove otherwise.
When visitors come to our country,
if we give them a warm welcome
they will want to come back.

Hey, cab driver, don't take advantage of them,
hey, salesman, don't overcharge them.
Whatever they bring
it's for the whole country.

We should never prove other than what we are known for:
when somebody comes to our country
welcome him, treat him right,
so after he leaves he'll want to come back.

The dirt, the waste, the bad smell
destroy and cause illness.
Then everybody will be afraid to come here.

When someone comes to our country
welcome him, treat him right,
so when he leaves, he will want to come back.

Pickpockets, crooks,
destroy,
then everybody will be afraid to come here.

Let's step back and look at ourselves,
and act like how we're known:
share our wishes and our forces with them
so when they leave, they will want to come back.
—Youssou N'Dour, "Tourista" (1994)

* * *

Fieldnotes: Riverside, California, 1995. I am preparing for my first trip to Senegal, listening to Youssou N'Dour's song "The Tourist." I let myself be transported by the happy tune and imagine myself on a busy street in Dakar: "No worries: Youssou protect me from pickpockets." I swirl happily. "No worries: Youssou protect me from greedy taxi drivers." I turn the other way not to get too dizzy with more spinning. The lyrics sound so reassuring in California. They help me imagine that on my arrival to Senegal I will find good-willed Senegalese citizens who will welcome me and treat me right: I will not be overcharged, I will not be harassed to share my wealth, rather I will be served with generosity. I spin and jump once more to celebrate Youssou as the guide of the people and the voice of wisdom leading all the honest Senegalese to create a tourist's paradise. I grab at the cover of Youssou N'Dour's CD to show you: here he stands, giving us his back and stepping with open arms into the golden light of a setting sun. The caption, "Youssou N'Dour," is written across the length of his arms, while another caption, located at the level of his feet, reads: "The Guide (*Wommat*)."

Youssou N'Dour is for many Senegalese the most beloved singer of the country, appealing across generations because of the wisdom of his lyrics, supported by his good character and behavior. N'Dour founded his first group—the Super Etoile—in 1979. His popularity and fame has risen steadily, and he has become not only a national star but one of the great protagonists of world music.[1] He is a model citizen—successful, honest, unpretentious, free of vices (like smoking, drinking, or pursuing love affairs), and generous. His moral integrity, maintained through many years of public scrutiny, make him a legitimate guide of the people.

The hospitality of this country, this is how we're praised.
The singer's singing the hospitality of Senegal,
the rapper is telling about the hospitality of Senegal,
the writer is writing about the hospitality of Senegal.

Youssou N'Dour sings in Wolof about the hospitality of the Senegalese people. An English translation of these lyrics is included in the liner notes, for the benefit of the foreign consumer/potential tourist. The anonymous translator uses "hospitality" for the Wolof *terànga,* a translation that is both correct and, for obvious practical reasons, succinct. *Terànga* in Wolof does not simply convey hospitality, however, but covers a semantic field associated with the morality that governs interactions between hosts and guests and the circulation of gifts among a wide network of relations. *Terànga* as a specific form of generosity accrues the social standing of those who lavish gifts on relatives, friends, and acquaintances, materially and symbolically asserting their ability to give away wealth for the well-being and entertainment of others. Material giving entails a symbolic exchange: the host gives away material goods or services and receives the moral approval of the community and gains in social status (Sylla 1994). The moral value of exchange is measured by *terànga*—the degree of generosity that a person possesses.[2] The paths along which generosity flows are socially delineated to strengthen community solidarity and the support of well-established social networks. Assane Sylla, in *La Philosophie Morale des Wolof,* gives several examples of the kinds of social exchange that accrue one's *terànga:*

- the parents of a young woman, who have received a gift in money or objects by her fiancée, return part of the gift to the parents of the fiancée.
- a wife offers periodically to her parents-in-law a delicious meal (*rerru goro*).
- a wife offers a sum of money to her sister-in-law on the occasion of her marriage or a baptism of her children (*añu njeké*).
- a person gives money to a friend or relative on the occasion of a funeral (*jaxal*).
- a person returning from a trip brings gifts to friends and relatives (*sëricë*). (1994:86)

Each of these gifts allows the giver to prove the extent to which he or she is generous and potentially increases his or her moral standing. The list continues, but the point I want to make here is that *terànga* assumes shared social codes of exchange as well as shared moral codes of judgment. Sylla argues that *terànga* establishes competition among those of equal social status, who vie to outdo each other's *terànga* and increase their respectability according to the group's standards. At the same time, a lack of *terànga* brings a lack of respect in one's own social circle and a moral isolation that can take the form of severe sanctions if the breach in reciprocity and mutual obligations has been profound. Sylla describes the most severe of these sanctions—*toroxte*—in terms of "the loss of one's social position, of one's fortune, and of one's moral credit . . . the maximum degree of shame" (1994:88). The confiscation of material wealth by community members, elicited by a serious breach in community relations, is symbolic of the social retrieval of "moral credit" that a righteous member of the community enjoys among his fellows. *Terànga* denotes not only generosity but accountability, while the recognition of *terànga* as a virtue speaks of the importance of assistance as a form of moral currency that establishes a moral credit line that can be cashed in at times of need. In other words, *terànga* ensures the flow of wealth among social networks and guarantees voluntary gift giving as a form of social security amidst a steadily deteriorating economy in a chronic state of crisis.

My enhanced appreciation of the meaning of *terànga* as something more complex than "hospitality" was brought about by my displacement from California to Dakar. This recontextualization destabilized the happy interpretation of N'Dour's song that I had wishfully embraced in California. I will thus enter again the ethnographic present, to introduce the reader to my new encounter with N'Dour's "The Tourist" and the musing it elicited.

> *Dakar, Senegal, 1996.* It's Saturday evening, and the old mother, the two male wage earners, four of the young women of the household, and I have gathered to watch TV after dinner. Flickering on the screen in and out of focus (the reception in the house is not very good) I see Youssou N'Dour smiling and singing "The Tourist" against the background of a fancy hotel. One image in particular grabs my attention and my stomach: Youssou is singing in front of a ten-meter buffet framed by a swimming pool and by the sea, which appear in the more distant landscape.
>
> Who has ever seen so much food? Meters and meters of table thick with shrimps, lobsters, fried fishes, steamed fishes, pork, chicken, lamb, green salads, potato salads, bean salads, shredded carrot salads, pastas, soups, breads, fruits, desserts, and colored drinks. My eyes become bigger than my stomach! My stomach becomes bigger than a hut! I wonder if I am dreaming. I know for sure that nobody in this room but me has ever come close to so much food in all their lives, not even at a marriage or at a funeral! Not to say that the family is poor: they live in a good neighborhood, they own their own

house, they eat two meals a day as well as breakfast, and the daughters of the house have many beautiful dresses. But so much food! Am I hallucinating, still hungry after the evening meal? Remembering? Because I saw such a banquet when I went to the Club Mediterraneé at Cap Skirring, in the Casamance. I had followed the local Ballet thorough the back entrance of the facility until we walked into the core area of the estate: a huge and extravagantly shaped swimming pool, surrounded by a large sunbathing area with an open bar, and a series of buildings sporting a theater, a disco, and a central dining room, with banquet tables covered with food. While the Med "guests" finished their dinner, the dancers of the Ballet dressed and warmed up to perform around the swimming pool. And now again, flickering on the TV screen, I see the same icons of wealth and leisure—the pool and the banquet table. The luxury of the environment leaves no doubt that the tourists in N'Dour's song can only be rich foreigners or Senegalese politicians and superstars. Any other Senegalese on the premises would most likely be workers, and it is these workers that N'Dour is addressing in his song.

N'Dour draws on the codes of *terànga* to re-dress the morality of those working within the tourist economy. *"Hey cab driver, don't take advantage of them. Hey salesman, don't overcharge them. Whatever they bring, it's for the whole country."* His words of admonition toward cab drivers and salesmen who should exercise restraint and not charge gullible tourists "too much" resonate against the wasteful abundance set off by the images on the screen. I imagine that like me, the other viewers in the living room have visions of fat tourists gorging themselves on the mounds of food and indulging in all sorts of pleasures routinely denied to the Senegalese masses. N'Dour's smile is uncanny, ironic. It looks like a glossy advertisement and a veiled invitation to charge those tourists as much as possible!

The happy tune that sounded so (wishfully) comforting in California seems plainly ludicrous in Dakar. Set against the tourist economy of the city, Youssou N'Dour's song echoes the Senegalese government's rhetoric of *encombrement humaines,* developed in the 1970s. The Senegalese government considered poor Senegalese a nuisance to tourists and attempted to eliminate the poor rather than poverty, in order to make Dakar more attractive to foreigners. Similarly, N'Dour's lyrics suggest that poverty is not bad because of the suffering it causes to the poor but because it scares away potential tourists: "The dirt, the waste, the bad smell, / destroy and cause illness. / Then everybody will be afraid to come here." N'Dour's lyrics seem to fault the poor for illness and pollution while calling upon *terànga's* strict moral codes to suggest that workers in the tourist economy sacrifice for the benefit of the tourists, sharing their strength with them, so that they will come back for more.[3]

The dancers of the Ballet Mansour practice this form of *terànga* as they perform weekly in the most luxurious hotels of Dakar and the surrounding areas, providing a constant cultural referent in the tourist economy.[4] The Hotel Terànga, located in a strategic position off a central plaza in downtown Dakar, is among the hotels that regularly host the Ballet's performances. Every Sunday, as the hosts of the hotel are served a lavish lunch on a terrace overlooking the ocean, the members of the Ballet perform before them. Between bites, the guests consume the spectacle, while others are pulled out of a nearby swimming pool and the surrounding chairs by the call of the drums to gather around the performers. This is as close to "Africa" as many of them will get. Like the environment of the Club Mediteranée at Cap Skirring, the Hotel Terànga provides all the comfort and entertainment that a tourist may desire within the confines of the estate. Carefully choreographed trips to the outside can also be purchased. Yet, outside of the sealed environment of tourist enclaves, encounters with the population are hard to control. These encounters inevitably take the form of "hustling," as members of the informal economy try to capitalize on the few precious moments in which the tourists are away from the strict supervision of tour managers to make a sale.

While in Dakar, I often saw the tourists at the Hotel Terànga on little white roofless buses that took them around the Cornice (the large area of the city that surrounds the hotel), trekking from the Sandaga market on one side and the Village Artisanal on the other. The tourists could not even step off the bus without being surrounded by vendors heavy with souvenirs. These tourists, who spent more than a hundred dollars a night at the hotel, bargained fiercely about the price of merchandise and expected to be sold items at local prices.

Local wages were also paid to the performers of the Ballet Mansour who entertained the foreign guests at the Hotel Terànga. Dancers earned two thousand CFA Francs for each performance (the equivalent of four dollars at the time of my research) at the hotel or any of the other luxurious resorts of Dakar in which the Ballet operates. Since dancers got to perform once or twice a week, with the best dancers performing a maximum of four times a week, the best-paid members of the Ballet earned thirty-two thousand CFA Francs a month (about sixty-four dollars). In this context, how does *terànga* work? What is the meaning of *terànga* in relation to the tourist economy?

I have argued that in the contemporary context *terànga* is a virtue that compels the individual to distribute gifts and favors that ensure the survival of a community under a chronic state of crisis. Within such an environment, even if a dancer's wage is barely sufficient for the satisfaction of the most basic necessities, it is often divided and distributed on social occasions. This practice of circulating earnings adds an affective value to money. Money is not only measured in economic terms, over which dancers, like other members of society, have little control; the fluidity with which money travels across a network of relations converts hard currency into affective ties and mutual responsibilities. A sickness, a divorce, deteriorating terms of trade in the global market, a crisis in the governmental structure—any of these factors can push an individual to the brink of catastrophe, putting pressure on a budget already stretched to maximum capacity. At such times, the possibility of counting on others' *terànga* is essential for survival.

Economic insecurity is endemic even among the most secure positions in the formal economy like government jobs. Even members of the National Ballet of Senegal, who earned more money than the dancers of the Ballet Mansour and possessed a minimum of social security as government employees, were reminded of their vulnerability to unstable economic and political conditions during the months following the municipal and regional elections on November 24, 1996. The month preceding the elections, the government sponsored its own candidates (of the Socialist party) through a series of political rallies and gatherings throughout the city. While Ballets of the popular neighborhoods of Dakar got to earn some money by performing at political rallies in support of the Socialist party, members of the National Ballet were left with no salary for three months. Dancers had to rely on a network of family and friends to survive without pay. Also, job insecurity increased in the public and private sectors because reforms in labor regulations and policies introduced with the first Structural Adjustment Programs of the early 1980s made it easier for employers to lay off workers (Somerville 1997). Thus while older members of the National Ballet benefit from assured life employment, younger members enter the Ballet on a yearly contractual basis.

Dancers, to make ends meet, share *terànga* with members of their social network, whom, as Sylla remarks, are their equals in social status. But can they enter into the circle of reciprocity that *terànga* implies with members of the tourist economy, as Yossou N'Dour proposes in his song? *Terànga* works as a reciprocating generosity because it implies an act of faith in the goodwill of others to come forth with a similar spirit when the occasion arises: yesterday's host will be in the position of guest and become the socially legitimate recipient of the other's generosity. Do members of Ballets incur a social debt to be repaid at some indeterminate time in the future by the tourists, when they will travel to First World nations as tourists themselves, or working as permanently foreign "guests"? Do they increase their moral status by

performing "honestly" in the capitalist economy and the system of global inequalities that it entails? When dancers perform somersaults and back flips on the cement surrounding hotel swimming pools, when they dance hard and cut their bare feet on the glass left by drunken tourists at the hotel, when they return to homes with no electricity or running water and eat plain rice for dinner and nothing for breakfast, do they gain prestige in the eyes of the tourists? Do they become the honorable members of society that the recognition of *terànga* bestows on those who perform it? These are rhetorical questions: the answer can only be in the negative. The appeal to *terànga* in the context of the tourist economy ensures that the tourists will be provided with the cheapest and kindest services by the local population, who can thus secure them a degree of luxury they may not be able to afford when vacationing in the First World. In this context, *terànga* serves as a code word of appeal to the exploited workers of the tourist economy to be content with their lot and to view the exploitation with gratitude, as a way to prove their moral worth and their capacity to sacrifice for the "common good": "Whatever they bring, it's for the whole country." N'Dour's song, in this context, performs a hegemonic function by translating in terms that are meaningful to the Wolophone population the political ideology of the state elite.

However, the concept of *terànga*, even if it is distorted from its original meaning, helps us understand the relationship of the Senegalese elite to international institutions such as corporations and banks. During the three decades of Senegal's independent era, the political elite has entertained tight reciprocal relations with international financial institutions that have ensured mutual profits at the expense of the Senegalese masses. In this context, *terànga* highlights ties of dependent reciprocity between Senegalese and foreign institutions. A brief review of monetary policies can elucidate these ties.

Since the late 1960s crisis in the agricultural sector, the Senegalese government has borrowed financial capital from foreign institutions, entering a spiraling cycle of dependency. By 1980, the ratio of debt service to exports was close to 29 percent (Somerville 1997:19). In 1979 Senegal signed the first Structural Adjustment loan with the World Bank and agreed to the first International Monetary Fund economic and financial recovery plan. Senegalese membership in the Franc Zone helped stave off the most austere "recovery" measures until the early 1990s. For example, in 1989 the government benefited from President Francois Mitterand's debt-forgiveness initiative that cancelled two billion Francs of Senegalese debt (Van De Walle 1991). At the same time, membership in the Franc Zone also produced an overvaluation of the CFA Franc, which had remained tied to the French Franc for the value of fifty

CFA to one Franc since 1948 (Van De Walle 1991:387). If this policy had some favorable effects during the 1970s, in the 1980s, due to a sharp rise in the value of the Franc relative to the U.S. dollar, the CFA became overvalued in the international market. The overvaluation benefited the urban bourgeoisie, who were able to purchase imported goods at a rate they could not otherwise afford, while it undermined local agricultural production and the weak manufacturing sector, which could not compete with cheaper imports.

The 1990s saw the end of France's privileged assistance to its former colonies and the end of the parity system in place since 1948. In 1994 the rate was changed to one hundred CFA Francs for every French Franc. This sharp devaluation decreased the purchasing power of the population, placing significant strain on the urban underclasses that had come to swell Dakar in response to the agricultural crisis.[5] At the same time, Structural Adjustment policies decreased access to civil service, job security, and social assistance. While the Senegalese masses sank into a deepening crisis, the higher echelons of government officials kept themselves afloat through their ties of *terànga* with foreign donors.[6] Rather than following the austerity regime imposed upon the general population, the politicians continued spending by allowing international financial institutions to plunder the economic resources of the nation to underwrite their own luxurious lifestyles. Significant to our discussion of *terànga* in a political context, the Senegalese elite funneled portions of French aid back to French political parties, with the obvious expectation that the cycles of reciprocity would continue. In this context, *terànga* makes the Senegalese government accountable to international financial institutions while leaving its own citizens unprotected. The ties of solidarity between the government and its own citizens are broken (if they ever existed) while the political class bargains with international institutions at the expense of its own nation.

Competing interests also besiege the relationship of Ballet dancers with Ballet directors, who are differentially positioned in relation to company earnings. Below, I will delineate these conflicts as they played out in the Ballets that I researched. I will then focus on the Ballet Mansour and the narrative produced by one of its dancers to further examine how Ballets' insertion in the tourist economy influences artistic creativity and artists' careers.

Ballets, Social Contracts, and Spirals of Exploitation

A Ballet's position in the economy determines in large part the degree to which the interests of company members and directors converge or diverge,

creating amicable or hostile working relations between them. In the unstable economic environment in which Ballets operate, a Ballet's members and directors enter into a precarious relationship of mutual and uneven dependence, each gambling on the skills of the other to fight for a place in the economy and earn a living through dancing. While dancers rely on their director's connections and networks to procure performance contracts, the director relies on a stable membership of skilled dancers to build a solid repertory and promote the company on the local and international performance markets. In this context, while dancers do not pay for their training, which allows them to accumulate precious cultural capital they could not otherwise afford, they rehearse without a salary in the hope of later gains, when the company will secure performing and touring contracts. Yet even when contracts are obtained, it rests on the director's discretion to distribute payment between dancers, musicians, and choreographers, rather than allocating money for instruments and costumes necessary for the company, or to secure a permanent rehearsal space and attend to other company needs. If dancers become unhappy with the financial arrangements, they will leave the company in search of better opportunities with another Ballet. These dynamics were exemplified by the four Ballets I researched.

While the National Ballet of Senegal and the Ballet Mansour continually lost dancers to First World nations, the Ballet Kaddu gi was losing dancers to better Ballets. In contrast, the Ballet Fambondy had been able to retain most of its dancers for its six years of existence. The pecking order of Ballets in relation to the urban market of Dakar and the international market explains these dynamics and the greater or lesser degree of conflict present within Ballets.

Because all members of the National Ballet of Senegal are government employees, they receive a monthly salary, whether they perform or not, although they make more money when touring. Furthermore, the differences in salary between the members and the directors of the Ballet are mediated by the state and do not cause friction within the company. In contrast, the other three Ballets are private institutions, and no third party mediates between directors and dancers. Within these Ballets, as in all others of the city, dancers receive money only when money is earned through the group's performances.

At the time of my research, the Ballet Mansour was exceptionally positioned to take part in the tourist economy, having a monopoly of contracts in all of the major tourist hotels of Dakar, while the Ballet Fambondy and the Ballet Kaddu gi were not inserted within the formal labor market. The Ballet Kaddu gi, as a function of its relative newness (two years) and its marginality in the economy, was caught in a vicious cycle: As dancers gained skills by participating in the Ballet's rehearsals, they left for Ballets that offered a more secure promise of economic reward. The continuous turnover of dancers prevented the directors from building a company strong enough to sustain a commodifiable repertory. If the lack of economic prospects produced high rates of defection, however, it also made for a shared sense of camaraderie, since nobody profited above others from the Ballet's activities. Equality was also stressed by the Ballet's founders, who served simultaneously as its choreographers and directors/managers: while experience and expertise made Adama Diallo and Ndiuwar Thiam the leaders of the group, they welcomed the choreographic contributions of dancers. This unanimity of purpose and consensual work ethic was stressed by the group's choice of name: *kaddu gi* literally means "word," "voice," "speech," or "sentence," but figuratively it connotes the united voice of the people gathered in a general assembly.[7] The name Kaddu gi emphasizes the importance of consensual agreement within a deliberating political body. A social group, gathered to deliberate on important political matters, after a process of debate, achieves consensus and commits to common action: it emerges as one voice.[8]

The Ballet Fambondy, unlike the Ballet Kaddu gi, was ready to enter the formal economy at the time of my research. The director of the Ballet, Djibril Sane, due to his experience in Senegal and abroad as the choreographer and founder of several Ballets, had been able to gather around him a group of talented and committed dancers, many of whom had been members of the Ballet since its creation in 1990. In fact, several dancers had been working with Sane before 1990 as members of another Ballet. Having worked together for several years, Sane and his dancers had built a sizeable and original repertory. Hence the Ballet had gained some contracts for performances for local audiences (at political rallies and at the Theatre Daniel Sorano, where it performed for an audience of state functionaries' school children). With the money earned, the Ballet was able to purchase expensive musical instruments as well as the many costumes necessary for a professional show. Dancers and musicians in the Ballet held Sane in high esteem and had no interest in leaving the company at a time when their hard work seemed ready to come to fruition, especially as Sane was expertly negotiating the most coveted opportunity of all: touring in a foreign country (usually Europe, but also the United States or Japan). Yet, if the group's aspirations were to be frustrated, it would be hard for Sane to hold on to all of the members and demand the professionalism and commitment that has pushed them to give so generously.

The Ballet Mansour, as a successful private enterprise, confronted dancers with greater monetary rewards and more conflicting aspirations than the other private Ballets under consideration. Mansour Guèye founded the Ballet that carries his name (also known as the Ballet d'Afrique Noire) in 1957, inspired by the Ballet of Keita Fodeba. Mansour, a dancer who had performed as a member of the National Ballet of Senegal, at the time of my research acted as the general director and producer of the company. Since its inception in 1957, the company has grown to include three overlapping groups operating in Dakar and five more companies operating in Spain and the Canary Islands. In Senegal, three full-time choreographers created three different shows, which were performed by two groups of dancers, rotating among the resorts of Dakar and the surrounding areas. In addition to them, since 1994 Mansour gathered an additional three choreographers, a composer, and the best dancers to work on the production of a Mande epic.

Mansour Guèye reinvested many of the Ballet's profits in the company itself, not only by expanding the number of dancers and choreographers that work under its auspices but also by providing the infrastructure necessary for its smooth running. In 1995 Mansour completed the construction of a beautiful studio for the company located in the neighborhood of Ñaari Tali.

The Ballet Mansour never benefited from government grants and paid taxes regularly to the state. Thus, all the investments in the company enterprise have been fueled by its commercial operation and as such were built on the labor of dancers and musicians. Yet, by reinvesting profits in the Ballet, employment was secured in an unstable economic environment and growing professional opportunities were provided for its most talented dancers. This state of affairs has produced tensions between the professional interests of the dancers and the economic reality to which they were subjected. This tension was most directly expressed by Souleymane, one of the dancers of the Ballet. He was the only member of the company who explicitly complained about working conditions, both to the director of the Ballet and to me. In our interview, he related the working conditions of the Ballet to larger economic forces, which can guide us in questioning the relation of economic retribution to creativity.

> FRANCESCA: You do not want to leave like all the others? [I was referring to the many artists who leave a Ballet while on tour to make a living in a First World country.]
> SOULEYMANE: To leave for Europe? I do not want? I do want . . . but, if I leave . . . I do not want to do something . . . I do not know. If I leave for Europe I want to go to show to the Europeans that we

are Africans. . . . Because the Europeans they dance exact, on tapes they dance perfectly well. Yes. But we, we dance badly. Yes.

F: It depends. There are people who dance well.

s: We do not dance well, but we can dance well. Do you know why we dance badly? Because we, now, until now, we are not free. We think of nothing but money. We want to become rich with that *jembe.*

F: You do not dance well because you are not free.

s: Yes. Because always our manager is there, or people that tell us to do it fast, do it fast because there are contracts. So there is no harmony, no civilization, there is not something that you feel, that you are free to do. Because you—Francesca—you want to dance, and I am there, your stage manager, or your producer, I am there, and I tell you do it fast, make it fast because I am in a hurry. So you cannot, you cannot do something that will be comfortable. To be comfortable you need that your manager, your producers, or your dance director in the Ballet lets you do all that you want, but in order. Then you can dance to express your civilization, your ethnicity. And that is what I want, I want to express our purity. One is free. We, we are afraid of nothing. Why be afraid? Of what to be afraid? To have people applaud us? Or to have the Europeans applaud us? No. We do not need that to tell us that we are strong, that we dance well. No. There are some Europeans who do not know, so we have to show them that we are civilized, that we are men ready to love, to feel maternal love, to love our parents. We are not animals—UGH! We are not pets.

Souleymane asserts that while Europeans dance well (at least on tape, for he has not seen live performances), Africans dance badly. He first relates this asymmetry to the economic asymmetry between the West and Africa, asserting that artistic production under economic duress cannot but be of bad quality ("We are not free. We think of nothing but money"). Then he more specifically addresses the working conditions that he confronts as a member of the Ballet, pressured by managers, producers, and artistic directors to deliver a product for European consumption. As we know from chapter 7, Souleymane had pursued dancing with a Ballet in search of an African identity, free, as he argues above, of contaminating external influences. Yet his engagement with ethnic dance in the Ballet Mansour was frustrated by his confrontation with the tourist milieu in which the Ballet operates. The racism of European spectators exoticizes performers into pets—trained and docile animals performing tricks for the pleasure of the audience. Against this exploitative and denigrating environment he proclaims his moral and artistic independence—"We do not need that [the applause of the Europeans] to tell us that we are strong, that we dance well." At the same time, he expresses the desire to redress racist stereotyping: "We have to show them that we are civilized, that we are men ready to love, to feel maternal love, to love our parents." Maternal love is construed by Souleymane as the quality that sets humans apart from animals ("we are not pets") and further represents the commitment towards one's own parents, rather than one's own "masters." That is a measure of civilization. Significantly, in this context, Souleymane consciously equates ethnicity with civilization: "Then, you can dance to express your civilization, your ethnicity." His statement contradicts Euro-American conceptualizations of African ethnicity that have equated it to a localized phenomenon associated with the lowest forms of culture and social organization. The racist ideology that configures African performers as pets also asserts that African ethnicities have never possessed or "arisen" to civilization. In contrast, African ethnicity and its association with tribalism are in Souleymane's perspective subsumed under a higher and more universal category of culture: "civilization."

Souleymane argues that the task of the artist is to express his or her own cultural specificity, which cannot be accomplished under oppressive conditions. He goes on to relate his experience of exploitation as a dancer within a contemporary African Ballet to larger patterns of exploitation:

> SOULEYMANE: If I want to have my own style and somebody else tries to guide me, I will not be able to create my own style. Because style is not something of slavery.
> FRANCESCA: It is the creative spirit.
> S: It is the free spirit. A slave cannot have style because when somebody hits you and beats you, you cannot have style [we laugh]. You will be afraid. But when you are free, you are *free*, and now there is no longer slavery, now you are *free*, you jump, you dance, you do everything, and you have your own *style*.

Slavery in Souleymane's view is both a concrete historical experience and a figure of oppression and repression. Through the deployment of the concept of slavery, he seems to argue that just as a dancer cannot have style if he or she is not in control of the creative process, so a whole people cannot express their cultural specificity unless they are in control of the historical process and the material conditions of production. To express a true cultural identity, an ethnicity, as Souleymane calls it, the artist and the society at large must know self-determination. Souleymane further relates slavery to historical amnesia:

SOULEYMANE: We need to produce something like musical comedy, like Sunjata, do you know Sunjata?

FRANCESCA: Yes.

s: Sunjata is a legend. Men, like *sëriñ* Touba or Lat Dior, there are some men that died and that were our ancestors, and they lived in the past, and now the choreographers, the dance professors go to visit the ancestors and show that to the people. As if I was dead two hundred years ago and now one showed my life on the stage. Do you know what I mean?

F: Yes.

s: "That guy, there is our grandfather!" And now I show his work—the play—and people look. But now people do not do that any longer. They only think about leaving for the States or for France, just go on tours. But there are shows where the whites, they . . .

F: What?

s: They laugh at us. Because they say, "But that guy, what does he do?" Because all that we dance, it is not that, all that we do it is not so. . . . If it was something of the past, all right, it would be good, because it is good for us to know what our ancestors did. But people are there producing things, people have some rhythms, but something they have created to make money. Yes. Because there are some rhythms that you listen to and you know that they are not true. There are some rhythms that you feel they are not true. Have you felt that? There are rhythms that people play, and it is not that. Because if a guy plays that TA TA TATA [he claps his hands], okay, he played that. But there are some rhythms that you listen to and you know they come from *afar,* and those are the rhythms that are important. There are people who sabotage, and people who do not know and they want to make money. Impostors, thieves, that do not know either how to dance or how to play, or they know how to drum but they do not know how to dance, and they always look for profit. There are many in the U.S., in Holland, they do not know anything and they come PAF! they open up a school. It is not that. We need, we the Africans, we need

to do research with civilized people. Mathematicians, ethnologists, all of those, and we show something that is about us, something that comes out of us, that shows our art, our African civilization. Because we, besides art, we have nothing. Because we
were slaves. But before being slaves we were cultivators, black-
smiths, weavers, leather workers, and griots. [Pause]
It is slavery that made us crazy. One was taken to the States, the
other to England, the other to France, and all this *metissage*, all
was lost, one no longer knew who he was. People knew nothing,
one was afraid, one was not free. . . . We are here, we are not sure
of what we have done! We are not sure because we are hungry,
we need money, we are not comfortable. And we need to be left
with our culture, because if people want to buy it, one is not
going to do something sure. Because our culture is not to be
sold, our culture is not for sale, but it is to be planted, to be
sown. It is something to be taught and not to be commercialized.
. . . You need to talk to people to tell them that they must work
with strength, in the family, and show something that is sure,
that is not superficial, that they try to look for the ancestors who
will give them suggestions.

Souleymane situates the everyday economic reality of Senegal within a
single historical framework that extends back from the Atlantic slave trade
and continues through the colonial period up to the postcolonial present.
He expresses the historical consciousness that slavery was the central process
that dramatically integrated Africa into the global capitalist dis/order (to use
Samir Amin's [1992] characterization), a process that continues to violently
operate, albeit in different forms.[9] Souleymane keeps returning to the com-
mercialization of dance and its relation to poverty by focusing on the historical context of slavery as the source of economic and cultural uncertainty.
Hunger and poverty produce cultural impostors ready to sell ad hoc artistic products created solely for profit.

Souleymane's reference to *metissage* is particularly significant, and like his
deployment of the concept of civilizations, it suggests that he is drawing on
and reinterpreting key concepts of Senghor's Négritude. Senghor exalted
metissage as the positive mixture of European and African cultures that would
bring forth the civilization of the universal. Furthermore, he actively promoted *metissage* as a component of "an open Négritude" and as the necessary path toward the building of a modern African culture fit for the new in-

dependent nation: "In that, such open Négritude is a humanism. It has enriched itself enormously from the contributions of the European civilization, and it has enriched it" (Senghor 1964b:8). Contrary to Senghor's vision of *metissage* as a mutually enriching exchange between Europe and Africa, Souleymane argues that it was brought about by slavery and the violent expropriation of people and cultures. This violence resulted in historical amnesia and cultural disorientation in the motherland: "It is slavery that made us crazy. One was taken to the States, the other to England, the other to France, and all this *metissage,* all was lost, one did no longer know who he was. People knew nothing. One was afraid, one was not free. We are here, we are not sure of what we have done! We are not sure because we are hungry, we need money." In Souleymane's narrative, the enforced deportation of slaves out of Africa is superimposed upon contemporary migration patterns: Africa, from where he speaks, and the United States and Europe, representing the triangular poles of the slave trade, merge into the single geography of contemporary migration. Souleymane collapses historical time into a single causal determination, linking slavery and contemporary poverty.

Souleymane also articulates his distance from Senghor's model of universal cultural modernity, in which all the cultures from different parts of the world contribute to create a single global culture. Souleymane suggests instead that the sciences of "civilized people" should be employed to preserve and develop African art:

> You know, here in Senegal there are not many men who try to move forward, to develop African art. Because, you know, with African art there are but illiterate people, self-taught people. There are people who do not know how to read and how to express . . . that do not know how to do mathematics with dance. So it is because of that that we the Africans are always stagnating, we are underdeveloped with art. It cannot develop. We need help. The Japanese, the Russians, the Americans, the Africans, we need to come together to create strength. We need to produce something like musical comedy, like Sunjata.

In Souleymane's vision, foreigners should contribute to the creation of a truly African art form. Contrary to the vision of interculturalism argued for by Senghor and popular in contemporary North American artistic circles that promote a "melting-pot" version of culture, Souleymane proposes a model in which human and cultural resources from around the globe are put at the service of African artists, so that they can produce the pure art that he values. Again he brings economics into his cultural discourse, arguing that

Africans are underdeveloped artistically because they are poor and illiterate. His reference to mathematics, which may appear obscure in the context of a discussion about dance, was made clearly relevant in the following passage:

> The pure art is in the villages, it is a choreography, a choreography that is not a choreography of counts. One does not count. But a choreography that one feels, a choreography with the calls of the drums. Because we Africans, we cannot count art, but one *feels;* one *feels* the choreographic movements. One knows that one has to change [the dance steps]. It is now with academic art, at the conservatory and with professors of dance, like Maurice Béjart, do you know him? . . . With modern dance and classical dance that one puts choreography in mathematics, to be able to understand it and to be able to sell it so that people will buy it.

Souleymane draws our attention to the relationship of dancing to polyrhythms, which in ethnic-centric dance forms is articulated through complex drumming patterns and singing rather than counting. While modern dance and ballet work with counts, African dancers respond to the call of the drums. "Feeling" the choreographic movements means to create "a choreography with the calls of the drums" rather than through mathematical formulas. Yet, Souleymane associates putting choreography into mathematics with the ability to teach and sell dance. Significantly, many African dance teachers in the West adopt the "mathematical" approach to dance that Souleymane identifies, putting counts to dance phrases in order to teach in accord with the expectations of their students. Maurice Béjart is one of the "mathematicians" with whom Soulemayne dreams of collaborating. Yet, this collaboration, unlike the work produced by Mudra Afrique, which seems to have embodied Senghor's idea of cultural *mettissage,* in Souleymane's vision should produce "musical comedy, like Sunjata."

Souleymane's definition of musical comedy is radically different from Euro-American uses of the term. For him, musical comedy is historical drama, centered on towering figures in Senegalese history. In Souleymane's perception, good art comes from "afar" and needs to be extracted from the ancestors as historical memory: "The dance professors go to visit the ancestors and show that to the people." History is configured in Souleymane's narrative as the male-centered experience of ancestors ("our grandfathers") who gave shape to political events. Significantly, Lat Dior and *sëriñ* Touba (Amadou Bamba Mbaké) are both figures that stand engraved in Senegalese popular memory as heroes against the French colonizers.

Lat Dior (1842–86) was the last monarch of the Kajor (Wolof) kingdom, which together with the kingdoms of Waalo, Baol, Siin, and Salum was part of the Jolof Empire (1200s–1500s) until its disintegration in the middle of the sixteenth century. Boubacar Barry (1998) has characterized the Kajor kingdom as the paradigmatic example of *ceddo* regimes, warring military regimes intent on raiding neighboring states to sell captives to European slave traders. Lat Dior was the last representative of the Kajor monarchy, as the *ceddo* regimes disintegrated with the shift of the area's economic base away from the Atlantic slave trade and toward peanut production for export. The French, intent upon building a railroad line from Dakar through Saint-Louis to facilitate the transport of peanuts, cut through the center of Kajor's territory (Clark and Phillips 1994). Lat Dior organized resistance against the French from 1860 to 1886, when he was defeated and killed in the battle of Dekhele (Barry 1998:196–99, 223–29). It is ironic that Lat Dior is celebrated in Senegal as a great hero against European colonizers, while Kajor's nefarious and violent involvement in the Atlantic slave trade is silenced in popular memory.

Amadou Bamba Mbaké (1850–1927), colloquially called *sëriñ* Touba, was the founder of the Mouride brotherhood, and before Lat Dior's death he had been a frequent visitor to the kingdom. With the death of Lat Dior, Bamba became a central figure around which popular sentiments of resistance against the French coalesced. Bamba was a spiritual leader and became known for his peaceful resistance against the French, who, for fear of his influence upon religious followers, deported him into exile in Gabon from 1895 to 1902, and then again in Mauritania from 1903 to 1907 (Clark and Phillips 1994:189–91). Amadou Bamba is an omnipresent icon in the city of Dakar, where his image is painted on store fronts, makeshift signs, houses, buses, taxis, and cars.[10] Amadou Bamba's miracles and his clever defiance against the French, who kept him captive during his time of exile in Gabon, are the subject of daily conversations and animated discussions among contemporary Dakarois. Yet his subsequent collaboration with French authorities, like the organization of disciplined recruits to be sent off to aid the French in World War I, is not discussed.

The third historical hero mentioned by Souleymane is Sunjata Keita (Maghan Konaté), the founder of the Mali empire (1200–1500). Sunjata has been one of the most celebrated figures in West African orature, and the Sunjata Epic is a central element in the repertory of Mande griots.[11] The figure of Sunjata fulfills the ideological function of representing a great historical past that acts as a source of identification in the present along an unbroken line of associations, reducing colonialism to an irrelevant historical parenthesis. The association of historical consciousness with a vast musical repertory further makes the Sunjata Epic an attractive and respected source of choreographic inspiration.

It is not surprising that the director of the Ballet Mansour, Mansour Guèye, chose the epic as the showpiece that would launch his troupe to international notoriety. Given the seriousness of the enterprise and the respect toward Mande repertory that the epic entails, Mansour elicited the assistance of the choreographers Jean Pierre Leurs, Mamadou Diop, and Oscar Aboubacar Camara and the musical composer Guimba Diallo to produce an original redendition of the epic, which they called the *Manding Epic.* Mansour in 1994 gathered the best dancers of his companies to work on this piece, and Souleymane was among those selected to participate. While he did not discuss his work on the epic with the Ballet in our interview, it is obvious that it fulfilled his vision for a dance genre that would express a "pure ethnicity" and a "Black African civilization." Before turning to consider why Souleymane did not want to say that his work with the Ballet fulfilled his search for a meaningful dance expression, I would like to briefly examine the historical narrative presented by the Ballet.

The Ballet's rendition of the *Manding Epic* begins in the late twelfth century with the depiction of Sumangaru Kante's attack on the Mandinka kingdom and his rule over the Mandinka people until Sunjata Keita's intervention. The invention of the *balafon,* which with the *kora* stands as the most renowned instrument of the Mande, is attributed in the Ballet's version of the epic to Sumangaru Kante (of the Sosso people), in conformity with African orature. The Sosso dominated the Malinke from the end of the twelfth century until their liberation by Sunjata Keita in 1230. The *balafon* was then appropriated by the Malinke and was subsequently played at the courts of Malinke kings; to this day it is played by Malinke griots. The Ballet Mansour, in its version of the epic, presents the history of the *balafon* and prominently features the instrument in the program. Yet, what makes the epic most original is the centrality accorded to Abu Bakari, the main protagonist of the Ballet Mansour's performance. While Sunjata Keita has been celebrated in innumerable oral accounts and has been the subject of much historical research, Abu Bakari is an obscure historical figure. After the reign of Mansa Uli (a son of Sunjata) and that of his brothers Wati and Khalifa, Bakari (who was either a son or grandson of Sunjata) inherited the throne of the Mali empire in the early fourteenth century (Imperato 1977). According to the Ballet's epic, Bakari left the coast of West Africa around 1307 with a fleet of two thousand ships to sail to North America. He arrived safely in the New World and peacefully met with indigenous inhabitants. Although he sent emissaries back to recount his peaceful exploits, he himself never returned to his homeland.

The Ballet's focus on the figure of Bakari wrenches the "discovery" of America away from European history and claims it for African history. Bakari is a threat to European historiography, and to insert his figure within the collective memory of African, European, and American people amounts to a Copernican revolution in history. For professional historians, to merely confront the possibility of the veracity of Bakari's exploits with serious research amounts to professional suicide. Thus, Bakari stands as an obscure historical figure, with no deeds attached to his name. The boldness required to present Bakari as a central protagonist of the Ballet's *Manding Epic* shows the respect for oral history that the Ballet's choreographers and directors are willing to assert, as well as their commitment for a political-cultural project intent upon asserting the protagonism of African societies in world history.

At the time of my research in Dakar, Mansour Guéye often spoke to the dancers about the importance of the epic as an attempt to move away from the "entertainment" programs performed at tourist hotels and toward launching the company on an international career. The emphasis on the seriousness of the program was evidenced by the presence of the three choreographers and the musical director, who worked assiduously with the company for several years. The promise of success was used by the director to motivate dancers, who worked hard and received no retribution for rehearsals. At the same time, since the company operated as a private institution and received no funding from the government, the money to produce the epic (to pay for the choreographers, to purchase the costumes, and so on) was coming from the company's earnings at tourist enclaves, a fact that was not missed by the dancers. Souleymane's refusal to speak directly about his satisfaction with being involved in the production of the epic can be interpreted as an expression of his conflicting experience in the Ballet: the work that involved him in the making of the *Manding Epic,* fulfilling his artistic dreams, stood in sharp contrast with his work as a dancer at tourist hotels, where he felt exoticized as a pet and exploited as a dancer. In this context, the same directors that exploited him as a dancer also offered him the opportunity to grow as an artist, a fact that may have made him unwilling to openly praise his superiors. All members of the Ballet Mansour who participated in the making of the *Manding Epic* were caught in this uneasy position and the explosive tension among company managers and company members that it entailed. This situation partly accounts for the massive defections of members of the Ballet on their first international tour of the epic.

The Ballet Mansour (touring under its original name, Ballet d'Afrique Noire) premiered its work in a twelve-week tour in the United States. The tour ended dramatically at the Zellerbach Theater in Berkeley, California, on April 9, 2000, when seventeen company members "disappeared" after the performance. What accounts for this en masse defection?

The coverage of the event in the *San Francisco Chronicle* (April 13 and 14, 2000) speculates that the artists left because of their dissatisfaction with their contract. Kevin Fagan's article in the April 14 issue of the *Chronicle* quotes a woman "who wished to remain anonymous" and who "befriended the dancers" as saying: "'The reason the dancers defected is they were making $140 a week for their performances, and this did not include meals. They rehearsed five years for their show, and when they got to this country they were expecting to make a little bit of money—but the promoters and whatever pretty much hoarded the money.'" The same article quotes the manager of ICM Artists Ltd.—Jane Hermann—who booked the Ballet as saying: "'I can't tell you how much we paid the company because that is confidential, but it was enough to put in line with the pay of American dancers. . . . They were treated right, stayed in nice hotels. I think that when the dust settles, we'll find out something else was at the bottom of it all.'" Kim Curtis of the *San Diego Union Tribune* speculates about the "something else" by questioning the political conditions in Senegal, only to conclude that the country "has been relatively stable in recent years" and had ended forty years of Socialist party rule earlier in January. None of these three newspaper articles speculates about the economic conditions of Senegal and the dancers' living conditions in their own country. By simply blaming the directors of the company for the dancers' defection and failing to consider the economic deprivation of Senegalese artists, the U.S. media avoided confronting spectators with uncomfortable questions about world inequalities and their implications in the theater. In contrast, this narrow focus was forcefully rejected by Souleymane, who was well aware of the relation between his own exploitation as a dancer in the Ballet and larger patterns of exploitation with historical roots centuries deep.

I have also argued that a Ballet's position in the economy determines patterns of defection: members of poorer and less competent Ballets strategically capitalize on the dance training they receive to vie for a place in the National Ballet of Senegal and in the Ballet Mansour, which offer the best positions for professional dancers in the national market. Members of these two Ballets, however, if they have artistic and economic aspirations beyond their present predicament, do not see any better prospect than to emigrate to a First World nation. For the touring members of the Ballet Mansour, what would their prospects be once they returned home? The most fortunate members of the Ballet earned sixty-four dollars a month for their work in Senegal. While on tour, assuming that dancers got paid what was reported in the paper, $140 a week, they earned more than double what they made for a month of work in Dakar. More than a symptom of their exploitation by the company manager, this difference is an effect of global inequalities. It indexes the differences in income between workers of developed and underdeveloped nations. Aware of these differences, many dancers consider their participation in a Ballet as a long-term immigration strategy. Although motivated by a true love for dance, they are willing to endure years of strife and unrewarded work in Ballets to gain a chance to tour internationally, and by so doing to enter the well-guarded borders of First World nations.

For members of the underclasses who do not possess the necessary economic resources to gain a tourist visa[12] and who do not possess the money to buy a dangerous illegal entry into the capitalist centers of the world, Ballets offer a means of "escape" that seems relatively safe and within their reach. Ballets also offer a way of accumulating precious cultural capital that can be put to use as a way of making a living in the new country. Dancers of the Ballet Mansour enacted such a strategy. Having accumulated sizeable cultural capital through their years of hard labor on the *Manding Epic* and the other programs performed by the Ballet, at the first "opportunity" they escaped to the United States. As illegal immigrants, they will rely on their dance training as a resource for survival and sustenance. I wish them luck.

Conclusion:
Négritude Reconsidered

In this final chapter I will reexamine the relationship between the interpretation of ethnicity offered by the National Ballet of Senegal on the stage of the theater and the interpretation of ethnicity offered by Négritude ideology on the stage of national politics. To do so we need to interrogate the ways in which Négritude, as the ideology of the Senghorian state, was integrated into the project of nationhood—what in chapter 2 I call the second phase of Négritude. In his earliest elaboration of the concept, Senghor defined Négritude as the "ensemble of the cultural values of the Black world," clearly referring to the indigenous, ethnic-centric cultures of the country.[1] What role, then, did ethnicity play in the nation's cultural politics?

Just as the project of Négritude during the struggle of decolonization was inserted into a larger universalist project (the civilization of the universal), with the coming of independence Négritude was articulated within a dual dialectic of *enracinement* and *overture*. Within this dialectic, Senghor reasserted the ideological stance of western ethnologues vis-à-vis African ethnicities. He assigned African ethnicities to the pole of *enracinement*. Thus, ethnicity came to stand for introverted closure; it marked a movement inward, a turning away from the world, albeit a rooting down. In this articulation, ethnic identity stands in contradiction to "modern" citizenship in so far as it can only represent localized identities insufficient by themselves as the basis for the construction of a common national culture inserted within a wider international world.

For Senghor the project of national integration could not be animated through the articulation of ethnic identities, but rather it required the mediation of universalist elements—*overture*—embodied by the French cultural world and its universalist values. This view is expressed clearly in Senghor's discussion of language and its role in education:

> We can, at the present moment, establish this general principle: that the study of West Africa and France constitute the two poles of instruction in French West Africa, and that this *bicephalism* will be found at all levels. As one will proceed, the African pole will lose its attraction in favor of the French pole. It is necessary to start with the milieu of the Negro-African civilizations, in which the child will be immersed. The child must learn to know and express knowledge first in his maternal language, then in French. Little by little, he will expand the circle of the universe, where, man, he will engage tomorrow. With his race, he will [also] need a subtle and richer knowledge of French. This is to say that *bicephalism* means bilinguism. (Senghor 1964b:14)

In Senghor's view, education in African languages and about African cultures cannot make a complete adult. Rather, French is considered necessary for the intellectual growth of a proper citizen capable of taking upon himself the task of building a meaningful future. The African world is conflated into a narrow universe, the world of a child with its limited spatial coordinates, while French stands in for universal knowledge, which alone can insert the African into the modern world.

Senghor's theorization of bilingualism signaled the way in which Négritude was to be implicated in the project of nation building and influenced his government's approach to language policies. We can now consider the interplay of language policies and the language of politics to gain a better understanding of the way in which Négritude figured within Senghor's vision of the nation.

At the eve of independence in 1960, Senegalese society inherited a national school system modeled after the French and structured during the colonial period (under Faidherbe at the end of the 1880s) to educate the elites of all French West Africa. At the end of Senghor's presidency, after twenty years of governance (1960–80), the French educational system continued to function primarily as a means of integration into the state bureaucracy rather than as a form of popular education. Furthermore, because mastery of French was still necessary to enter the political structure, it served to mask the exclusion of "unqualified" popular elements from the domain of politics. In this context, the prime interface of political discourse between the government and civil society was the western-educated stratum of the urban intelligentsia (Diaw 1993). The figure of Senghor himself embodied emblematically this nexus, as he was the president of the country, the head of the Socialist party, and a leading man of letters (Diaw 1993). Yet, just as in colonial times, political opposition to the government was forged from the urban intellectual stratum, so with independence, political opposition came from the educated elite and a militant student movement. In fact, only those fluent in French could take part in the political debate—which was carried out in French and centered on negotiating western conceptions of democracy in an African context—while the masses, by virtue of their inability to speak and understand French, were excluded from such a debate (Schaffer 1998). The peasantry and other popular social groups had to rely on the *marabouts* (the religious authorities of Islamic brotherhoods) to translate politics not only into the local languages but also into an idiom that would make political sense of their predicament. Significantly, Leopold Sédar Senghor had defeated Lamine Guéye in the run toward political independence from France precisely because of his capacity to rally support among the religious brotherhoods in control of peanut production.

In this context, under the Senghorian government it was the educated elite and a militant student movement that asserted the need for the democratization of politics and the Africanization of the school curricula. These demands exploded in full force in 1968 when strikes at Dakar's university immobilized instruction and spread to the lower educational structure not only in Dakar but in other cities as well (Sylla 1993b). Protest came in a climate of political authoritarianism, in which the Senghorian government had established a de facto single-party rule that forced all political opposition underground (Diop 1993).

The students and teachers' movement demanded among other things that the indigenous languages of the country be recognized as national languages. In response to popular pressure, the Senghorian government in 1971 declared six indigenous languages the official languages of Senegal: Wolof, Pulaar, Séréér, Joola, Manding, and Sarakholé-Soninké, which together represent the languages spoken by the majority of the population (close to 90 percent).[2] In 1975 the state ratified an official orthography for Wolof and Séréér, while the other four languages are still awaiting such measures. Senghor's timid support for African languages as the appropriate vehicle of primary education never materialized into actual policies.

Popular protest continued for more than a decade and culminated in the political crisis of the 1980s with Senghor's resignation. In spite of political liberalization and the ratification of a national charter for educational reform, Diouf's government (1981–2000) also failed to institutionalize any significant change in the educational system. None of the Senegalese languages are taught in the national education system, save for limited pilot programs in a few schools (Sylla 1993b). From elementary school up to the highest reaches of the educational system, all instruction is conducted in French, and all textbooks are written in French.

In this context, the classification of the six African languages as "official" remains rather ambiguous, as the relationship of these six languages to written language and scholastic education is practically nonexistent. The national census of 1988, which can account for the full effect of Senghor's presidency, estimates that the literacy rate for the six national languages as well as Arabic reached 6 percent, with Arabic presumably accounting for the greatest bulk (Schaffer 1994:106). The literacy rate in French, while much higher, was still very low: the census states that of the country's population aged six years or older, only 26 percent were literate in French (102). This figure hides regional and gender imbalances as well as the fact that literacy rates for adults have dropped, because French is not used by the majority of the population outside of school or government posts, and the circulation of written material (books and journals) has been limited. With such high rates of illiteracy enduring almost unchanged in contemporary Senegal, it is not clear how meaningful political participation in the affairs of the nation can be possible.

Powerful intellectual figures, such as the historian Cheikh Anta Diop and the filmmaker and writer Ousmane Sembène, proposed an alternative to the timid integration of Négritude into the cultural life of the nation pursued by Senghor by supporting the use of Wolof in the national education system. Diop, to prove beyond doubt that Wolof was an apt language for general education, translated Einstein's theory of relativity as well as the *Communist Manifesto* into Wolof and published the journal *Siggi* partially in Wolof (O'Brien 2002:150). These erudite demonstrations were clearly a polemical engagement with Senghor's notion of the infantile connotations of African languages.[3] Sembène, who is multilingual, also actively supported the use of Wolof and other indigenous languages in the press, the school, and the judiciary,[4] voicing opposition to the Senghorian government not only through his films and novels but also through the journal *Kaddu*, which he cofounded with the linguist Pathè Diagne. In direct confrontation with the political opinions expressed by the journals, the Senghorian government in 1977 ratified severe sanctions against breaches in the official orthography of Wolof established by the government in 1975, prohibiting the use of double consonants, as in the titles of the journals. The despotism of the prohibition proved that even at the level of orthography the Senghorian government favored the conventions developed by French scholars over the work done by Senegalese linguists at the Centre de Linguistique Appliquée de Dakar (O'Brien 2002: 151–53).

The government used the delay in establishing written orthography for all of the six official languages as an excuse to forestall their introduction in the school system, arguing that it could not privilege one African language over the others. Similarly to the government rhetoric, Donal Cruise O'Brien, in his essay "The Shadow Politics of Wolofization," argues that the government's delay was justified by a concern that privileging Wolof over other national languages could lead to "a para-politics of primordialism" (1998:42). O'Brien argues that the government's refusal to privilege Wolof as the national language allowed for a peaceful Wolofization, which was de facto taking place in postcolonial Senegal.[5] Can we be content with such a complacent analysis? Certainly, as Diop and Sembène argued, the introduction of Wolof in the educational system would have been a great step toward democratizing scholarization, which alienated many precisely because it was carried out in French. To safeguard against "primordialism," rather than inaction the government would have done better to have ensured an equitable distribution of resources to foster linguistic diversity and promote Senegalese languages at different levels of institutionalization (on radio and television, in the print media, in the schools, in cultural centers, at cultural events, and so on). Rather than a neutral procedure, the continued use of French served as a barrier against democratization.

The authoritarian and exclusionary impulse of the Senghorian government was clearly visible in relation to party politics. Under Senghor's presidency all political opposition was forced underground until the constitutional revisions of 1976 and 1978, which legalized the activities of the Parti Démocratic Sénégalais, the Parti Africaine de l'Indépendence, and the Mouvement Républicain Sénégalais as legitimate opposition parties.[6] It was not until the political crisis of 1980, which culminated in Senghor's resignation, that political pluralism without restriction was made constitutional, and it was not until 2000, after several electoral reforms, that the Parti Démocratic Sénégalais displaced the Socialist party's continued hegemony.

Rather than presenting the popular forces as the historical agents of this democratizing process, the canonical literature on Senegal has depicted Senghor as the president-hero who, unlike the president-dictators of other African nations, was able to peacefully lead the country to democracy by a slow and benevolent liberalization process (Fatton 1987; O'Brien 1998). Such evaluations are predicated on western conceptualizations of African ethnicity of the kind we have explored under the Order of the Other: ethnicity is equated with a "primordial" tendency to violence and authoritarism. According to this logic, a too-quick liberalization of the Senegalese political process would have set loose these primordial tendencies. Senghor, however, knew the limits of how much liberalism his own people could take and calibrated the advance toward democracy to a pace that was bearable and peacefully sustainable.

In contrast to this interpretation, I assert that Senghor skillfully manipulated the negative Eurocentric conception of ethnicity to justify his political authoritarianism. Senghor, as the major ideologue of the Senegalese Socialist party, constructed Africa as a symbol of purity and innocence standing against the evils of capitalist society. He then used Négritude to support an ideology of African socialism that assumed a smooth coherence between romanticized African communal values and Marxism. Nativism and Marxism could productively merge to justify Senghor's brand of African socialism: the alterity of the Negro-African served to guarantee that his socialist credentials were rooted in an uncontaminated "unanimism" (Hountondji 1996; Mbembe 2002). This assumed coherence allowed Senghor to displace the centrality of class struggle from national politics and to focus solely on the colonial classes as the "enemy" of the people. The supposed unanimism of traditional African societies served to justify single-party rule and hide the regime's authoritarianism under the guise of an indigenous "politics of consensus" (Diaw 1993; Schaffer 1998).

Furthermore, Senghor's Négritude, in its bicephalous paradigm, misnamed one of the speaking "heads" of the Senegalese nation. In its historical reality, the "African" pole of Senghor's bicephalous conception is not represented by an idyllic ethnic community but by the powerful structure of Islamic brotherhoods. As noted in chapter 4, it was the "heads" (*khalifas*) of Islamic brotherhoods who, from the moment of independence throughout the Senghorian presidency, supported the Socialist party and acted as a link between the government and civil society. It is within the frame of Islamic religiosity that ethnicity was able to figure within the horizon of national politics. In this context, ethnic forms of organization and values remained subsidiary to the structure and organization of the Islamic brotherhoods on one side, and to the secular and French model of law and the state on the other side.

We can now return to the stage of the theater and the representation of ethnicity offered by the National Ballet of Senegal. As I argue in chapters 1 and 3, the performances of the National Ballet of Senegal represent Senegalese national identity as a cluster of ethnic identities centered around the trope of the village. We are confronted with a seemingly paradoxical situation: While ethnicity is foregrounded on the stage of the theater as the dominant identity of the Senegalese nation, on the stage of national cultural politics ethnicity is marginalized. From within the national context, African Ballets are among the few educational institutions where ethnic-centric culture is foregrounded, taught, and disseminated. In addition, Ballets offer a unique cultural space that asserts a polycentric model of cultural production: the majority of Ballets represent the dance and music complexes of several of the ethnic groups of Senegal, and membership in any Ballet is generally delinked from ethnic identity. Thus a polyethnic group of dancers comes to learn a polyethnic dance repertory, a process that was often commented upon favorably by the dancers I spoke with.

Because Ballets share a commitment to integrating ethnic cultural elements exclusively with other ethnic elements, they are thought of as representing "traditional" culture. Precisely because of their polyethnic representation of "traditional" culture, however, they open up a novel space of cultural production. Within this context, while some Ballet choreographers prefer not to mix dance and music genres from different ethnicities, others look for novel combinations, negotiating new ethnic and aesthetic rules for the creative merging of styles. The extent to which the mixing of previously separate ethnic repertories is supported by a deep knowledge of those repertories greatly determines dancers' and musicians' reaction to and judgment of such mixing. If the mixing of styles is perceived to come from a superficial knowledge of genres, it will be judged negatively. However, if creative experimentation is supported by a solid knowledge of tradition it will be welcomed. In this context, furthermore, the temporal dimension of tradition in relation to ethnic dance repertory acquires a different valence from that given to tradition on the proscenium stage. If from the perspective of white spectators the vague temporality of dances reinforces negative stereotypes of Primitive Africans forever tied to an immutable (and outdated) past, from the perspective of Ballet dancers it allows a connection to a world of knowledge marginalized in their own educational system. The national education system makes little room for ethnic-centric culture and fractures the youth's sense of continuity with an indigenous tradition by the use of French as the language of instruction. In contrast, the circle of dancers and drummers claims the relevance of the past for the present, calling center-stage the spirits of the ancestors, with their knowledge and their way of communicating. The recursive aspect of polyrhythmic drumming serves as a positive metaphor for historical time, opening up the communication with the past and tearing loose the fabric of colonial culture. For many of the youth, dance and music have the power to blast through the Francophone education, (re)calling them to a culture more consonant with their social and historical identity.

The youth that comes from the popular classes realistically recognizes the limits of an education in French as a means of mobility "upward" into the middle class, or outward into an international professional world. African Ballets offer them a much more realistic means of escaping the predicament of poverty through the possibility of utilizing the ethnic-centric cultural patrimony (and matrimony) of dances to make a living at home and abroad. Ethnic-centric culture, far from representing an introverted world, becomes a resource of integration into an international network of recognition and migration.[7]

To the youth of the 1990s, Francité, rather than representing the vast horizon of modernity, stands in for a closed and narrow world, a dead end and a historical anachronism. The youth of Dakar in the practice of daily living reject Senghor's *overture* toward the French world and instead search for meaningful "global" cultural references that are more in tune with the reality of the new world order as well as with their own sociocultural needs. In this context, the urban youth consider cultural elements from North America more desirable than French elements. In fact, not only does the contemporary "world" speaks English, the new language of power and empire, but also African American music and dance have proven their power in conquering the globe and influencing the cultural practices of the youth all over the planet. No matter how mythologized the story of African American success becomes, it offers a more appealing and coherent path of integration into the global reach of modernity than Senghor's Francité can ever promise.

Yet Senghor's love for art and his celebration of Négritude were often acknowledged positively by Ballet dancers and in fact constituted a kind of rhetoric with which they could support their own love for dance against an otherwise indifferent or even hostile environment (think of Souleymane's narrative in chapter 7). Senghor is warmly remembered by performers as the president-poet, in contrast to Diouf, the president-technocrat who demonstrated little interest in the arts.

In the present moment, the desire of the youth to see their cultural world supported and recognized rather than neglected in the name of more pressing economic priorities is now turned, hopefully, to the Wade presidency. Time will tell if the new government will indeed materialize its intentions to give more support to the cultural needs of its citizens.

Notes

Introduction

1. The term "ballet," as used by Francophone Senegalese speakers, refers to a dance company as well as to a dance piece choreographed for performance by African Ballet troupes. For clarity I will use the lowercase to refer to ballet as a dance form and the uppercase to denote an African Ballet dance company.

2. Franko refines this theorization of the expressive process with a more complex analysis of successive generations of modern dancers. His aim is to question the facile generalizations that have characterized modernist dance history.

3. For a discussion of the Black Atlantic, see Gilroy (1993).

4. I am particularly indebted to Kobla Ladzekpo in the Ethnomusicology Department at the University of California at Los Angeles and the drummers of the National Ballet of Senegal for this understanding.

5. I refer to drums rather than drummers because one drummer may play more than one drum simultaneously, producing more than one layer of sound.

6. The writings of Léopold Sédar Senghor (1964b:287–91) and Keita Fodeba (1957) most strongly support this interpretation.

7. Dance studies and dance critics did not systematically face their own class and cultural biases until the 1990s (see, for example, Foster 1995, 1996; Franko 1995; Savigliano 1995, 1996; Desmond 1997).

8. I pluralize Wolof and Mandinka words using the English *s* throughout. I do so for simplicity, since plural forms in Wolof and Mandinka would not be recognizable to English readers.

9. *Sabar* dancing historically belongs to the Wolof and the Séréér ethnic groups, yet because of the process of Wolofization, the Séréér's contribution to the *sabar* complex tends to be subsumed under the Wolof's.

10. I capitalize certain common nouns throughout the text to suggest that such categories connote a stereotype, or an ideologically constructed type of human.

Chapter 1: The National Ballet of Senegal at a Theater in California

1. I make such an assumption because of the location and structure of the theater, the price of the tickets (eighteen, twenty-five, or thirty-two dollars), and the program of performances offered throughout the year.

2. "Native" is a term linked to colonization. It was used to define the jural and political status of the colonized. The opposition between native and nonnative was not primarily based on geographical displacement and cultural distance; it was a political distinction defining the power of one group over the other. Contemporary uses of the term "native ethnographer," which refers to an ethnographer doing research in his or her own culture, obscures the political content of the term. The fact that ethnographies are rarely written in native languages (the languages of indigenous nations and Third World peoples) stands as a reminder that the legacy of colonialism still shapes ethnographic practice and publishing.

3. The baobab tree is significantly called *l'arbre à palabre* because people regularly gather under its majestic structure to talk and discuss community or personal matters (Bouly Sonko, personal communication with the author, Dakar, March 1997).

4. See Gere (1995) for an example of how the term "ethnic dance" has been replaced by "world dance."

5. I have taken the term "ethnologic" from Mudimbe (1988) and Amselle (1990), who use it to summarize the logic and theoretical posture of ethnography and ethnology. I will discuss this issue fully in chapter 2.

6. See Foster (1986) for a general discussion of frames and their influence on spectators.

7. The importance of representing Senegalese culture through performance, replacing western ethnography with African choreography, was elaborated by Senghor in his Négritude ideology. I address this topic at length in Chapter 2.

8. Sekou Touré, quoted in www.paam.arc.co.uk/paam/ballets/home.html (accessed July 1999).

9. This strategy was inspired by Savigliano (1997) and Tobin (1998:202–24).

10. I have slightly modified Abiola Irele's translation (see Irele 1990:76).

11. A twenty-one-string instrument played across the Mande area (southern Senegal, the Gambia, Mali, Guinea-Bissau, and northern Guinea).

12. A one-string instrument of the Tambacunda region in eastern Senegal.

13. The nomadic Peul, also known as Fulbe, live across a large geographical area, spanning from the westernmost nation of Senegal all the way across to Cameroon.

14. The exchange of money during celebration is associated with the roles of griots as mediators between social groups. The complexity of griots' social role and its changing configuration in contemporary West African societies will be addressed in chapters 4, 7, and 8.

15. I learned later that this is the *koumpo*.

16. They perform the *cin*.

17. From an interview with Bouly Sonko (Dakar, March 1997), I learned that the *koumpo* as well as the other spirits onstage are benevolent spirits associated with fertility and joy. They like to play with the young girls and scare them at times, but they are good spirits. The point I want to make here is that this information is not available or easily accessible to non-Senegalese spectators.

18. Mary Jo Arnoldi has similarly characterized the performance of specific grass masquerade figures among the Kirango in the Segou region of Mali as a type of "shape-shifting dance" (1995:90).

19. This one-legged stilted spirit is called *chakaba*.

20. On a different version of the program Jean Pierre Leurs and Bouly Sonko are both given credit for the choreography.

21. *Pangols* is a Séréér word that refers to the cult of the ancestors within the family lineage (Bouly Sonko, personal communication, Irvine, California, February 1998).

22. The report on the evil power of the crocodile bladder appears as demented because the author presents it as a plain and transparent reality, which needs no cultural decoding to be understood. Yet this discourse, associated with witchcraft, is highly metaphorical and idiomatic, requiring a great deal of cultural translation to be comprehensible to outsiders. For an excellent overview of contemporary studies on witchcraft in Africa, see *African Studies Review* 41.3 (1998).

23. The term "animist" has a derogatory connotation that conveys the bias of the Muslim majority against indigenous religions.

24. For an exemplary study of Senegalese precolonial history that accounts for the great political and economic complexity of the region, see Barry (1998).

Chapter 2: African Dance, Africanist Discourse, and Négritude

1. The assumption made here is that history in Africa began with colonialism. It was only in the 1940s that Euro-American scholars no longer denied African history prior to the arrival of colonizers (Mudimbe 1994:21–22).

2. The ruthlessness of Belgian domination in the Congo was later to become a shameful chapter in the history of European colonization. For a discussion of the relation between symbolic and political violence in the colonizing process, see Mbembe (2001:29–65).

3. Sovereign power properly belonged to the seventeenth century and was associated by Foucault (1977) with the display of public torture and terror as signs of monarchic power. Butchart argues that the display of the power to punish and torture was complemented in the colonies with a display of positive power, such as the power to heal. Fabian (2000) stresses how early European ethnographers in Africa staged their entrance into the field through the deployment of marvelous techniques of display.

4. The spectacularization of European might set against the choreographed presence of the colonized was powerfully popularized through the World Fairs and Ex-

hibitions (from 1889 to 1937), which attracted millions of onlookers (see Greenhalgh 1988). The exhibitions combined the display of the wonders of the industrial age with the ostentatious exhibition of human captives and goods from the colonies. The corporeality of African dancers was staged in opposition to the mechanical achievements of the "great" European civilizations, carrying the weight of representation for the black race and the unbearable lightness of the flesh pitted against the enormous machines and architecture of the white race.

5. Sachs was born in Germany in 1881 and taught at the University of Berlin from 1919 to 1933. He also taught as an adjunct professor at Columbia University from 1953 to 1959.

6. This last consideration, with its attention to unconscious behavior, does not properly belong to the Order of the Same (which, according to Mudimbe, was the dominant paradigm up until the 1920s) but expresses an interest in the African as psychological subject that developed in the 1930s and continued to bloom in the 1960s and 1970s in its racist manifestations as well as in the form of resistance expressed in the Black Consciousness movement, Négritude, and the revolutionary psychology of Fanon (see Butchart 1998, chap. 7).

7. This discourse will focus on the figure of the genius choreographer as the fundamental unit of analysis of dance studies.

8. I have here reinterpreted and enlarged Hountondji's concepts of extraversion and unanimism. See Hountondji (1996, chaps. 2, 3, and 4 and pp. 227–37).

9. See Hountondji (1996) and Mudimbe (1988) for a full discussion of this topic.

10. *Liberté I: Négritude et Humanisme* (1964); *Liberté III: Négritude et Civilisation de l'Universel* (1977); *Liberté V: Le Dialogue des Cultures* (1993); and *Ce Que Je Crois: Négritude, Francité, et Civilization de l'Universel* (1988).

11. See Wilder (1999:49).

12. During the greater length of the colonial period in the territorial area that was to become Senegal (1865–1944), only residents of the four urban *communes* of Saint-Louis, Gorée, Rufisque, and Dakar were granted French citizenship. Colonial subjects outside the four *communes* had no political rights but were subjected to forced labor and taxes. For more information on this subject see Diouf (1999) and Crowder (1962).

13. Unless otherwise noted, all translations from French are mine.

14. Senghor's first poetry collection is *Chants d'Ombre* (1945); his edited volume, *Anthologie de la Nouvelle Poésie Négre et Malgache de Langue Francaise,* was published in 1948, followed by *Ethiopiques* (1956), *Nocturnes* (1961), and later volumes of collected poetry. For an analysis of Senghor's literary production, see Irele (1990) and Kesteloot (1991; 2002).

15. The powerful reinterpretations of mimesis provided by Taussig (1993) and Bhabha (1994) critique the simplistic conceptualization of mimicry produced under the Order of the Same.

16. The identification of rhythm as the aesthetic quality and organizing syntax that structures African artistic production across forms was to become the central the-

sis of Robert Farris Thompson's famous book *African Art in Motion: Icon and Act* (1974). Thompson nevertheless does not even mention Senghor. He explores the continuity between African sculpture and dance, and his writings continue to be among the best analytical works on African dance.

17. See also Hountondji (1996) and Amselle (1990).

18. See Fanon (1952; 1963), Cabral (1969), Towa (1971), Adotevi (1972), Mphahlele (1974), Hountondji (1996), and Ly (1982).

19. For a similar yet more satirical critique of Négritude, see Ousmane Sembène's *Xala* (1976).

20. See chapter 4 for a brief discussion of the secessionist movement.

21. For an in-depth discussion of the festival and its implication for Négritude ideology, see Jules-Rosette (1998:87–98).

22. Achille Mbembe is the scholar that most closely follows Mudimbe's analysis of African studies and updates it into the twenty-first century (see Mbembe 2002). *On the Postcolony* (2000) brilliantly theorizes the space of marginality and violence that Mudimbe alludes to.

23. For studies that reconceptualize tradition and historicize indigenous practice, see Ranger (1983; 1993), Comaroff (1985), Arens and Karp (1989), Amselle (1990), Apter (1992), Drewal (1992), Comaroff and Comaroff (1992; 1993), Diagne (1993), Kaspin (1993), Stoller (1995), Diawara (1996), Ranger and Werbner (1996), Aliyu (1997), McLaughlin (1997), Okafor (1997), Strother (1998), Werbner (1998), and Masquelier (2001). For studies on African popular cultures see Coplan (1985; 1994), Arnoldi (1987; 1995), Barber (1987, 1997), Barber, Collins, and Ricard (1997), Jules-Rosette (1984; 1987), Fabian (1990; 1996; 1998), Waterman (1990), Gunner (1994), Veit (1996), and Askew (2002).

24. For notable theorizations of new turns in ethnographic practice in the wake of postmodernism, see Appadurai (1996) and Marcus (1998).

25. See Jules-Rosette (2002:604).

26. I am appropriating Savigliano's choreocritic voice here (see Savigliano 2003 for a brilliant example of the ethnographic use of such a voice).

Chapter 3: The National Ballet of Senegal at the National Theater in Dakar

1. *Marabout* is a French adaptation of an Arabic term that refers to a Muslim religious leader, scholar, or cleric.

2. The Sorano is home not only to the National Ballet but also to the National Dramatic Ensemble and the Lyrical Traditional Ensemble, which regularly perform and rehearse in the theater.

3. *Toubaab* is a Wolofization of *toubib* ("doctor" in colloquial French), a term used throughout Senegal to refer to French people and by extension all white people. The word tends to carry a negative connotation.

4. The *musóór* is a headpiece that is tied around the head and answers to complex aesthetics in women's attire.

5. These are the circles of *sabar* dancing and *seruba* dancing.

6. I echo Adotevi's critique of Négritude in *Négritude et Négrologues* (1972).

7. The troupe is now touring a new program, entitled *Kuuyamba.*

8. See Butchart (1998), chap. 7, for a discussion of this operation in the context of South Africa.

9. Paulin Hountondji (1996) has cogently criticized the concepts of modernization, westernization, and acculturation in relation to African subjects.

10. I deliberately use the French term *fétiche,* which connotes the magical African object—the "amulet"—produced by the *féticheur,* the healer. I want to underscore the similarity between the fetish, understood in a Marxist sense, and the *fétiche.*

11. This is, of course, the reverse problematic of the homogenization of "Africa" into one conceptual entity. Here the West is constructed as one homogeneous cultural, political, economic, and historical space in spite of the significant differences among the countries that make up the "West" and the geographical ambiguity of the boundary itself.

12. The construction of ancient Egyptians as blacks is problematic in that it projects backward contemporary racial categories. Yet these authors are correct to argue that the politics of race are at the center of this historiographic project and account for radical rewritings of ancient history.

Chapter 4: *Sabar* Dancing and a Women's Public Sphere

1. *Taalibes* are religious followers associated with a specific *marabout,* who can act as an intermediary between his *taalibes* and *Yalla* while imparting to them religious wisdom and education. Young children are often brought to live with a *marabout* to receive such an education, learning the Koran and important Islamic principles. These young *taalibes* go on daily alimony quests to collect money to buy food and to provide for their everyday needs and those of the *marabout.* In a situation of steadily deteriorating economic conditions, the young *taalibes* of the capital are often forced to spend most of their days begging in the streets, amidst the danger and the pollution of passing cars and the rough social environment of street corners. For a portrait of the difficulties and joys of a young *taalibe,* see Mansour Sora Wade's short film *Picc mi* (1992).

2. In 1996–97, five hundred CFA Francs were roughly equivalent to one dollar. Thus twenty-five CFA Francs were equivalent to five cents.

3. Precise statistics are hard to come by in light of the few systematic studies conducted. Furthermore, data analyzed in published materials can be much older than the publications themselves. Van Djik's statistics are based on data from 1977. In light of the deteriorating economy throughout the 1980s and 1990s, we can reasonably assume that the informal sector has remained stable if not swelled during the last two decades.

4. Statistics concerning unemployment vary greatly according to the social group under consideration. Duruflé (1994) reports a 12 percent unemployment rate for

heads of households (predominantly men) in Dakar (1991 statistics), while Bop (1995) reports a 39 percent unemployment rate among Dakar's women (1988 statistics). For women between the ages of twenty and twenty-four Diop (1996) reports an unemployment rate of 44 percent and a rate of 35 percent for males of the same ages (1991 statistics).

5. According to the World Bank's 1994 estimates, 89 percent of the Senegalese population is excluded from any form of medical assistance (Diop 1996:74). Other economic indices provide information about the poverty of Dakarois. For example, only 47 percent of Dakar's households are connected to the city sewer system, while in the *banlieues* of Dakar the figure drops to a dramatic 4 percent. The national average is 7 percent (Diop 1996). For a fuller discussion of poverty in Dakar and the government response to it, see Diop (1996).

6. Each of these factors is the result of complex dynamics, warranting extended studies. For more information on the agricultural sector and its relation to the colonial context, see O'Brien (1971); for information on Senegal's government policies in the agricultural sector (since independence), see Delgado and Jammeh (1991).

7. The tourist industry provides dubious economic benefits to the Senegalese population. For an excellent study on this subject, see Schlechten (1988). For a brilliant critique and ironic account of the government's attempts to clean the streets of Dakar, see Aminata Sow Fall's novel *The Beggars' Strike* (1981).

8. In 1997 I witnessed a military officer destroying the meager stand of an illegal trader along a major Dakar street. During the same period I also saw the HSM market being cleared of all its nonregistered traders. The market was thus considerably reduced in size.

9. I quote from the abridged English edition here and below.

10. For a more detailed discussion of this topic, see Ministére de la Femme (1993). A team of Senegalese scholars conducted the study, with the Population Council acting as executing agency.

11. For a discussion of Wolof griots as musicians in a contemporary context, see Tang (2000), Panzacchi (1994), and Leymaire (1978). For a discussion of Mande griots, see Ebron (2002), Charry (2000), Hoffman (2000), Diawara (1996), Drame and Senn-Borloz (1992), and Camara (1992). For a general discussion of griots across societies, see Hale (1998).

12. This division intersects with other systems of social stratification, like class. In precolonial times, caste divisions were inserted within larger social hierarchies, producing complex economic and political stratifications. For example, in the ancient Wolof kingdoms the *garmi* (royal families) occupied the top of the social hierarchy, followed by the *jàmbur* (notables), the *baadoolo* (the mass of the peasantry), the *ñeeño* (the artisans), and at the very bottom the *jaam* (slaves). Slaves of royal families could occupy important social positions, however, above the *baadoolo* (Barry 1998). The *géér* included in this schema the *garmi,* the *jàmbur,* and the *baadoolo,* which were juxtaposed to the *ñeeño,* while the slaves remained external to the sys-

tem of patronage established between these two castes. For a discussion of Wolof pre-colonial societies, see the excellent works of Abdoulaye Diop (1981; 1985) and Barry (1998).

13. For a wonderful discussion of the complicated social, moral, and economic negotiations of reciprocal obligations at family events, see Aminata Sow Fall's novel *Le Revenant* (1982).

14. For a definition of *mbalax*, see "Soirée Sénégalais at LT" below.

15. *Soirées* are dance events held in the clubs of the city.

16. This is the case with the Séréér, whose contribution to the *sabar* dancing idiom is often silenced or rather assimilated to a more general discussion of the Wolof. The logic that governs such discursive assimilation rests on the more general Wolofization of the Séréér.

17. These languages are Wolof, Pulaar, Séréér, Mandinka, Joola, and Soninkè.

18. Islam was introduced in Senegal by the Almarovid in the eleventh century, but it spread among the majority of the Senegalese population during the end of the nineteenth century. Four Sufi Brotherhoods are present in Senegal: the Mouridiyya, the Tidjaniyya, the Qadiriyya, and the Layene. For in-depth analyses of the Mouridiyya, see O'Brien (1971) and Coulon (1981). For a more general discussion of Islam in Senegal, see Coulon (1983) and Callaway and Creevey (1994).

19. As noted in chapter 1, Tekrour was a multiethnic empire in the River Valley of northern Senegal and acted as a nexus for the trans-Saharan trade to the north as well as the east-west regional trade. Historical documents remarking the existence of Tekrour date to the eleventh century (up to the thirteenth century), yet the political entity of Tekrour is probably older.

20. Because of the strong Wolof presence outside of the four *communes*, this colonial policy has not produced the kind of "tribalization" of politics that plagues other African nations.

21. For a discussion of the political implications of the division between citizens and subjects in colonial Senegal at the moment of national independence, see Diouf (1994:100–102).

22. Amadou Bamba Mbaké (1850–1927) was the founder of the Mouride brotherhood, which garnered a following from the Wolof population. Members of the Wolof ethnicity still constitute the majority of the brotherhood, yet communities of different ethnicities belong to the Mourides. In particular, the Islamicization of the Séréér in the peanut basin and their involvement with peanut production has led scholars to talk of the Wolofization of the Séréér.

23. The Muslim population has been estimated to comprise about 90 percent of the total Senegalese population at the eve of independence and to have increased to 95 percent by 1992 (Callaway and Creevey 1994:24).

24. The Movement of the Democratic Forces of the Casamance has historical roots in pre-independent Senegal but was constituted in its present form in 1982. During that year it made its demand for independence known to the Senegalese government

through a peaceful demonstration in Zinquinchor, the regional capital of the Bassa Casamance. Leaders of the movement were arrested, and government repression has continued for many years, with a heavy military presence in the Bassa Casamance. For more information on the Casamance question, see Barbier-Wiesser (1994).

25. The independence movement is articulated in regional and ethnic terms. While several ethnic groups live in the Casamance, the most numerous of which are the Joola and the Manding, the movement for independence has garnered its members mostly from the Joola people. The Islamization of the Manding can explain the ethnic focus of the movement.

26. This statement may be too drastic, because the participation of men in the dancing circle of *sabars* is a debated and continually negotiated occurrence. The issue warrants in-depth research. Historically, men did dance the *sabar,* and some *sabar* rhythms and events call for the participation of males only (Mohamed Mboji, following my presentation at the African Studies Association annual meeting in Philadelphia, November 1999). For example, the *simb*—the character of the lion hunter (and the event that features him)—is only danced by men, while the *làmb*—the rhythm for the wrestling matches—is danced by the male wrestlers in the ring.

27. Male *géwëls,* as guardians of the dance traditions of the country (together with women *géwëls*), do dance the *sabar* masterfully, a fact that can support Camara's notion of a fluid gender identity for male griots.

28. Again I need to remind the reader of the contextual nature of these statements, which are linked to the urban milieu of Dakar and the period of 1995–96. Dakar's *sabars* cannot be taken unproblematically as representative of *sabars* in general, including the issue of men's versus women's participation. Rather, the similarities between linguistic Wolofization and the *sabar* are once again useful in that the Urban Wolof of Dakar is different from the *Wolof bu xoot* (deep Wolof) of the interior, and similarly the *sabars* of Dakar are different from the *sabars* of other regions. Thus, while the participation of men in *sabar* dancing is "traditional," the interplay within the sexes in the urban environment has changed the rules of male participation.

29. The *funanà* is one of the musical genres of Cape-Verde.

30. Women of my generation or younger also play the *sabar* drums, most notably the daughters of Doudou N'Diaye Rose, one of the most respected and internationally famous *sabar* player in the country. The group takes the name of Doudou N'Diaye Rose et Ses Rosettes to mark the presence of women drummers. At Saint-Louis, I met Lamine Koura et Ses Kourettes, another *géwël* family in which the father—Lamine Koura—has taught his daughters to play the *sabar* drums. Yet in none of the events I attended in Dakar did I see a woman play drums. The groups that include female drummers tend to perform at concerts and musical events rather than the social events and street *sabars* that are the topic of my analysis.

31. Heath (1994) makes a similar point while analyzing women's *sabar* performances at political rallies.

32. The film *Karmen Geï* by Gaï Ramaka (2001) is a striking divergence from this

pattern, and it has caused considerable scandal in Senegalese environments. For a critical analysis of the film, see Castaldi (2003).

33. The erotic energy of *sabars* finds its way, tamed, onto the television screen. In a paper presented at the meeting of the African Studies Association in Philadelphia in 1999, I offered a more nuanced reading of music videos. Yet the main argument stands the same.

34. *Khalifa* is the head of a Muslim brotherhood or one of its branches, with considerable political and religious power over the community of believers.

35. O'Brien (1971) has written extensively on the ideology of submission within the Mouride order. See also Schaffer's discussion of the concept and practice of *ndigal* (1998:106–14). Heath has noted the similarity between a bride's submission to her husband and a disciple's submission to his or her *khalifa*, which also characterizes the relationship of a *taalibe* to his or her *marabout*.

36. Soxna Diaara—celebrated in Fatou Guewel's song—is for many Mourides the prototype of good womanhood, and the popular recounting of her life underscores her extraordinary *sutura* (see Roberts and Roberts 2003:155–58).

37. I thank Mohammed Mboji, visiting professor of African history at Cornell University, for making this remark in response to my presentation of a section of this chapter to the meeting of the African Studies Association in Philadelphia (1999).

38. For a fuller discussion of this topic, see Amadiume (1988) and chapter 5 in this volume.

39. Concerning the bilateral descent system of the Wolof, Abdoulaye-Bara Diop writes: "Biological kinship is closer on the side of the uterine lineage; it is within it that one finds affection, protection, and deep solidarity in case of emergency: sickness (*jagadi*), misfortune (*naqar*), poverty (*jekkadi*), great difficulty (*tiis*)" (1985:24). This statement seems to support my interpretation.

40. The concept of *fitna*, for example, associates social disorder with female beauty and thus supports the need to restrain women's social circulation least they seduce men and disrupt the stability of (male) society. Fatima Mernissi writes: "*[F]itna*, i.e. disorder chaos. (*Fitna* also means a beautiful woman . . . the connotation of a *femme fatale* attraction which makes men lose their self-control. In the way Kacem Amin used it *fitna* could be translated as chaos provoked by sexual disorder and initiated by the woman)" (1975:4). Obviously a discussion of Islamic sexual morality warrants more consideration than I am able to give it here.

41. This interpretation is suggested by the filmmaker Gaï Ramaka and has been strongly resisted by the Senegalese mainstream.

42. Some ethnic groups practice female circumcision in the name of the Islamic religion (the Manding and the Tukulours), while other groups who are strongly Islamicized do not (the Wolof). What accounts for these differences?

43. A consensus on the subject of the relationship between gender equality and ethnicity seems to exist among scholars and Senegalese lay people alike, asserting that the Joola of the Casamance provide a model of society that is less hierarchical—and thus

less patriarchal—than that of any other ethnic group in Senegal. This interpretation supports Amadiume's theoretical model, which relates the presence of matrifocal units in a society with anti-state and decentralized social systems and with autochthonous religious systems (independent from Islamic and Christian religions). Not incidentally, the Joola are among the least Islamicized ethnic groups in Senegal. To my knowledge, the only comparative study of gender equality and ethnicity in Senegal is Callaway and Creevey (1994).

44. In 1996 this translated to about two to four dollars.

45. The word *mbalax* is used to connote a popular-music genre as well as a prominent rhythm in the *sabar* complex. The name of the rhythm has come to qualify the musical genre, because the *mbalax* rhythm is the *sabar* rhythm that constitutes the basis of *mbalax* music.

46. *Mbalax* music was established in Dakar in the 1970s club scene and came out of a fusion between Afro-Cuban and *sabar* music. For a discussion of *mbalax,* see Truher (1997).

47. The *grand boubou* is one of the many Senegalese dresses. It is composed of three pieces: a wraparound gown (*sër*), a grand blouse, and a headpiece (*musóór*).

48. People from low-income neighborhoods, like the ones attending the event tonight, almost never buy bottled drinks. Only special occasions would justify such an expense. Furthermore, "good" Muslims do not drink alcohol, but those who do, do so discreetly. Thus it is much better to exit the discotheque to purchase an alcoholic drink than to do so in front of other people.

49. The aesthetic of dressing up elegantly is called *sañse* in Wolof.

50. Author's consultation with Lamine Koura, Saint-Louis, Senegal (February 1996).

51. See chapter 8 for a discussion of this Ballet.

Chapter 5: Tales of Betrayal

1. Thiossane is one of the most well-known clubs of Dakar. It is owned by Youssou N'Dour, who regularly performs there. *Thiossane* means tradition/culture.

2. The capitalization of categories of identity serves two purposes. As in previous chapters, I use it as an alternative to quotation marks to signal that such categories of identity are socially constructed even when they are not explicitly discussed as such. Yet, in the stories themselves, these categories (White, Black, Woman, Feminist, Girl, Mother) are not contested or argued against, so they refer to prototypical, stereotyped figures rather than specific persons. When two categories mark the same subject, as in White woman or white Woman, the category that is capitalized is is foregrounded in the narrative, while the lowercased aspect remains in the background. This usage helps us recognize that subjects always strategically position themselves within socially constructed categories of identity, at times foregrounding some categories over others, and yet living with and from them contemporaneously (we cannot separate gender from race or class as they come already "mixed") as well as always exceeding such categorizations.

3. See chapter 8 for an elaboration of this point.

4. Legally the couple can get married, but Muslim morality frowns upon such unions, discouraging their formation.

5. The incisive comments on the politics of feminism of my friend and colleage Riselia Duarte-Bezerra, as well as Visweswaran's (1994) theorization of betrayal in the ethnographic process, have greatly influenced the writing of this chapter.

6. See Amadiume (1988, 1997); Hooks (1990); Spivak (1990, 1999); Mohanty, Russo, and Torres (1991); Visweswaran (1994); Guillaumin (1995); McClintock (1995); Savigliano (1995, 1996, 2003); El Saadawi (1997); Oyewùmí (1997); Chaudhuri and Pierson (1998).

7. For a more general illustration of the presence of such narratives in the mainstream media and the political use to which they have been put, browse through the issues of *Times* or *People* published at the time of the U.S. war on Afghanistan and in the aftermath of September 11, 2001.

8. With the disintegration of communism, more and more of the Second World is becoming incorporated into the Third World.

9. In the African context, the division between formal and informal economies, and subsistence versus cash agriculture, is much more meaningful for gender analysis than the divide between the private and public domain that has structured feminist debates in the West. This point has been made by African and Africanist scholars for more than a decade, but it has not been heard by the western feminist mainstream.

10. While this accusation against western feminists has been made for at least a decade within the academy, not enough has changed to void it. Rather, the bombastic imperialism of the United States at the turn of the twenty-first century sadly exemplifies the popularity of a kind of "imperial feminism" that appeals to Europeans and Euro-Americans.

11. The evolutionary narrative, with its hierarchy of values, takes us from a primitive and promiscuous matricentric system in which fatherhood is not recognized, to a domesticated patriarchal promiscuity in which men engage in polygamous marriages, to the final stage of development that sees nuclear families centered on a monogamous couple as the civilized human ideal. For a full discussion of the racism implicit in this narrative, see Amadiume 1997:71–88 and 101–5).

12. Amadiume argues that such a gender balance is a product of decentralized social systems that are anti-state and democratic. The Joola of the Casamance seem to conform to this pattern.

13. Callaway and Creevey pose many serious questions about the relationship between Islam, sexual morality, women's rights, ethnicity, and state policies.

14. On Sarah Bartmann, see Gilman (1985), Abrahams (1998), Strother (1999), and Magubane (2001). On the portrayals of African prostitutes, I have in mind Jean-François Werner's *Marges, Sexe, et Drogues à Dakar: Enquête Etnographique* (1993), which was prominently displayed in all the major bookstores of Dakar in 1996, the time of my research.

15. See Savigliano (2003:209–24) for an analysis of this type of white (post)feminist woman in the context of tango tourism in Buenos Aires.

16. See also El Saadawi's discussion of polyandry in pre-Islamic societies (1997:74).

Chapter 6: The Circulation of Dances on and off the Stage

1. Scholars of African arts and performance have argued against Nicholls's evolutionary schema for at least ten years. See, for example, the lengthy discussion on African popular arts in the *African Studies Review* 30.3 (September 1987). Perhaps the antipathy between the U.S. Afrocentric school (to which Nicholls seems to adhere) and Africanist ethnographers prevents the flow of ideas and a much-needed dialogue between these two camps. In spite of my critique of Nicholls, I share his heartfelt concern about the effects of globalization on African artists and his desire to see African dances remain relevant to the education of African youths.

2. Senghor talked of this hybrid process as a *metissage* (see, for example, Senghor 1964b).

3. This is also the case for the solo dances of the *seruba* complex—for example, the *lenjengo*—and the *econcon*.

4. The interview was conducted in English. I take sole responsibility for mistakes and misinterpretations.

5. See chap. 4, n. 46 above for a definition of *mbalax*.

6. *Khaley* literally means child; *khaley nguewel* thus means the child-griot or the young griot. That Aziz, a masterful dancer and drummer, calls himself a child underscores the greatness of the family to which he belongs.

7. The *sabar* repertory is composed of an ever-growing number of dances. Other dances of the *sabar* complex that I came to know include *baar mbaye, ñaari gorong, lëmbël, yaaba,* and *yaaba composé.*

8. I use the feminine pronoun because, as discussed in chapter 4, the generic dancer is indeed female. Yet a male dancer can also take the center of the circle, and the same dynamics with the drummer would apply.

9. I did not record my interview with Aziz Faye. I took notes as we talked and filled in gaps in the notes immediately after we spoke. I then read back my transcription to Aziz for his approval.

10. A *ndigal* is an injunction from a *marabout* to his *taalibes,* and as such it must not be disobeyed.

11. McNee (2000) cites in her bibliography Keita Abdoulaye's master's thesis, which is dedicated to the treatment of *taasu* (Université de Cheick Amta Diop de Dakar, 1986). I did not have a chance to read it.

12. Tang (with whom I had no communication) completed her dissertation on the *sabar* Wolof only a few months after I completed mine. She discusses the *bàkk* from the drummers' point of view, echoing and complementing my analysis. I have chosen to focus only on the points that arise from my research in the hope that Tang will publish her own work.

13. For example, Samba Diop, in his book on the oral history of Waalo, mentions the *bàkk* as "a praise poem dedicated to a wrestler or being sung by a wrestler" (1995:264).

14. In the Mande tradition, for example, the *kora* "speaks" (Prince Djiabate, personal communication with the author, Los Angeles, November 2000).

15. Because it belongs to the Séréér and Manding ethnicities as well as the Wolof, the *tama* can "speak" Manding, Séréér, or Wolof depending on the social context in which it is played.

16. Aziz says "we" because he sometimes plays with his brother's group.

17. *Mu* by itself is also the narrative pronoun for the third-person singular (for example: *mesuma gis Astou mu fecc* [I have never seen Astou dance]; *begg naa mu ñew* [I want him or her to come]).

18. For an excellent discussion of Urban Wolof, see Swigart (1994; 2000).

19. Griots' speech is replete with innuendos built on multiple communicative layers. *Tink's* also plays on the phonemic closeness to *tank* denoting the leg and the gluteus.

20. In my interviews with dancers, I found that anything coming from the generation before them was considered "old."

21. For a good discussion of the role of the mass media in relation to griots' practices, see Diawara (1996).

22. Peter Abilogu, teaching dances from Nigeria, Sandor Diabankouezi, teaching dances from the Congo, and Malang Bayo, teaching dances from Senegal, more or less used the same words.

23. See chapter 4 for a detailed and specific description of the passage from stillness to dancing as the marker of good improvisers.

24. The privileging of Wolof dance forms as "Senegalese" is also under way in Dakar's discotheques, where Soirées Sénégalaises feature live *mbalax* and *sabar* groups to the exclusion of other ethnic forms.

25. Author's interviews with Vieux Màgget Diallo, Dakar, Senegal, 1996.

26. Author's interview with Sedou Massaly, Dakar, February 1997. Massaly was the lead dancer of the Ballet Fambondy in Dakar.

27. Tiérou uses the Ouelou language—his mother tongue—to define these three circles: the *glo*, the *caillo*, the *gla* (1989:57–62). As a master dancer who belongs to a lineage of specialized performers that guard the "Wise Masks" of western Ivory Coast, Tiérou speaks knowledgeably of his own dance tradition, yet he does so in general terms, as if it were the tradition of the whole continent (the title of the book—*The Eternal Law of African Dance*—is a good indication of this generalizing tendency). This slippage between the particular and the generic African is less annoying theoretically than the slippage performed by Afrocentric scholars like Nicholls because Tiérou consistently speaks of the same social context in the Ivory Coast, while Nicholls draws examples from a wide array of unrelated social and historical contexts. Tiérou's consistency allows other scholars to assess whether his discussion of the Ivorian context can be applied to other African contexts. I find it to be useful in clarifying the Senegalese context.

28. Author's interviews with Bouly Sonko, Dakar, Senegal, 1996 and 1997.

29. For a discussion of the difference between entertainment dances and more sacred/secret ones among the Bamana of Mali, see Arnoldi (1995:18–24).

30. Each *rab* has a particular song and rhythm, and since there are many *rabs* in the spiritual pantheon, days can go by before the sick person falls possessed by the spirit whose song is being played.

31. At the time of my research in 1997, a *ndëp* was held for several consecutive days in the neighborhood of Ñaari Tali, right next to a busy bus stop.

32. Throughout the book, I have used pseudonyms for dancers, while I have kept the real names of choreographers. In doing so I have respected the choreographers' wishes and avoided the ethnographic premise of the Order of the Other, which failed to recognize agency among individual African artists. At the same time, even though dancers spoke to me with the agreement that their name would appear in association with their interviews, I have decided to protect their anonymity.

Chapter 7: Urban Ballets and the Professionalization of Dance

1. See chapter 8 for a discussion of the Ballet Mansour.

2. The presence of musicians other than drummers is particularly relevant for dances outside of the *sabar* complex. For dances of the Mande complex, a *balafon* player often accompanies the drum ensemble, while for Peul dances, one or more flutists play along with drummers.

3. For an excellent discussion of polyrhythm in African drumming and musicology, see Agawu (2003:71–96).

4. For a discussion of *bàkks* as markers of a *géwël* family's or a *Mbalax* group's identity, see Tang (2000:189–200).

5. I take the term "Mandification" from Thomas Hale (1998:327), who uses it to refer to the overrepresentation of *jàlí* (Mande griots) in the literature on griots as well as in the circuit of (Francophone) African world music.

6. The Mande complex originated with the Mali empire in the early thirteenth century and spread its influence through successive waves of migration. Historiographical considerations beyond the scope of my expertise lead scholars to include different ethnic groups under the Mande umbrella. For example, Andrew Clark and Phillips Lucie (1994:187) include the Soninke and the Jaxante within the Mande, in addition to the Bambara and Malinke, while Sory Camara (1992:1) includes the Soninke, Bambara, Joola, Malinke, Bobo, Bozo, Busa, Bisa, Kuranto, Toma, Mendé, Turan, and Dan, followed by an unsettling "et cetera." To add to the confusion, while some scholars use the terms "Malinke," "Manding," and "Mandenka" interchangeably (the first being a French version of the term, the second an English version), others argue that "Manding" or "Mandenka" refers to a larger entity than the Malinke ethnicity, which includes the Bambara and in some cases the Joola.

7. Peul dancers performing with the Ballet Mansour and the National Ballet of

Senegal were all in their fifties and even sixties. The dances they performed are particularly demanding, as they call for back flips, headstands, and dramatic balancing acts on calabashes. In the Ballet Mansour, after the performance of the Peul, who act as a separate group from the rest of the company, an announcer would reveal the age of the dancers to the audience, always eliciting cries of surprise and admiration.

8. Drummers reported urinating blood as a sign of overwork.

9. Sory Camara argues that two types of relations among *hórós* allow for the kind of licentious talking, joking, or mediating responsibilities typical of *jàlí*. The first involves interclan *sànàkuñà* relations, which have been discussed in the anthropological literature as joking relations. The second involves a set of protective and affectionate relations within the domestic sphere (see Camara 1992:35–50).

10. Sory Camara, who has written the most authoritative book on West African griots, offers a typical example: He dedicates only two pages to a discussion of griots' dancing, which is actually more than many of his colleagues have written on the subject. See Camara (1992); Leymarie (1978); Drame and Senn-Borloz (1992); Panzacchi (1994); Diawara (1996); and Hale (1998).

11. The fact that Ismael mentions that he was noticed because of his lighter skin suggests that colonial racial politics are still at work in Senegal. This is also suggested by the fact that many Dakarois women engage in the practice of *xeesal*, the whitening of the skin through the use of dangerous creams. While men do not perform *xeesal*, Ismael's remark suggests that the aesthetics of whiteness are also relevant vis-à-vis the male gender.

12. Mudra Afrique is a dance school founded in 1977 by the internationally renowned choreographer Maurice Béjart and directed by his protégée Germaine Acogny. For a discussion of the school, see Acogny (1980). When Mudra was closed in 1983 due to financial difficulty, Acogny returned to France to work with Béjart and to continue developing her own choreographic style and teaching. In 1995 she was back in Senegal, establishing a new school: the Centre International de Danses Traditionnelles et Contemporaines Africaines à Toubab Dialaw. The center was not yet in operation when I visited it in 1996, but it has been actively functioning since 1998. Acogny's presence in Senegal is bringing a new impetus to ethnic dance and fostering innovative collaborations with partners in Africa and the larger world.

13. The National Conservatory is the only government institution dedicated to dance education in the country, yet it is better known for its music training than for its dance studies. The school offers instruction in ballet, modern, and African dance. Several Ballet dancers expressed the opinion that the conservatory is weak in the teaching of ethnic dance, with the exception of the *sabar* complex.

Chapter 8: Exploiting *Terànga*

1. The name of the group in 1979 was actually the Etoile de Dakar, which had been in existence since the 1960s. When the group broke up, N'Dour took it over, and

two years later he changed its name to Super Etoile. See Bender (1991) for more information.

2. A common praise for those displaying generosity is *ku xam terànga la,* which literally means "that person knows *terànga*" (Sylla 1994:87).

3. N'Dour's involvement in the Set Setal movement provides a more positive example of his influence. The movement encouraged the youth of Dakar to care for the environment without waiting for government intervention and incited the youth to clean up and beautify the city with a series of murals. For a history of the movement, see Bugnicourt (1991).

4. For example, the Ballet has been performing at Le Meridien President, located at Pointe des Almadies, since Le Meridien's inauguration in 1995; at the Savana Hotel; and for twenty years at the Hotel Terànga.

5. Djibril Diop Mambety captures the moment of the 1994 devaluation in his short film *Le Franc* (1994) by depicting a poor Dakarois's dreams of a good life at the very time in which devaluation measures are announced to the general population. The surreal quality of the film makes it a brilliant critique of the whims of monetary policies, which are so detached from the influences of ordinary citizens and yet so intimately determining of their daily lives.

6. See, for example, Van De Walle (1991:403).

7. Author's interview with Ndiuwar Thiam, Dakar, Senegal, November 1996.

8. For the political importance of consensus in Wolof's conceptions of democracy, see Schaffer (1998:57–61).

9. This same point is eloquently made by Wallerstein (1979; 1986) and Amin (1970; 1971; 1973).

10. See Roberts (2003) for a beautiful sampling of such images.

11. For a historical study of the Mali empire, see Cissé and Kamissoko (1988). For a discussion of the epic in relation to the *kora* repertory of Mande griots, see Charry (2000).

12. Visa requirements vary but in general need to be supported by demonstrated financial resources well beyond the means of the general population.

Conclusion

1. Senghor (1964b:9).

2. See Swigart (2000:96).

3. Senghor's deployment of Séréér in his poetry did not take away from the colonial undertones of his theorization and implementation of language policies.

4. In an interview with Sada Niang (1993:92), Sembène pointed to the absurdity of the use of French rather than Wolof in the Senegalese courts: "When you go to court the magistrates are Wolof and speak Wolof, the accused are Wolof and speak Wolof, but these two groups speak only through interpreters. Any statement made by the accused in Wolof is fully understood by the presiding judge, the trial judge,

and the lawyers, but still somebody has to provide French translation for them. Isn't that ridiculous?"

5. In 1988 Wolophones comprised 71 percent of the population, with 44 percent of speakers being classified as Wolof, by the late 1990s the number of Wolophones grew to 90 percent, while the number of Wolof people remained pretty much the same (Swigart 1992:23). For the other official languages the distribution among ethnic groups was as follows: Pulaar was spoken by 24 percent of the population, with 23 percent classified as Peul and Tukulour; Séréér was spoken by 14 percent of people, with 15 percent of the population belonging to the Séréér ethnicity; Joola was spoken by 6 percent of Senegalese, with 5.5 percent belonging to the Joola; Manding was spoken by 6 percent of the population, with 5 percent being classified as Manding; Sarakholé-Soninké was spoken by 1 percent of the population, and no figures are given for ethnic affiliation (Diagne 1993:58). By the late 1990s, apart from the noted increase in Wolophones, the percentage of people speaking the other five languages has probably varied little into the present. The only exception may be Pulaar, which was more aggressively pursued as a marker of a common identity by two ethnic groups (the Peul and Toucouleur) who united as one linguistic community in partial reaction to Wolofization, and which may thus have increased a little (Swigart 1992; O'Brien 1998:37).

6. For a fuller discussion of Senghorian politics, see the essays in Diop (1993), as well as Diouf and Diop (1990) and Hesseling (1985).

7. Several dancers of the National Ballet of Senegal lamented that they are more appreciated and well known abroad than in Senegal. Dancers in other Ballets echoed this remark, saying that it was not until they toured abroad that they realized the value of their dance training, in material and in cultural terms.

References

Abilogu, Peter. 1982. "Igbe Izimize: Traditional Dance of the Urhobo of Nigeria."
Master's thesis, University of California at Los Angeles.

Abrahams, Yvette. 1998. "Images of Sarah Bartmann: Sexuality, Race, and Gender in
Early Nineteenth-Century Britain." In *Nation, Empire, Colony: Historicizing Gender and Race.* Ed. Nupur Chaudhuri and Ruth Pierson. 220–36. Bloomington:
Indiana University Press.

Acogny, Germaine. 1980. *Danse Africaine.* Berlin: Reiter-Druck.

Adotevi, Stanislas. 1972. *Négritude et Négrologues.* Paris: Union Générale d'Éditions.

Agawu, Kofi. 2003. *Representing African Music: Postcolonial Notes, Queries, Positions.*
New York: Routledge.

Aldrich, Robert. 1996. *Greater France: A History of French Overseas Expansion.* New
York: St. Martin's Press.

Aliyu, Sani Abba. 1997. "Hausa Women as Oral Storytellers in Northern Nigeria."
In *Writing African Women: Gender, Popular Culture, and Literature in Africa.* Ed.
Stephanie Newell. 149–56. London: Zed Books.

Amadiume, Ifi. 1987. *Male Daughters, Female Husbands: Gender and Sex in an African Society.* London: Zed Books.

———. 1997. *Reinventing Africa: Matriarchy, Religion, and Culture.* London: Zed
Books.

Amin, Samir. 1970. *L'Accumulation à l'Echelle Mondiale: Critique de la Théorie du
Sous-développement.* Dakar: IFAN.

———. 1971. *L'Afrique de l'Ouest Bloquée: L'Economie Politique de la Colonisation,
1880–1970.* Paris: Les Éditions de Minuit.

———. 1973. *Le Développement Inégal: Essai sur les Formations Sociales du Capitalisme Périphérique.* Paris: Les Éditions de Minuit.

———. 1992. *Empire of Chaos.* Trans. Locke Anderson. New York: Monthly Review
Press.

Amselle, Jean-Loup. 1990. *Logiques Métisses: Anthropologie de l'Identité en Afrique et Ailleurs.* Paris: Éditions Payot.

Amselle, Jean-Loup, and M'bokolo Elikia. 1985. *Au Coeur de l'Ethnie: Ethnies, Tribalisme, et État en Afrique.* Paris: Éditions la Découverte.

Antoine, Philippe, and Jeanne Nanitelamio. 1995. "Peut-On Échapper à la Polygamie à Dakar?" *Les Dossiers du Centre Francais sur la Population et le Developpement (CEPED)* 32 (September): 1–35.

Appadurai, Arjun. 1996. *Modernity at Large: Cultural Dimensions of Globalization.* Minneapolis: University of Minnesota Press.

Apter, Andrew. 1992. "Que Faire? Reconsidering Inventions of Africa." *Critical Inquiry* 18.1 (Autumn): 87–104.

Arens, W., and Ivan Karp, eds. 1989. *Creativity and Power: Cosmology and Action in African Societies.* Washington, D.C.: Smithsonian Institution Press.

Arnoldi, Mary. 1987. "Rethinking Definitions of African Traditional and Popular Arts." *African Studies Review* 30.3 (September): 79–84.

———. 1995. *Playing with Time: Art and Performance in Central Mali.* Bloomington: Indiana University Press.

Askew, Kelly. 2002. *Performing the Nation: Swahili Music and Cultural Politics in Tanzania.* Chicago: University of Chicago Press.

Badji, Awa. 1997. Interview. Dakar, Senegal (March).

Balibar, Etienne. 1991. "Class Racism." In *Race, Nation, Class: Ambiguous Identities.* Ed. Etienne Balibar and Immanuel Wallerstein. 204–16. London: Verso.

Balibar, Etienne, and Immanuel Wallerstein, eds. 1991. *Race, Nation, Class: Ambiguous Identities.* London: Verso.

Balzar, John. 1995. "Africa: In a Paranoid Land, Contagion of Fear Spreads." *Los Angeles Times,* February 4, A2.

Barber, Karin. 1987. "Popular Arts in Africa." *African Studies Review* 30.3 (September): 1–78, 105–32.

———. 1997. *Readings in African Popular Culture.* Bloomington: Indiana University Press.

Barber, Karin, John Collins, and Alain Ricard, eds. 1997. *West African Popular Theatre.* Bloomington: Indiana University Press.

Barbier-Wiesser, François, ed. 1994. *Comprendre la Casamance: Chronique d'une Intégration Contrastée.* Paris: Éditions Karthala.

Barry, Boubacar. 1998. *Senegambia and the Atlantic Slave Trade.* Cambridge: Cambridge University Press.

Bayart, Jean-François. 1993. *The State in Africa: The Politics of the Belly.* London: Longman.

Bender, Wolfgang. 1991. *Sweet Mother: Modern African Music.* Chicago: University of Chicago Press.

Bernal, Martin. 1987. *The Fabrication of Ancient Greece.* Vol. 1 of *Black Athena: The Afroasiatic Roots of Classical Civilization.* London: Free Association Books.

———. 1991. *The Archeological and Documentary Evidence*. Vol. 2 of *Black Athena: The Afroasiatic Roots of Classical Civilization*. London: Free Association Books.

Bezerra, Riselia Duarte. 2000. "Sambations: Samba and the Politics of Syncopation." Ph.D. dissertation, University of California at Riverside.

Bhabha, Homi K. 1994. *The Location of Culture*. London: Routledge.

Boddy, Janice Patricia. 1989. *Wombs and Alien Spirits: Women, Men, and the Zar Cult in Northern Sudan*. Madison: University of Wisconsin Press.

Bop, Codou. 1995. "Les Femmes Chefs de Famille à Dakar." *Afrique et Developpement* 20.4 (Numéro Spécial de l'Institut sur le Genre): 51–67.

Boye, A. E. K. 1993. *Etude sur les Conditions Sociales et Juridiques des Femmes Soutien de Famille au Sénégal*. Dakar: Bureau Regional du Population Council.

Bugnicourt, Jacques. 1991. *Set Setal: Des Murs Qui Parlent; Nouvelle Culture Urbaine à Dakar*. Dakar: ENDA Tiers Monde.

Butchart, Alexander. 1998. *The Anatomy of Power: European Constructions of the African Body*. London: Zed Books.

Cabral, Amilcar. 1969. *Revolution in Guinea: Selected Texts*. New York: Monthly Review Press.

Callaway, Barbara, and Lucy Creevey. 1994. *The Heritage of Islam: Women, Religion, and Politics in West Africa*. Boulder, Colo.: Lynne Rienner Publishers.

Camara, Sory. 1992. *Gens de la Parole: Essai sur la Condition et le Role des Griots dans la Société Malinké*. Paris: Éditions Karthala.

———. 1996. "La Tradition Orale en Question." *Cahiers d'Etudes Africaines* 34.144 (4):763–90.

Castaldi, Francesca. 1999. "Sabar Rhythms and the Choreography of a Female Public Sphere in Dakar, Senegal." Paper presented at the African Studies Association, Philadelphia. November 11–14.

———. 2003. "Subalterity and Eroticism in Gaï Ramaka's *Karmen Geï*." Paper presented at the African Popular Music Workshop. African and African-American Studies Research Project, University of California at San Diego. February 21.

Césaire, Aimé. 1947. *Cahier d'un Retour au Pays Natal*. Paris: Présence Africaine.

Charry, Eric. 2000. *Mande Music: Traditional and Modern Music of the Maninka and Mandinka of Western Africa*. Chicago: Chicago University Press.

Chaudhuri, Nupur, and Ruth Pierson, eds. 1998. *Nation, Empire, Colony: Historicizing Gender and Race*. Bloomington: Indiana University Press.

Chernoff, John. 1979. *African Rhythm and African Sensibility: Aesthetics and Social Action in African Musical Idioms*. Chicago: University of Chicago Press.

Cissé, Youssouf, and Wâ Kamissoko. 1991. *Soundjata: La Gloire du Mali*. Paris: Éditions Karthala.

Clark, Andrew, and Lucie Phillips, eds. 1994. *Historical Dictionary of Senegal*. 2d ed. London: Scarecrow Press.

Comaroff, Jean. 1985. *Body of Power, Spirit of Resistance*. Chicago: University of Chicago Press.

Comaroff, Jean, and John Comaroff. 1992. *Ethnography and the Historical Imagination.* Boulder, Colo.: Westview Press.

———. 1993. *Modernity and Its Malcontents: Ritual and Power in Postcolonial Africa.* Chicago: University of Chicago Press.

Copeland, Roger, and Marshall Cohen, eds. 1983. *What Is Dance? Readings in Theory and Criticism.* Oxford: Oxford University Press.

Coplan, David. 1985. *In Township Tonight! South Africa's Black City Music and Theatre.* London: Longman.

———. 1994. *In the Time of Cannibals: The Word Music of South Africa's Bosotho Migrants.* Chicago: University of Chicago Press.

Coulon, Christian. 1981. *Le Marabout et le Prince: Islam et Pouvoir au Sénegal.* Paris: A. Pedone.

———. 1983. *Les Musulmans et le Povoir en Afrique Noire.* Paris: Éditions Karthala.

Crowder, Michael. 1962. *Senegal: A Study in French Assimilation Policy.* London: Oxford University Press.

Dagan, Esther. 1997. "Origin and Meaning of Dance's Essential Body Position and Movements." In *The Spirit's Dance in Africa: Evolution, Transformation, and Continuity in Sub-Sahara.* Ed. Esther Dagan. 102–21. Westmount, Quebec: Galerie Amrad African Arts Publications.

Delgado, Christopher, and Sidi Jammeh. 1991. *The Political Economy of Senegal under Structural Adjustment.* New York: Praeger.

Desmond, Jane, ed. 1997. *Meaning in Motion: New Cultural Studies of Dance.* Durham, N.C.: Duke University Press.

Diagne, Souleymane. 1993. "The Future of Tradition." In *Senegal: Essays in Statecraft.* Ed. Momar Coumba Diop. 269–90. Dakar: CODESRIA.

Diaw, Aminata. 1993. "The Democracy of the Literati." In *Senegal: Essays in Statecraft.* Ed. Momar Coumba Diop. 291–323. Dakar: CODESRIA.

Diawara, Mamadou. 1996. "Le Griot Mande à l'Heure de la Globalization." *Cahiers D'Etudes Africaines* 34.144 (4): 591–612.

Diop, Abdoulaye. 1981. *La Societé Wolof: Les Systemes d'Inegalité et de Domination.* Paris: Éditions Karthala.

———. 1985. *La Famille Wolof.* Paris: Éditions Karthala.

Diop, Cheikh Anta. 1954. *Nations Nègres et Culture.* Paris: Éditions Africaines.

———. 1960. *Les Fondements Culturels Techniques et Industriels d'un Futur État Fédéral d'Afrique Noire.* Paris: Présence Africaine.

———. 1967. *Antériorité des Civilisations Nègres: Mythe ou Vérité Historique?* Paris: Présence Africaine.

———. 1974. *The African Origin of Civilization: Myth and Reality.* Trans. Mercer Cook. Westport, Conn.: Lawrence Hill.

———. 1978. *Black Africa: The Economic and Cultural Basis for a Federal State.* Trans. Harold Salemson. Westport, Conn.: Lawrence Hill.

———. 1987. *Precolonial Black Africa.* Trans. Harold Salemson. Westport, Conn.: Lawrence Hill.

———. 1989. *The Cultural Unit of Black Africa: The Domains of Matriarchy and of Patriarchy in Classical Antiquity.* London: Karnak House.

Diop, Momar Coumba. 1993. "From 'Socialism' to 'Liberalism': The Many Phases of State Legitimacy." Introduction to *Senegal: Essays in Statecraft.* Ed. Momar Coumba Diop. 1–27. Dakar: CODESRIA.

———. 1996. *La Lutte contre la Pauvreté à Dakar: Vers la Définition d'une Politique Municipale.* Accra, Ghana: Programme de Gestion Urbaine, Bureau Regional pour l'Afrique.

Diop, Samba. 1995. *The Oral History and Literature of the Wolof People of Waalo, Northern Senegal.* Lewiston, N.Y.: Edwin Mellen Press.

Diouf, Makhtar. 1994. *Sénégal: Les Ethnies et la Nation.* Paris: Éditions l'Harmattan.

Diouf, Mamadou. 1999. "The French Colonial Policy of Assimilation and the Civility of the Originaires of the Four Communes (Senegal): A Nineteenth-Century Globalization Project." In *Globalization and Identity: Dialectics of Flow and Closure.* Ed. Birgit Meyer and Peter Geschiere. 71–98. Oxford: Blackwell.

Diouf, Mamadou, and Momar Coumba Diop. 1990. *Le Sénégal sous Abdou Diouf.* Paris: Éditions Karthala.

Drame, Adama, and Arlette Senn-Borloz. 1992. *Jeliya: Etre Griot et Musicien Aujourd' hui.* Paris: Éditions l'Harmattan.

Drewal, Margaret Thompson. 1992. *Yoruba Ritual.* Bloomington: Indiana University Press.

Duruflé, Gilles. 1994. *Le Sénégal Peut-il Sortir de la Crise? Douze Ans d'Ajustement Structurel au Sénégal.* Paris: Éditions Karthala.

Ebron, Paulla. 2002. *Performing Africa.* Princeton, N.J.: Princeton University Press.

El Saadawi, Nawal. 1997. *The Nawal El Saadawi Reader.* London: Zed Books.

Evans-Pritchard, Edward. 1937. *Witchcraft, Oracles, and Magic among the Asande.* London: Oxford University Press.

Fabian, Johannes. 1990. *Power and Performance: Ethnographic Explorations through Proverbial Wisdom and Theater in Shaba, Zaire.* Madison: University of Wisconsin Press.

———. 1996. *Remembering the Present: Painting and Popular History in Zaire.* Berkeley: University of California Press.

———. 1998. *Moments of Freedom: Anthropology and Popular Culture.* Charlottesville: University Press of Virginia.

———. 2000. *Out of Our Minds: Reason and Madness in the Exploration of Central Africa.* Berkeley: University of California Press.

Fall, Aminata Sow. 1981 [1979]. *The Beggars' Strike, or the Dregs of Society.* Trans. Dorothy Blair. Harlow, Essex: Longman.

———. 1982. *Le Revenant.* 3d ed. Dakar: Nouvelles Éditions Africaines.

Fanon, Frantz. 1952. *Peau Noire, Masques Blancs.* Paris: Éditions du Seuil.

———. 1963 [1961]. *The Wretched of the Earth.* Trans. Constance Farrington. New York: Grove Press.

Fatton, Robert. 1987. *The Making of a Liberal Democracy: Senegal's Passive Revolution, 1975–1985.* Boulder, Colo.: Rienner Publishers.

Faye, Aziz. 2000. Interview. Los Angeles (June).

Findling, John, ed. 1990. *Historical Dictionary of World's Fairs and Expositions, 1851–1988.* New York: Greenwood Press.

Fodeba, Keita. 1957. "La Danse Africaine et la Scéne." *Présence Africaine* 14–15 (June-September): 202–9.

Fortes, Meyer. 1959. *Oedipus and Job in West African Religion.* Cambridge: Cambridge University Press.

Foster, Susan. 2001. "Closets Full of Dances: Modern Dance's Performance of Masculinity and Sexuality." In *Dancing Desire: Choreographing Sexualities On and Off the Stage.* Ed. Jane Desmond. 147–207. Madison: University of Wisconsin Press.

———, ed. 1996. *Corporealities: Dancing Knowledge, Culture, and Power.* London: Routledge.

———, ed. 1995. *Choreographing History.* Bloomington: Indiana University Press.

———. 1986. *Reading Dancing: Bodies and Subjects in Contemporary American Dance.* Berkeley: University of California Press.

Foucault, Michel. 1972. *The Archeology of Knowledge and the Discourse on Language.* Trans. Sheridan Smith. New York: Pantheon.

———. 1973. *The Order of Things: An Archaeology of the Human Sciences.* New York: Vintage.

———. 1977. *Discipline and Punish: The Birth of the Prison.* Trans. Alan Sheridan. New York: Pantheon.

Franko, Mark. 1995. *Dancing Modernism/Performing Politics.* Bloomington: Indiana University Press.

Frobenius, Leo. 1909. *The Childhood of Man: A Popular Account of the Lives, Customs, and Thoughts of the Primitive Races.* London: Seeley and Co. Ltd.

———. 1936. *Histoire de la Civilisation Africaine.* Paris: Gallimard.

———. 1938. *African Genesis.* London: Faber and Faber.

Fusco, Coco. 1994. "The Other History of Intercultural Performance." *Drama Review* 38.1 (Spring): 143–67.

Gere, David, Lewis Segal, Patrice Clark Koelsch, and Elizabeth Zimmer, eds. 1995. *Looking Out: Perspectives on Dance and Criticism in a Multicultural World.* New York: Schirmer.

Gilman, Sander. 1985. "The Hottentot and the Prostitute: Toward an Iconography of Female Sexuality." In *Difference and Pathology: Stereotypes of Sexuality, Race, and Madness.* 76–108. Ithaca, N.Y.: Cornell University Press.

Gilroy, Paul. 1993. *The Black Atlantic: Modernity and Double Consciousness.* London: Verso.

Gottschild, Brenda Dixon. 1996. *Digging the Africanist Presence in American Performance: Dance and Other Contexts.* Westport, Conn.: Greenwood Press.

Greenhalgh, Paul. 1988. *Ephemeral Vistas: The Expositions Universelles, Great Exhibitions, and World's Fairs, 1851–1939.* Manchester: Manchester University Press.

Guillaumin, Colette. 1995. *Racism, Sexism, Power, and Ideology*. London: Routledge.

Gunner, Liz, ed. 1994. *Politics and Performance: Theatre, Poetry, and Song in Southern Africa*. Johannesburg: Witwatersrand University Press.

Hale, Thomas. 1998. *Griots and Griottes: Masters of Words and Music*. Bloomington: Indiana University Press.

Harrison, Jane. 1983. "From Ritual to Art." In *What Is Dance?* Ed. Roger Copeland and Marshall Cohen. 502–6. Oxford: Oxford University Press.

Heath, Deborah. 1992. "Fashion, Anti-fashion, and Heteroglossia in Urban Senegal." *American Ethnologist* 19.1 (February): 19–33.

———. 1994. "The Politics of Appropriateness and Appropriation: Recontextualizing Women's Dance in Urban Senegal." *American Ethnologist* 21.1 (February): 88–103.

Hesseling, Gerti. 1985. *Histoire Politique du Sénégal: Institutions, Droit, et Société*. Paris: Éditions Karthala.

———. 1994. "La Terre, à Qui Est-elle? Les pratiques fonciéres en Basse-Casamance." In *Comprendre la Casamance: Chronique d'une Intégration Contrastée*. Ed. François Barbier-Wiesser. 243–62. Paris: Éditions Karthala.

Hinsley, Curtis. 1991. "The World as Market Place: Commodification of the Exotic at the World's Columbian Exposition, 1893." In *Exhibiting Cultures: The Poetics and Politics of Museum Display*. Ed. Ivan Karp and Steven Lavine. 344–65. Washington, D.C.: Smithsonian Institution Press.

Hoffman, Barbara. 2000. *Griots at War: Conflict, Conciliation, and Caste in Mande*. Transcribed and translated with Kassim Koné. Bloomington: Indiana University Press.

Hooks, Bell. 1990. *Yearning: Race, Gender, and Cultural Politics*. Boston: South End Press.

Hountondji, Paulin. 1996 [1976]. *African Philosophy: Myth and Reality*. 2d ed. Bloomington: Indiana University Press.

Imperato, Pascal. 1977. *Historical Dictionary of Mali*. Metuchen, N.J.: Scarecrow Press.

Irele, Abiola. 1990 [1981]. *The African Experience in Literature and Ideology*. Bloomington: Indiana University Press.

Jackson, Michael. 1989. *Paths toward a Clearing*. Bloomington: Indiana University Press.

———, ed. 1996. *Things as They Are: New Directions in Phenomenological Anthropology*. Bloomington: Indiana University Press.

Johnson-Odim, Cheryl. 1998. "Actions Louder Than Words: The Historical Task of Defining Feminist Consciousness in Colonial West Africa." In *Nation, Empire, Colony: Historicizing Gender and Race*. Ed. Nupur Chaudhuri and Ruth Pierson. 77–93. Bloomington: Indiana University Press.

Jules-Rosette, Benneta. 1984. *The Message of Tourist Art: An African Semiotic System in Comparative Perspective*. New York: Plenum.

———. 1987. "Rethinking the Popular Arts in Africa: Problems of Interpretation." *African Studies Review* 30.3 (September): 91–98.

———. 1992. "Conjugating Cultural Realities: Présence Africaine." In *The Surrep-

titious Speech: Présence Africaine and the Politics of Otherness, 1947–1987. Ed. V. Y. Mudimbe. 14–44. Chicago: University of Chicago Press.

———. 1998. *Black Paris: The African Writers' Landscape.* Urbana: University of Illinois Press.

———. 2002. "Afro-Pessimism's Many Guises." *Public Culture* 14.3 (September): 603–5.

Kaspin, Deborah. 1993. "Chewa Visions and Revisions of Power: Transformation of the Nyau Dance in Central Malawi." In *Modernity and Its Malcontents: Ritual and Power in Postcolonial Africa.* Ed. Jean Comaroff and John Comaroff. 34–57. Chicago: University of Chicago Press.

Koura, Lamine. 1996. Interview. St.-Louis, Senegal (March).

Kesteloot, Lilyan. 1991. *Black Writers in French: A Literary History of Negritude.* Trans. Ellen Conroy Kennedy. Washington, D.C.: Howard University Press.

———. 2002. *Histoire de la Littérature Négro-Africaine.* Paris: Éditions Karthala.

Langer, Susan. 1953. "Virtual Power and the Magic of the Circle." In *What Is Dance?* Ed. Roger Copeland and Marshall Cohen. 28–57. Oxford: Oxford University Press.

Larrain, Jorge. 1994. *Ideology and Cultural Identity: Modernity and the Third World Presence.* Cambridge, Mass.: Polity Press.

Leclerc, Gérard. 1972. *Anthropologie et Colonialisme: Essai sur l'Histoire de l'Africanisme.* Paris: Fayard.

Lévy-Bruhl, Lucien. 1910. *Les Fonctions Mentales dans les Société Inférieures.* Paris: Librairie Félix Alcan.

———. 1922. *Mentalité Primitive.* Paris: Librairie Félix Alcan.

Lewis, Lowell. 1995. "Genre and Embodiment: From Brazilian Capoeria to the Ethnology of Human Movement." *Cultural Anthropology* 10.2 (May): 221–43.

Leymarie, Isabelle. 1978. "The Role and Function of the Griots among the Wolof of Senegal." Ph.D. dissertation, Columbia University.

Linares, Olga. 1992. *Power, Prayer, and Production: The Jola of Casamance.* Cambridge: Cambridge University Press.

Ly, Abdoulaye. 1982. *Feu la Négritude: Notes sur une Ideologie Neocoloniale.* Dakar: Xamle.

Magubane, Z. 2001. "Which Bodies Matter? Feminism, Poststructuralism, Race, and the Curious Theoretical Odyssey of the 'Hottentot Venus.'" *Gender and Society* 15.6: 816–34.

Mambety, Djibril Diop, dir. 1994. *Le Franc.* Film. San Francisco: California Newsreel.

Mansour, G. 1980. "The Dynamics of Multilingualism: The Case of Senegal." *Journal of Mulitilingual Development* 1: 273–93.

Marcus, George. 1998. *Ethnography through Thick and Thin.* Princeton, N.J.: Princeton University Press.

Marcus, George, and Fred Myers, eds. 1995. *The Traffic in Culture: Reconfiguring Art and Anthropology.* Berkeley: University of California Press.

Martin, John. 1983. "Metakinesis." In *What Is Dance?* Ed. Roger Copeland and Marshall Cohen. 23–27. Oxford: Oxford University Press.

Masquelier, Adeline. 2001. *Prayer Has Spoiled Everything: Possession, Power, and Identity in an Islamic Town of Niger*. Durham, N.C.: Duke University Press.

Mbembe, Achille. 2001. *On the Postcolony*. Berkeley: University of California Press.

———. 2002. "African Modes of Self Writing." *Public Culture* 14.1 (January): 239–74.

M'Bow, Penda. 1989. "Religions et Statuts de la Femme." *Fippu* (April): 45.

McClintock, Anne. 1995. *Imperial Leather: Race, Gender, and Sexuality in the Colonial Context*. New York: Routledge.

McLaughlin, Fiona. 1997. "Music for Modern Muslims: Islam and Popular Music in Senegal; the Emergence of a 'New' Tradition." *Africa* 67.4: 560–81.

McNee, Lisa. 2000. *Selfish Gifts: Senegalese Women's Autobiographical Discourses*. Albany: State University of New York.

Mernissi, Fatima. 1975. *Beyond the Veil: Male-Female Dynamics in a Modern Muslim Society*. Cambridge, Mass.: Schenkam Publishing.

Ministére de la Femme, de l'Enfant, et de la Famille. 1993. *Senegalese Women by the Year 2015*. Abridged ed. Dakar: The Population Council.

Mohanty, Chandra. 1991. "Under Western Eyes: Feminist Scholarship and Colonial Discourses." In *Third World Women and the Politics of Feminism*. Ed. Chandra Mohanty, Ann Russo, and Lourdes Torres. 51–80. Bloomington: Indiana University Press.

Mohanty, Chandra, Ann Russo, and Lourdes Torres, eds. 1991. *Third World Women and the Politics of Feminism*. Bloomington: Indiana University Press.

Mphahlele, Ezekiel. 1974. *The African Image*. New York: Praeger.

Mudimbe, V. Y. 1994. *The Idea of Africa*. Bloomington: Indiana University Press.

———, ed. 1992. *The Surreptitious Speech: Présence Africaine and the Politics of Otherness, 1947–1987*. Chicago: University of Chicago Press.

———. 1988. *The Invention of Africa: Gnosis, Philosophy, and the Order of Knowledge*. Bloomington: Indiana University Press.

M'Veng, Engelbert. 1966. Introduction to *L'Art Negre: Sources, Evolution, Expansion*. Dakar: Exposition Organisé au Musée Dynamique à Dakar par le Commissariat du Premier Festival Mondial des Arts Negres.

Ndiaye, Raphaël. 1986. *La Place de la Femme Dans Les Rites Au Senegal*. Dakar: Les Nouvelles Editions Africaines.

N'Dour, Youssou. 1994. "Tourista." *The Guide (Wommat)*. Compact disc. EMI Virgin Music Publishing.

Niang, Sada. 1993. "An Interview with Ousmane Sembène by Sada Niang." In *Ousmane Sembène: Dialogues with Critics and Writers*. Ed. Sama Gadjigo, Ralph Faulkingham, Thomas Cassirer, and Reinhard Sander. 87–108. Amherst: University of Massachusetts Press.

Nicholls, Robert. 1996. "African Dance: Transition and Continuity." In *African Dance: An Artistic, Historical, and Philosophical Inquiry*. Ed. Kariamu Welsh-Asante. 41–62. Trenton, N.J.: African World Press.

O'Brien, Donal Cruise. 1971. *The Mourides of Senegal: The Political and Economic Organization of an Islamic Brotherhood*. Oxford: Clarendon Press.

———. 1998. "The Shadow-Politics of Wolofisation." *Journal of Modern African Studies* 26.1 (March): 25–46.

———. 2002. "Langue et Nationalité au Sénégal." In *La construction de l'Etat au Sénégal.* Ed. Momar-Couna Diop and Mamadou Diouf. 319–35. Paris: Éditions Karthala.

Okafor, Chinyere. 1997. "Gender Politics in West African Mask Performance." In *Writing African Women: Gender, Popular Culture, and Literature in Africa.* Ed. Stephanie Newell. 157–69. London: Zed Books.

Ottenberg, Simon. 1997. "Introduction: Some Issues and Questions on African Dance." In *The Spirit's Dance in Africa: Evolution, Transformation, and Continuity in Sub-Sahara.* Ed. Esther Dagan. 10–15. Westmount, Quebec: Galerie Amrad African Arts Publications.

Oyewùmí, Oyèrónké. 1997. *The Invention of Women: Making an African Sense of Western Gender Discourses.* Minneapolis: University of Minnesota Press.

Panzacchi, Cornelia. 1994. "The Livelihood of Traditional Griots in Modern Senegal." *Africa: Journal of the International African Institute* 64.2: 190–210.

Rabine, Leslie. 1997. "Dressing Up in Dakar." *L'Esprit Créateur* 37.1 (Spring): 84–107.

Ramaka, Gaï, dir. 2001. *Karmen Geï.* Film. San Francisco: California Newsreel.

Ramatou. 1997. Interview. Dakar, Senegal (January).

Ranger, Terence. 1983. "The Invention of Tradition in Colonial Africa." In *The Invention of Tradition.* Ed. Erie Hobsbawm and Terence Ranger. 211–62. Cambridge: Cambridge University Press.

———. 1993. "The Invention of Tradition Revisited." In *Legitimacy and State in Twentieth-Century Africa.* Ed. Terence Ranger and Olufemi Vaughan. 62–111. London: Macmillan.

Ranger, Terence, and Richard Werbner, eds. 1996. *Post-Colonial Identities in Africa.* London: Zed Books.

Roberts, Allen, and Mary Roberts. 2003. *A Saint in the City: Sufi Arts of Urban Senegal.* Los Angeles: UCLA Museum of Cultural History.

Sachs, Curt. 1937. *World History of the Dance.* New York: Norton.

Sane, Djibril. 1997. Interview. Camberene, Senegal (March).

Sartre, Jean-Paul. 1949. "Orphée Noir." *Présence Africaine* 6 (1st Trimester): 219–47.

Savigliano, Marta. 1995. *Tango and the Political Economy of Passion.* San Francisco: Westview Press.

———. 1996. "Fragments for a Story of Tango Bodies (On Choreocritics and the Memory of Power)." In *Corporealities: Dancing Knowledge, Culture, and Power.* Ed. Susan Foster. 199–232. London: Routledge.

———. 1997. "Nocturnal Ethnographies: Following Cortázar in the Milongas of Buenos Aires." *Etnofoor* 10 (1/2): 28–52.

———. 2003. *Angora Matta: Fatal Acts of North-South Translation.* Middletown, Conn.: Wesleyan Press.

Schaffer, Frederic. 1994. "Demokaraasi in Africa: What Wolof Political Concepts

Teach Us about How to Study Democracy." Ph.D. dissertation, University of California at Berkeley.

———. 1998. *Democracy in Transition: Understanding Politics in an Unfamiliar Culture.* Ithaca, N.Y.: Cornell University Press.

Schlechten, Marguerite. 1988. *Tourisme Balnéaire ou Tourisme Rural Intégré? Deux Modèles de Développement Sénégalais.* Fribourg, Switzerland: Éditions Universitaires.

Sembène, Ousmane. 1976. *Xala.* Trans. Clive Wake. Chicago: Lawrence Hill.

Senghor, Léopold Sédar. 1945. *Chants d'Ombre.* Paris: Éditions du Seuil.

———. 1948. *Anthologie de la Nouvelle Poésie Négre et Malgache de Langue Française.* Paris: Presses Universitaires de France.

———. 1956. "L'Ésprit de la Civilisation ou les Lois de la Culture Négro-Africaine." *Présence Africaine,* special issue: Le I.er Congrès International des Écrivants et Artistes Noirs (19–22 Septembre): 51–65.

———. 1961. *Nocturnes: Poèmes.* Paris: Éditions du Seuil.

———. 1964a. *On African Socialism.* Trans. and intro. Mercer Cook. New York: Praeger.

———. 1964b. *Liberté I: Négritude et Humanisme.* Paris: Éditions du Seuil.

———. 1971. *Liberté II: Nation et Voie Africaine du Socialisme.* Paris: Éditions du Seuil.

———. 1972. "Pourquoi une Idéologie Négro-Africaine?" *Présence Africaine,* special issue 82 (2d Trimester): 11–38.

———. 1977. *Liberté III: Négritude et Civilisation de L'Universel.* Paris: Éditions du Seuil.

———. 1988. *Ce Que Je Crois: Négritude, Francité, et Civilisation de l'Universel.* Paris: Bernard Grasset.

———. 1993. *Liberté V: Le Dialogue des Cultures.* Paris: Éditions du Seuil.

———. 1994. "Negritude: A Humanism of the Twentieth Century." In *Colonial Discourse and Post-colonial Theory: A Reader.* Ed. Patrick Williams and Laura Chrisman. 27–35. New York: Columbia University Press.

Somerville, Carolyn. 1997. "Reaction and Resistance: Confronting Economic Crisis, Structural Adjustment, and Devaluation in Dakar, Senegal." In *Globalization and Survival in the Black Diaspora: The New Urban Challenge.* Ed. Charles Green. 15–42. New York: State University of New York Press.

Sorell, Walter. 1967. *The Dance through the Ages.* New York: Grosset and Dunlap.

Souleymane. 1997. Interview. Dakar, Senegal (January).

Sow, Fatou. 1997. "Social Sciences in Africa and Gender Analysis." In *Engendering African Social Sciences.* Ed. Ayesha M. Imam, Amina Mama, and Fatou Sow. Dakar: CODESRIA.

Spivak, Gayatri. 1990. *The Postcolonial Critic: Interviews, Strategies, Dialogues.* New York: Routledge.

———. 1999. *A Critique of Postcolonial Reason: Toward a History of the Vanishing Present.* Cambridge, Mass.: Harvard University Press.

Stoller, Paul. 1995. *Embodying Colonial Memories: Spirit Possession, Power, and the Hauka in West Africa.* New York: Routledge.

Strother, Z. S. 1998. *Inventing Masks: Agency and History in the Art of Central Pende.* Chicago: University of Chicago Press.

———. 1999. "Display of the Body Hottentot." In *Africans on Stage: Studies in Ethnological Show Business.* Ed. Bernth Lindfors. 1–61. Bloomington: Indiana University Press.

Stuckey, Sterling. 1987. *Slave Culture: Nationalist Theory and the Foundations of Black America.* Oxford: Oxford University Press.

———. 1994. *Going through the Storm: The Influence of African American Art in History.* Oxford: Oxford University Press.

Swigart, Leigh. 1992. "Practice and Perception: Language Use and Attitudes in Dakar." Ph.D. dissertation, University of Washington.

———. 1994. "Cultural Creolization and Language Use in Post-colonial Africa: The Case of Senegal." *Africa* 64.2: 175–89.

———. 2000. "The Limits of Legitimacy: Language Ideology and Shift in Contemporary Senegal." *Journal of Linguistic Anthropology* 10.1 (June): 90–130.

Sylla, Abdou. 1993a. "Pratique et Théorie de la Création dans les Arts Plastiques Sénégalais Contemporains." Ph.D. dissertation, Université de Paris I, Sorbonne.

———. 1993b. "Reform Options for the Education System." In *Senegal: Essays in Statecraft.* Ed. Momar Coumba Diop. 370–419. Dakar: CODESRIA.

Sylla, Assane. 1994. *La Philosophie Morale des Wolof.* Dakar: IFAN Université de Dakar.

Tang, Patricia. 2000. "Masters of the Sabar: Wolof Griots in Contemporary Senegal." Ph.D dissertation, Harvard University.

Taussig, Michael T. 1993. *Mimesis and Alterity: A Particular History of the Senses.* New York: Routledge.

Tempels, Placide. 1969 [1945]. *Bantu Philosophy.* Paris: Présence Africaine.

Thiam, Ndiuwar. 1996. Interview. Dakar, Senegal (November).

Thompson, Robert Farris. 1974. *African Art in Motion: Icon and Act.* Los Angeles: University of California Press.

Tiérou, Alphonse. 1989. *Dooplé: Loi Éternelle de la Danse Africaine.* Paris: Editions Maisonneuve et Larose.

Tobin, Jeffrey. 1998. "Manly Acts: Buenos Aires, 24 March 1996." Ph.D dissertation, Rice University.

Towa, Marcien. 1971. *Léopold Sédar Senghor, Négritude ou Servitude?* Yaounde: Éditions CLE.

Truher, Sarah. 1997. "Dëgg-Dëgg Mooy Sa Doole: Mbalax as Mediator of Senegalese Cultural Identity." Master's thesis, University of California at Los Angeles.

Van De Walle, Nicolas. 1991. "The Decline of the Franc Zone: Monetary Politics in Francophone Africa." *African Affairs* 90.360 (July): 383–406.

Van Dijk, Meine. 1986. *Sénégal: Le Secteur Informel de Dakar.* Paris: L'Harmattan.

Vansina, Jan. 1994. *Living with Africa.* Madison: University of Wisconsin Press.

Veit, Erlmann. 1996. *Nightsong: Performance, Power, and Practice in South Africa.* Chicago: University of Chicago Press.

Visweswaran, Kamala. 1994. *Fictions of Feminist Ethnography.* Minneapolis: University of Minnesota Press.

Wade, Mansour Sora. 1992. *Picc mi.* Film. San Francisco: California Newsreel.

Wallerstein, Immanuel. 1979. *The Capitalist World-Economy: Essays.* Cambridge: Cambridge University Press.

———. 1986. *Africa and the Modern World.* Trenton, N.J.: Africa World Press.

———. 1991. "Social Conflict in Post-Independence Black Africa: The Concepts of Race and Status-Group Reconsidered." In *Race, Nation, Class: Ambiguous Identities.* Ed. Etienne Balibar and Immanuel Wallerstein. 187–203. London: Verso.

———. 1997 [1991]. *Geopolitics and Geoculture: Essays on the Changing World-System.* Cambridge: Cambridge University Press.

Waterman, Chris. 1990. *Juju: A Social History and Ethnography of an African Popular Music.* Chicago: University of Chicago Press.

Werbner, Richard, ed. 1998. *Memory and the Post-colony: African Anthropology and the Critique of Power.* London: Zed Books.

Werner, Jean-François. 1993. *Marges, Sexe, et Drogues à Dakar: Enquête Etnographique.* Paris: Éditions Karthala.

Wilder, Gary. 1999. "Practicing Citizenship in Imperial Paris." In *Civil Society and the Political Imagination in Africa.* Ed. Jean Comaroff and John Comaroff. 44–71. Chicago: University of Chicago Press.

Williams, Patrick, and Laura Chrisman, ed. 1994. *Colonial Discourse and Post-colonial Theory: A Reader.* New York: Columbia University Press.

Index

history: Abu Bakari's discovery of America,
193–94; ancient civilization, 67–68, 210n12;
colonialism and, 35–36, 207n1; as contended
space, 1–2; dance as articulation of, 3; gender
as informed by, 119; historically situated tradition, 63–64; memory as sedimentation, 11–12
homosexuality, 81, 90, 95–96, 167–70, 214n41.
See also sexuality
hoplà, 164
hórós, 158–59, 220n9
Hotel Terànga (Dakar), 179
humanism, 50, 54–55

immigration, 111–17, 195–96
improvisation: assigned authorship status, 138;
bàkk improvisation, 130–34, 141, 153,
217–18nn12–13; club dancing and, 93–101; as
drummer-dancer dialogue, 11, 141–42; pro-
fessionalization and, 152–54. *See also sabar*
complex
independence movements. *See* nation
intergenerationality. *See* generationality
International Congress of Black Writers and
Artists (Paris, 1956; Rome, 1959), 51
International Monetary Fund, 72, 180–81
Irory Coast, 154
Irvine Barclay Theater (California), 2
Islam: *dahiras,* 80–81; dance tradition and, 31,
170, 207n23; feminism and, 116, 121, 123; gender and, 84–91, 214n35; *marabouts,* 60, 85–86,
87; Mouride brotherhood, 77, 78–79, 86, 88,
191–92, 212n22, 214nn35–36; "Muslim Woman
in Dakar" photo, 65–67, 66; objections to
dance, 171–72; popular music and, 85–86;
sabar kinaesthetic and, 80, 84, 86–89; in Senegalese politics, 78–79, 199, 202; sexuality and,
116, 123, 214n40, 214n42; *taalibes,* 70, 80, 210n1;
Tidjaniyya order, 85
Ismael (pseud.), 164–67, 220n11
Ivory Coast, 218n27

Jackson, Michael, 167
jàlís, 153–54, 158, 162, 192, 219n5, 220n9
Jean Vilar Theater (Saint-Quentin, France), 21
jembe, 133, 168, 169, 170
Joachim, Paulin, 51
Joola: clan-based society, 79, 214–15n43, 216n12;
econcon as symbol for, 31; Joola language as
official language, 199–200; language distribution, 222n5; Mande ethnicity complex

and, 219n6; role in independence movement, 213n25
Jules-Rosette, Bennetta, 48–49, 51, 59

Kaddu, 200
Kaddu gi, 97, 148–49, 151, 162–63, 183–84
Kajor kingdom, 191–92
kankuran, 145–46, 148
kaolack, 129–31, 140
Karmen Geï (Ramaka, 2001), 213–14n32
Kasse, Alioune, 138–39
Keme Bourama, 64
kersa, 86
Khaley Nguewel, 129, 217n6
Khaware, 24
kinaesthetics, 80–82, 84–89
kinship. *See* family
Kirango, 207n18
Kohler, Wolfgang, 38
Konaté, Maghan, 188, 190–93
kora, 25, 26, 31, 193, 206n11, 218n14
koumpo, 28, 63, 145, 147, 207n17
Koumpo (National Ballet of Senegal perform-
ance), 27, 28, 63, 147
Koura, Lamine, 213n30
kutiro, 146

Lam, Kine, 165
làmb, 213n26
language: bilingualism as *bicephalism,* 198, 202;
drums and, 132–33, 218n15; as external vs. internal to dance, 3–4; literacy, 200; movement
analysis and, 136–38; Senegalese indigenous
languages, 199–201, 221–22nn4–5; Senegal
language distribution, 222n5; Senghorian
state and, 198; tribal languages, 29–30. *See
also* French language; Wolof language
lëmbël, 82
Lemzo Diamono, 129, 135, 138–39
lenjengo, 31, 146, 217n3
Leurs, Jean Pierre, 193
Lévy-Bruhl, Lucien, 52
Liberté series (Senghor), 49
La Linguère, 162
LT (Dakar nightclub), 91, 92–93, 148–49. *See
also* club dancing
Lucie, Phillips, 219n6

Maal, Baaba, 132
Mali, 154, 207n18

FRANCESCA CASTALDI is an independent dance scholar and researcher. She earned her Ph.D. in Dance History in Theory at the University of California, Riverside. The research presented in this book earned her the 2002 Award for Outstanding Research in African Studies from the African and African-American Studies Research Project, University of California, San Diego. Her work continues to interrogate the choreography of social identities, the everyday performance of corporealities, and the relationship between language and embodied experience.

The University of Illinois Press
is a founding member of the
Association of American University Presses.

———————————————————

Composed in 10.5/13 Minion
with Meta display
by Type One, LLC
for the University of Illinois Press
Manufactured by Sheridan Books, Inc.

University of Illinois Press
1325 South Oak Street
Champaign, IL 61820-6903
www.press.uillinois.edu